# Structure, Audience
# and Soft Power
# in East Asian Pop Culture

## TransAsia: Screen Cultures
### Edited by Koichi Iwabuchi and Chris Berry

What is Asia? What does it mean to be Asian? Who thinks they are Asian? How is "Asian-ness" produced? In Asia's transnational public space, many kinds of cross-border connections proliferate, from corporate activities to citizen-to-citizen linkages, all shaped by media—from television series to action films, video piracy, and a variety of subcultures facilitated by internet sites and other computer-based cultures. Films are packaged at international film festivals and marketed by DVD companies as "Asian," while the descendants of migrants increasingly identify themselves as "Asian," then turn to "Asian" screen cultures to find themselves and their roots. As reliance on national frameworks becomes obsolete in many traditional disciplines, this series spotlights groundbreaking research on trans-border, screen-based cultures in Asia.

### Other titles in the series:

*Cinema at the City's Edge: Film and Urban Networks in East Asia,* edited by Yomi Braester and James Tweedie

*Cultural Studies and Cultural Industries in Northeast Asia: What a Difference a Region Makes,* edited by Chris Berry, Nicola Liscutin, and Jonathan D. Mackintosh

*East Asian Pop Culture: Analysing the Korean Wave,* edited by Chua Beng Huat and Koichi Iwabuchi

*Horror to the Extreme: Changing Boundaries in Asian Cinema,* edited by Jinhee Choi and Mitsuyo Wada-Marciano

*Korean Masculinities and Transcultural Consumption: Yonsama, Rain, Oldboy, K-Pop Idols,* by Sun Jung

*The Chinese Exotic: Modern Diasporic Femininity,* by Olivia Khoo

*TV Drama in China,* edited by Ying Zhu, Michael Keane, and Ruoyun Bai

*The Pusan International Film Festival, South Korean Cinema and Globalization,* by SooJeong Ahn

*Japanese Cinema Goes Global: Filmworkers' Journeys,* by Yoshiharu Tezuka

*Southeast Asian Independent Cinema,* edited by Tilman Baumgärtel

### Series International Advisory Board

# Structure, Audience and Soft Power in East Asian Pop Culture

Chua Beng Huat

香港大學出版社
HONG KONG UNIVERSITY PRESS

Hong Kong University Press
14/F Hing Wai Centre
7 Tin Wan Praya Road
Aberdeen
Hong Kong
www.hkupress.org

ISBN 978-988-8139-03-3 *(Hardback)*
ISBN 978-988-8139-04-0 *(Paperback)*

British Library Cataloguing-in-Publication Data
A catalogue record for this book is available from the British Library.

10   9   8   7   6   5   4   3   2   1

Printed and bound by Paramount Printing Co. Ltd., Hong Kong, China

For Kuan Hsing, who makes events in Cultural Studies in Asia happen

# Contents

# Note on the Author

Chua Beng Huat is the head of the cultural studies in Asia research cluster at the Asia Research Institute, the convenor of the Cultural Studies Programs and head of the Department of Sociology at the National University of Singapore. He has held visiting professorships at universities internationally, including the Inaugural Distinguished Visiting Scholar Fellowship at Carolina Asia Center, University of North Carolina, Chapel Hill, USA. His publications relevant to cultural studies include, as author, *Life Is Not Complete Without Shopping* (2003; two printings), as editor, *Consumption in Asia: Lifestyles and Identities* (2000), *Elections as Popular Culture in Asia* (2007), and as co-editor, *Inter-Asia Cultural Studies Reader* (2007), and *East Asia Pop Culture: Analyzing the Korean Wave* (2008). He is the founding co-executive editor of the journal, *Inter-Asia Cultural Studies*.

# Preface

One of the offshoots of my work with the Inter-Asia Cultural Studies project has been the development of a research interest in East Asian Pop Culture. This research began serendipitously with a request from colleagues in the Geography Department at the National University of Singapore to present a keynote address for a Global Conference on Economic Geography, in December 2000. Although I was given the freedom to speak on a topic of my choice, I nevertheless felt that it must have something to do with geography.

To all Singaporeans, regardless of ethnicity, a sense that Singapore is part of the overseas Chinese community, the so-called global Chinese diaspora, seems obvious, unavoidable. Additionally the People's Action Party that has ruled Singapore continuously since 1959 believes that Confucianism, the bedrock philosophy of Chinese culture, had been instrumental to Singapore's economic success, as it supposedly had been for South Korea, Taiwan, and Hong Kong, and before that, Japan. By 2000, the Confucian or "Asian Values" thesis on capitalist economic development was in disarray, as a consequence of the 1997 Asian financial crisis. In this context, and in contradiction to this Confucian Greater China conceptualized by Tu Weiming (1991), in the keynote address I focused on Chinese-language pop culture that had been circulating since the beginning of the twentieth century in the Huaren communities across the region, discursively designating this as Pop Culture China.

The pop culture in every East Asian location has always been porous and receptive to the importation of and mixing with pop culture from not only within the region, but also from Europe and America. Indeed, the recent penetration of Japanese and Korean pop culture into Pop Culture China could not be missed. In the 1990s, Japanese "trendy" dramas were the rage on small screens across the regional. Koichi Iwabuchi convened an international conference at the International Christian University in Tokyo on trans-East Asian reception of Japanese trendy drama in 2001, to which Ien Ang and I were invited as commentators (Iwabuchi 2004). By the end of the decade, Japanese trendy dramas were being displaced and replaced by the Korean Wave. It was obvious that there was a larger field of East Asian Pop Culture at work, with Japanese and Korean pop culture treading through the network of Pop Culture China to reach a much bigger transnational audience/consumer market. I made a tentative step to map out the essential elements that are constitutive of a regional cultural economy that can be discursively and analytically designated as East Asian Pop Culture.

In 2002, an Asia Research Institute was established at the National University of Singapore. I was appointed a research fellow to develop a "cultural studies in Asia" research cluster, as one among a clutch of different research foci. In 2004, a small research agenda-setting workshop was convened, with individuals working in media and film studies from across Asia in attendance. This workshop set out a path for East Asian Pop Culture research, workshops and conferences at the Asia Research Institute. Researchers from postdoctoral fellows, to longer-term in-house research fellows, to short-term visiting fellows continue to be invited. Since then, the cluster has organized at least one international workshop a year on an aspect or a phenomenon in East Asian Pop Culture: new Southeast Asian cinemas (2004); the films of Hou Hsiao-Hsien (2005); Japanese and Korean television dramas (2005); the cinematic representation of the tropical urban/city, Asia pop music, and Asian cinematic practices (2006); media and medicine in Asia (2008), Pop Culture China (2009) and performing spaces in Asian cinema (2010); in addition, a year-long monthly public lecture series entitled "Violence in Contemporary Asian Films" was organized in 2006. Most of these workshops have resulted in the publication of the edited papers, either as monographs or in special issues of appropriate journals.

In all the workshops and conferences emphasis is always placed on finding both established and new voices among Asian-based scholars and on concepts emphasizing the "transnational" Asia/n. This produces three important consequences: first, a researcher is obliged to engage in an analysis of boundary crossings between the location of production and the location of consumption; second, by bringing together research on the reception of the same media products at different locations, multiple crossings are brought together for comparative analysis; and third, taking the analysis from different locations as a whole, a pan-East Asian "thing" emerges. Distilled from different audience receptions is not a simple "cultural proximity" or any shared cultural tradition, but an intermittent closeness and distance that conceptually, and most importantly, evinces the emergent possibility of a sense of the "pan-East Asia/n," which does not amount to a stable identity but, nevertheless, retains a certain coherence. Politically, this possibility runs contra to the impossibility of an East Asia in an international political arena of ongoing noisy rhetoric and exaggerated gestures of animosity that are rooted in the legacy of the brutal history of Japanese imperialism in Asia, in the first half of the twentieth century.

Comparative work on transnational East Asian Pop Culture is only possible through the meetings and work of a community of researchers from all the East

Asian locations. The heavy debt this book owes to them is obvious in the body of the text, in which they are heavily cited, and in the references. The list includes, among others, Yang Fang-chih, Eva Tsai, Kelly Hu, and Ko Yifen in Taiwan; Eric Ma, Anthony Fung, and Angel Lin in Hong Kong; Doobo Shim, Lee Dong Ho, Shin Hyunjoon, and Kim Hyun-Mee in Korea; Liew Kai Khiun, Wee Wan-ling, and Stephen Teo in Singapore; Koichi Iwabuchi and Yoshitaka Mouri in Tokyo; and Olivia Khoo, Audrey Yue, Wanning Sun, and Meaghan Morris in Australia. The absence of researchers from China in this list is a concern. Fortunately, here, we have the works of Michael Keane and his extensive group of Chinese colleagues for reference. I should add that Michael was a most hospitable host and friend during my short stint as a research fellow at Griffith University, Brisbane, Australia.

Some of the chapters in this book have morphed from earlier essays that were written for workshops and conferences and were previously published in journals and edited volumes. The permission of the publishers to disassemble and use extensive sections of these essays throughout the book is gratefully acknowledged: Routledge for Chapter 1, Blackwell Publishers for Chapter 2, Hong Kong University Press for Chapters 3 and 5, and Kyoto University Press for Chapter 6. I would like to thank Ms Wong Meisen for her research assistance in the final preparation of the manuscript; she was particularly helpful with Internet searches. The conference organizing work would not have been possible without the assistance of the highly effective and efficient event-team at the Asia Research Institute of Alyson Rozells, Valerie Yeo, Sharon Ong, and Henry Kwan. Finally, I am thankful for the research funding from the Asia Research Institute and the Provost Professorship that was essential throughout the journey of this book.

# Introduction

This book is an introduction to an emerging field of study, namely, East Asian Pop Culture. An inherent precondition of such a text is that a substantial amount of research and published material must already be available in the field before the writing can be undertaken. An introductory text is, therefore, fundamentally a parasitic text that draws on the existing material in order to attempt a relatively coherent mapping of the contours of the object of analysis. The indebtedness of such an endeavor to available material is even more pronounced in instances, such as this one, in which the analytic object has to be formulated in/from both comparative and regional perspectives. This is because rare is a single author who is equipped with the linguistic competency and cultural sensitivity required to understand the different regional sites, and is thus able to conduct research in all the significant locations that constitute the region as a unit, spatially and in other ways.

The basis of this text is a body of published empirical research work from a community of scholars who, though dispersed throughout the region, have been exchanging and collaborating intellectually, in workshops, conferences, and joint publications, for the past two decades, as the loose integration of the media industry in East Asia, particularly in the flows of television drama and pop music, became noticeable. These empirical studies of the different modes of production, distribution, circulation, and consumption in different regional locations are pioneering, seminal studies that opened up the emerging field both substantively and conceptually. They provide the necessary groundwork for not only comparative understanding of regional media activities but also the necessary ingredient for conceptual abstractions and concept formations that are the building blocks of a regional East Asian Pop Culture as a discursive formation. By examining specific structures, processes and practices, the chapters of this book address some of the conceptual issues in the formation of a field of investigation. As an introductory text, at best, it hopes to delineate some of the basic and broad outlines of the field and is therefore far from being exhaustive, let alone complete. The chapters of the book, which move from a preliminary conceptualization of an East Asian Pop Culture to the examination of some of the processes within it, to its current manifestation in regional cultural politics, are outlined below through a short history of the development, in the last two decades (1990–2010), of a loosely integrated field of research.

By the mid-1990s, in East Asia—made up of the People's Republic of China (henceforth China), Taiwan, Japan, South Korea (henceforth Korea), Hong Kong, and Singapore, on account of its seventy-five percent ethnic Chinese population— free-to-air cable and satellite television screens and computer screens with Internet streaming and the capacity to download were awash with Japanese television dramas. Japanese "trendy" dramas featured beautiful men and women who were young professionals, adorned in high fashion clothes, dining in upscale restaurants, living on their own in well-appointed apartments in the city (Iwabuchi 2004). By the beginning of the new millennium, Japanese television dramas began to face competition from Korean television dramas with the same formulae for romance but with main characters from a younger generation who remained entangled in familial relations, thus inserting an additional layer of drama—that between parents and grown children—and thereby mixing the romance and family-drama genres. Alongside the introduction of television dramas was also the influx of Japanese and Korean pop music and films (see Chapter 1). However, the conventional popularity of foreign-language pop music in any consumption location has always been limited to a smaller population of dedicated fans, largely because the majority of the potential audience do not possess the requisite language skills to appreciate the lyrics of the songs; this was also the case for Korean and Japanese pop music in East Asia. Films, on the other hand, are aimed at international markets of which the regional market is a significant segment; however, the number of Korean and Japanese films reaching the international market remains limited.[1] Ultimately, it is television dramas that have the greatest presence and impact on the regional cultural geography.

Each influx of dramas created media excitement, generating new transnational audiences in the region and, simultaneously, political anxieties in the importing locations regarding the "invasion" of foreign cultures. By the end of the first decade of the new millennium, however, the regional presence of Japanese and Korean television dramas had become routine in daily television programming and, therefore, a regular component of the daily viewing diet of the regional audience; surfing television channels in any major city in East Asia will bear this out. This is most observable in a place like Singapore which, because of its small domestic market, is essentially an importing and audience reception location.

The timing of the inflows of Japanese and Korean television dramas into the rest of East Asia was not accidental. First, it was partly a consequence of the radical changes in telecommunication technologies that enabled the rapid and massive expansion of television stations and changed the prevailing modes of transmission and reception from cable to satellite stations and to Internet downloads on computer screens. Second, by the late 1980s, the authoritarian regimes in the region, including China, began to liberalize their media industries, which resulted in the rapid development of television stations, legal and illegal, and the massive expansion of airtime that needed to be filled quickly and inexpensively. Imported serial television dramas were one of the most convenient vehicles to fill a substantial amount of airtime. The first wave of television dramas to cross national borders were Japanese dramas brought in physically in DVD form, without any consideration for copyright laws, to be aired on illegal cable television stations in Taiwan, in the mid-1980s. Subsequently, Korean dramas were legally bought by new stations in Hong Kong and Singapore—STAR TV and Channel U respectively—as alternative entertainment to compete with the already entrenched local stations which produced local dramas for the domestic media market.

To date, it has been overwhelmingly Korean and Japanese dramas that enter Taiwan, Hong Kong, Singapore, and urban China, that is, locations where ethnic Chinese make up the overwhelming majority of the population. There is very little flow in the reverse direction. This unequal condition is largely market-driven. Television drama that is dubbed and/or subtitled into a Chinese language in one location—primarily dubbed in Cantonese or Mandarin, and subtitled in simplified or complex script—can be re-exported to the other locations with a predominant ethnic Chinese population with no additional production costs. The massive ethnic Chinese market in East Asia—in China, Taiwan, Hong Kong, and Singapore—makes dubbing and subtitling a financially-viable undertaking. In contrast the much, much smaller Korean and Japanese markets make the dubbing and translation of Chinese languages programs unprofitable.

In addition to the size of markets, the entry and circulation of Japanese and Korean pop culture into locations with dominant ethnic Chinese populations have been facilitated by a historically well-established commercial structure through which Chinese-language pop culture has been produced, distributed, circulated, and consumed for close to a century. Since the 1920s, there has been an uninterrupted flow and circulation of Chinese-language pop music and films and, after the 1960s, television programs as well. Political and social instabilities in China since the turn of the twentieth century, when the decaying Qing dynasty faced military invasion from Western powers and imperial Japan, meant that film production progressively moved to Hong Kong. By the 1950s, with the consolidation of communism in China, Hong Kong emerged as the center for Mandarin and Cantonese film production. There was also a separate and short-lived development of a small production of Hokkien films, financed by overseas Chinese capital from the Philippines (Taylor 2008). The films were distributed throughout Southeast Asia which, with the closing of China's borders, emerged as the major market. Significantly, films from communist China continued to be imported to Singapore and Malaysia until the late 1950s, when these British colonial territories gained political independence. The new nations, abiding by the politics of the Cold War, banned films from all communist territories, including China.

During the 1950s and 1960s, the production of Chinese-language pop music and the making of Chinese-language singers were more diffused, and included Malaysian and Singaporean artists. However, by the 1970s, production had begun to concentrate in Hong Kong. In the 1980s, Hong Kong developed a new wave in Cantonese pop music, popularly known as Cantopop, which dominated the Chinese-language pop music scene (Erni 2007) for more than a decade. However, the economic liberalization of China from 1978 onwards precipitated a radical shift in the pop music market. The huge China market opened up opportunities for Mandarin pop music, such that by the end of the 1980s, even major Cantopop singers were recording Mandarin songs, and Taipei emerged as the center for Mandarin pop. The domination of Hong Kong and Taiwan in Chinese-language pop culture is reflected in the common use of the term *Gangtai* (港台) entertainment (Liew 2010; Moskowitz 2010) to refer to contemporary Chinese pop culture; a literal translation of Kong and Tai to signify Mandarin pop music from Hong Kong and Taiwan.[2] In spite of the shifting center, the overall structure and the paths of production, distribution, circulation, and consumption of Chinese-language pop culture remain quite stable and can be substantively and discursively constituted as Pop Culture China (see Chapter 2); a decentered, multilingual, multi-nodal, relatively well-integrated cultural economy that operates under the presumed "sameness" of a "common" Chinese cultural heritage (Tay 2009). Within this decentered but relatively integrated structure, China and Singapore remain largely locations of reception/consumption. In the case of China, at the end of the first decade of the twenty-first century, the commercial pop culture industry is still in its infancy; however, with its massive consumer market and production capacity, the media industry in China has already begun to compete with Taiwan and Hong Kong as centers of production of Chinese-language pop culture.[3] On the other hand, conditions in Singapore—specifically its multiracial population, use of English as the de facto lingua franca and relatively small ethnic Chinese population (approximately three million)[4]—pose insurmountable obstacles to the ability of its media and entertainment industries to compete in the regional market, condemning its artists to sojourn in the other centers of production and leaving Singapore to be largely a location of reception and consumption of imported media products, not only from East Asia but also South Asia and, of course, the United States (see Chapter 4).[5]

The multinational media enterprise, Shaw Brothers, illustrates the structure of Pop Culture China very clearly as it is central to the structure itself. Established as a film production company in Shanghai in the early 1920s, Shaw Brothers quickly moved its financial headquarters to Singapore by mid-decade, and produced largely Cantonese films in Hong Kong throughout the 1930s. From Singapore, the company fanned out to cities in Southeast Asia through the construction and acquisition of a network of movie houses and entertainment centers, which would exhibit its Hong Kong-produced films. After the disruptions of the Second World War, it rebuilt quickly in the 1950s and, by the 1960s, Mandarin had emerged as the primary language of its film production. By then, the centrality of Shaw Brothers in the structure of Pop Culture China was fully established: "it developed into what can be called a trans-Asia empire that included theme parks; dance halls; film studios of Chinese and Malay languages; a massive distribution network importing films from Hong Kong, India, Europe and the United States; and a circuit of more than 130 theaters throughout Southeast Asia" (Fu 2008: 3). As the nature of the media industry changed, Shaw Brothers abandoned filmmaking in the 1970s, and reduced its movie business to exhibition only. It turned to television production exclusively, establishing TVB; now one of the two established free-to-air stations in Hong Kong.

Culturally the multilingual character of Pop Culture China poses interesting questions for the transnational reception of Chinese-language pop culture. First, a media product from one of its constitutive locations with dialogue in the local language is often verbally incomprehensible to the audience in another constitutive location who speak a different language or "dialect." The dialogue would therefore have to be subtitled in standardized written script for those who can read, which is not everyone, across the entire Pop Culture China. Second, the same Chinese language may also have a different political, social and cultural status in different locations within Pop Culture China; for example, Cantonese, which is the lingua franca in Hong Kong, is a minority language in Singapore and almost completely absent in Taiwan. Meanwhile the Minnan (闽南语) or Fujian (福建话, also known as Hokkien) language has been appropriated by Taiwan independence supporters as the Taiwanese language (台语). The majority of ethnic Chinese in Singapore used to be Hokkien speakers but now the same language marks, and socially marginalizes, its speakers as without much, if any, formal education. Such complexities of the political, social, and cultural status of different Chinese languages in different locations unavoidably lead to different readings and receptions of the same films, drama narratives, and song lyrics. These differences are not, strictly speaking, the consequence of misunderstandings or any communicative failures; they are simply different local readings (see Chapter 3).

Without the massive and well-established Pop Culture China market and its audience that receives the Japanese and Korean pop cultures via different Chinese languages, flows and exchanges between Japan, Korea and other particular East Asian locations would be merely bilateral rather than regional. The nation-border crossings of Japanese and Korean pop culture into the rest of East Asia may thus be said to be their integration into the established structure of Pop Culture China, and together they constitute a larger entity of East Asian Pop Culture as a loosely integrated regional cultural economy. Within this general structure, the flows, circulation and consumption of pop culture products, that is, the processes that operate and mobilize the structure across national and cultural boundaries, raise many significant issues that warrant examination. Particularly, given the radically unequal flows and circulation, the impact of these processes is most pronounced, and thus most readily observable, in the different locations of Pop Culture China; unsurprisingly, most empirical analyses of consumption practices have been conducted by researchers within Pop Culture China locations.

On the consumption front, given that Korean and Japanese television programs are dubbed and subtitled in a Chinese language before being circulated through and received in Pop Culture China, the most immediate question that arises is: how do dubbing and subtitling impact the transnational audience's identification with or distancing from the actions and narratives on screen, during the reception process (see Chapter 5)? Beyond the individual audience are issues of the formation of transnational audience communities, such as conventional fan clubs and, with new communication technologies, online Internet communities which bypass the profits of producers and the censorship of the state. There is the question of the possibility, or likelihood, of the engendering of a pan-East Asian identity among regional transnational audiences. Finally, there are issues of cultural politics between the local audience of imported pop culture and those who view such importation as "cultural invasion" and "cultural imperialism," often implicitly or explicitly involving local state agencies (see Chapter 6).

On the production front, East Asian Pop Culture engenders the possibility of co-production, and generates opportunities for border-crossing employment of media professionals, including artists. The mixing of actors and actresses drawn from across the region—as in films in which Korean and Hong Kong actors and actresses co-star and the inclusion of ethnic Chinese singers in popular Korean boy-bands—to create pan-East Asian screen-and sound-products enables producers to tap an expanding market. Parenthetically, until now a successful formula for a pan-East Asian film or television drama seems to have eluded the regional media industries.

In terms of distribution, producers of East Asian Pop Culture ignore the massive China market at their own peril. For example, wary of the uncontrolled media piracy industry in China, Japanese producers have been reluctant to directly distribute their products there (Pang 2009). Nevertheless, Japanese pop culture, particularly animation and television dramas are well distributed and watched in China as they are readily available on pirated DVDs and/or the Internet. The result is a very significant loss of profit for the Japanese production companies without, however, diminishing the popularity of Japanese pop culture in China. In contrast, Hong Kong television and film producers were quick to tap into the southern China market almost immediately after, if not before, the handover of the island to China in 1997 (Fung and Ma 2002). After a brief period of dependency on Taiwan as a commercial intermediary, the state-owned but commercialized television companies in China began to import Korean dramas directly.

Withdrawal of state subsidies has forced the state-owned media enterprises in China to compete in the market. This has resulted in the rapid expansion of cable, satellite and relay television stations at the city and provincial levels, generating a greatly expanded, aggregated quantum of airtime that needs to be filled. Meanwhile, as a condition of joining the World Trade Organization (WTO) in 2002, China was required to open its domestic media industries to foreign competition. Importation of foreign television programs satisfied both of these conditions. By the end of the 2000s, China had surpassed Taiwan and Japan to become the biggest regional importer of Korean television dramas. However, it continues to regulate the flow of foreign imports through import quotas and the restriction of screening-time schedules on domestic stations. To bypass these restrictions, successful Korean companies, as well as other foreign producers, have begun to work with Chinese partners to co-produce Korean television dramas that can be framed as "local" Chinese products for the Chinese market; they subsequently export the China-made Korean dramas back to the Korean market (Lee D.H. 2008). These co-production arrangements have greatly benefited nascent Chinese companies, by improving both the quantity and quality of local products.

The dense traffic of pop culture products across East Asia has inevitably caught the attention of national governments in the region. Indeed, in the case of Korea, the government has elevated the economic status of pop culture to that of an export industry, assigning designated state agencies to coordinate the export effort. Significantly, the attention paid by governments in the region to pop culture extends beyond economic interests to interests in "cultural influence" and "cultural diplomacy." The idea that pop culture can be a resource for diplomacy was initially developed by American political scientist Joseph Nye. Drawing on the example of the global export of American consumerism, including Hollywood films and rock and roll music, Nye (2004) suggests that pop culture export is a vehicle through which the rest of the world comes to know and be attracted to the US. For this reason, he includes pop culture in a collection of social institutions, such as education and political ideology, that he considers to be effective instruments of a US "soft power," namely, the "ability" of pop culture to attract and influence its international audience to accept American views without coercion.

Evoking the concept of soft power, the Korean, Japanese, and Chinese governments have begun to talk publicly about their respective pop cultural exports as sources of soft power, provoking a regional soft power "competition." Their positions on this competition are reflective of their relative power in the region. The Koreans, with lingering memories of fifty years of Japanese colonization, think of an alliance with China to counter Japan, especially since its pop culture export to Japan has met with the jingoism and xenophobia of Japanese nationalists. The Japanese, under former prime minister Taro Aso, sought to place Japan at the center of manga and animation culture by establishing an International Manga Award for non-Japanese manga artists; the competition is judged by a panel of Japanese manga artists. Meanwhile, state officials in China, who see Chinese culture as the "root" culture of East Asia, refer to the Confucian tradition and set for themselves the "duty," if not the "right," to define what are "proper" East Asian cultural practices. In this last stance, the Chinese officials and public had been provoked by what they see as "cultural theft" by the Koreans. Two of the more controversial instances are illustrative. First, Korea has successfully petitioned UNESCO to recognize the rice dumpling festival, part of the Chinese *Duanwu* Festival (端午节), as Korean immaterial culture,[6] and second, the television drama *Jewel in the Palace* (大长今 2003) had, in the eyes of Chinese netizens, "audaciously" implied that acupuncture, a Chinese traditional medical practice, was Korea's own.[7] In this soft power competition, China has a trump card: again, its massive audience/consumer market. The desire to profit from this market has driven regional producers to co-produce in China. Unavoidably, this enables the state-owned partners in China to dictate to varying degrees the content of the final product, leaving foreign producers and their respective governments holding the short end of the ideological stick (see Chapter 7).

This brief narrative of the emergence and consolidation of the regionalization of media industries and pop culture in East Asia is but one illustrative instance of similar processes taking place at varying rates in different Asian regions. Broadly speaking, three other instances of regionalization deserve mention: in mainland Southeast Asia, that is, in Cambodia, Myanmar (also known as Burma), Laos and Thailand, Thai pop culture, including television dramas, has a dominant role regionally; in the Malay-speaking communities of island Southeast Asia, consisting of Singapore, Malaysia, Indonesia, the southern Philippines, and perhaps the Malay-Muslim provinces of southern Thailand, a Malay-language pop culture, with Indonesia being the major producer of television dramas, can be identified; and in South Asia, Indian pop culture dominates but, given that importation is severely regulated if not banned, local producers freely imitate the style of Indian pop culture, most noticeably the Bollywood movie format. Each of these instances has its particularities that deserve to be analyzed in their own right. For example, Burmese refugee entrepreneurs are key players and refugee camps an important conduit for the circulation of Thai-language television dramas (Jirattikorn 2008); Malay-language pop culture flows from an economically less developed Indonesia to a more prosperous Malaysia and Singapore;[8] while within India itself, regional film industries compete unyieldingly with Hindi-language Bollywood (Rajadhyaksha 2003; Raghavendra 2009). In view of these instances of regionalization, this introduction to East Asian Pop Culture should be read as a series of illustrations of some of the issues that should be examined not only within each region, but comparatively across regions in an inter-Asia framework.

# 1

# East Asian Pop Culture
## Mapping the Contours

Conventionally, mass entertainment—television, film, and pop music—is referred to as "popular culture." However, following Stuart Hall's (1994) proposition, the term "popular culture" should be reserved for the larger cultural sphere that encompasses the everyday life of the masses in contradiction to and contestation with elite culture, while "pop culture" should be used to refer to commercially-produced, profit-driven, media-based mass entertainment; so conceived, pop culture is but one segment of popular culture. American pop music, movies, and television programs loom large globally, penetrating all places where the local income level is high enough to enable the purchase of such products. The countries of East Asia which, with the exception of China, are all high-income countries in which there is no doubt that Hollywood movies are pervasive and predominant. Exaggerated by the visual ubiquity of advertisements for Hollywood films, which can be read as a generalized index of the domination of American pop culture, one prominent strand of public debate in East Asia concerns the impact of the liberal attitude—the cultural, moral, and political dimensions all rolled into one—portrayed in American pop culture. American liberalism is seen by some as questioning the conservatism of Asians and therefore, is to be encouraged, while others cast it as culturally and morally "corrosive" of "wholesome" Asian values. Yet, other than Hollywood's dominance in films, in all of East Asia local television programs garner a greater audience and local pop music receives more radio play than do the American equivalents, even in Singapore, where the default lingua franca is English. Any television channel surfing of free-to-air stations in any East Asian city will bear this out. Preoccupation with American pop culture takes attention away from the dense pop culture traffic among every major urban center in East Asia—Hong Kong, Taipei, Singapore, Shanghai, Seoul, and Tokyo.

Pop culture from different centers flows and crosses porous national and cultural boundaries and is routinely distributed throughout the entire region. However, until the 1990s, traffic had been rather thin. Taking the case of Korea as an example, according to Shim (2005: 239–240), from 1971 to 1988 twenty-eight

Taiwanese, three Japanese, two Filipino, and one Indian film were screened in the cinemas. With reference to television "countries of the Asian region as a whole have a relatively low dependence on imported programming, and a relatively very low dependence on intra-regional program trade" (Waterman and Rogers 1994, quoted in Shim 2005: 240). The situation has changed radically since the early 1990s as the regional traffic of pop culture, especially television dramas, has intensified. Now, advertisements of pop culture products and events from East Asian centers are routine features in major newspapers and magazines in the region. The trials and tribulations of pop stars and celebrities make up part of the daily gossip of fans in the different locations. Pop culture reviewers often face barrages of complaints from fans of the stars—singers and actors of both the big and small screens—if they pen negative reviews of the fans' pop "idols."[1] Producers not only have the regional market in view but they also source for finance, production professionals and artists across East Asia. The thick and intensifying traffic of finance, production personnel, products, and consumers across regional, linguistic, and national boundaries lends substance to the concept of East Asian Pop Culture as a loosely-integrated network of regional media industries and related practices which exceed any framing that focuses on a particular location, as in the case of a national cinema or a particular auteur filmmaker.[2] One of the tasks at hand for Cultural Studies in Asia is to conceptualize the shape and contour of this expanding regional cultural phenomenon.

One notable pioneering academic analysis of this regional phenomenon is that of the penetration of Japanese pop culture in East and Southeast Asia by Iwabuchi, who was well aware that the regional production, circulation, and consumption of pop culture in East Asia was an "underdeveloped area in the study of cultural globalization" (2002b: 50). This work provides important insights into the industrial strategies that have been adopted by Japanese pop culture production companies in their attempts to penetrate the Asian regional market since the early 1990s. He concluded that, for the pop music industry, "Japanese ventures for cultivating pan-Asian pop idols have only been, at best, partially successful" (Iwabuchi 2002b: 107). Since the record company, Pony Canyon, "retreated from Asian markets in late 1997" (ibid.), even "partially successful" may be an optimistic conclusion. In contrast, Japanese television melodramas featuring young urban professionals were very popularly received regionally during the latter half of the 1990s. For example, in Taiwan, Iwabuchi (2002b) found that popular reception was based on a sense of coevalness between the Taiwanese audience and the Japanese represented on screen—Taiwanese people feel that they share a modern temporality with the Japanese. This coevalness is the dynamic vector in generating and sustaining a sense of "cultural proximity" for the Taiwanese audience with a drama-mediated representation of Japan/the Japanese (Iwabuchi 2002b: 122). In contrast, in examining the Japanese audience's reception of pop culture imported from elsewhere in East

Asia, he found that the Japanese audience's reception was based on a "refusal to accept that it [Japan] shares the same temporality as other Asian nations" (Iwabuchi 2002b: 159). Instead, reception was mediated by a sense of nostalgia for Japan's own past as seen in the present of other locations in Asia.[3] The analysis of these two empirical instances provides us with insights into differences among local audiences watching pop culture imported from elsewhere in East Asia. The popularity of Japanese urban dramas motivated Iwabuchi to organize possibly the first international conference on East Asian Pop Culture, "Feeling Asian Modernities: TV Drama Consumption in East/Southeast Asia" in 2001, the papers of which were subsequently published as *Feeling Asian Modernities: Transnational Consumption of Japanese TV Dramas* (Iwabuchi 2004). In late 2005, as the Korean Wave swept through the region, a workshop on transnational Korean and Japanese television dramas in East Asia was organized at the Asia Research Institute in Singapore, which resulted in the publication of *East Asian Pop Culture: Analyzing the Korean Wave* (Chua and Iwabuchi 2008). Bringing together empirical reception studies of Japanese and Korean television dramas, these two volumes provide some of necessary information for regional comparisons that are constitutive of East Asian Pop Culture substantively and as a field of research.

## Doing Pop Culture Studies in East Asia: A Conceptual and Methodological Note

As I have suggested elsewhere:

> The life of a consumer product is very short. It is meant to be so in order to keep the factory that produces it working, the workers employed, its consumers happy but not for long, and the economy moving. This brevity of existence is a constraint on critical analysis of any consumer object, singularly or in constellation as a trend or a lifestyle. The problem is that by the time the analyst figures out the critical angle for commentary, the object in question would have already been consumed and committed to the trash-heap. Consumed and rejected, or unsold and rejected, either way it is discarded... the brevity of life of a consumer object and of a consumer trend makes it unavoidable that all published materials on consumer products and trends are by definition "historical." (Chua, 2003: vii)

The same is true of pop culture, which is essentially a mass entertainment consumer product. Film, television programs, and pop music—the data one is working with—are often already off the screen long before any analysis is completed. Consequently, many of the readers of the analyses will not have seen the film or television program nor heard the music; that is, the readers are not familiar with the products which engaged the analyst. For these reasons, analytic interest should not be restricted to the content of the products themselves, although they necessarily constitute some of the empirical material for analysis. The larger analytic interest should be oriented towards the structures and modalities through which the products partake in the political, social, cultural, and economic material relations within the different locations where the products are produced, circulated, and consumed.

## Cultural Economy

The emergence of East Asian Pop Culture, where economic interest has been realized through the production of culture as commodity, may be said to be part of the trend in global capitalism, where "the continuing rise of cultural industries based on the mass commodification of culture had breathed new life into the economy, created all manner of new forms of enterprise, and played a major role in economic regeneration in many parts of the world" (Amin and Thrift 2004: xii). This continuing rise in the mass commodification of culture constitutes one of the foundations of the emergence of the "cultural economy" as a new field of academic research. Strangely, in spite of this, the mass entertainment industry has not been included as a matter of course in this emerging field.[4] This may be a consequence of academic disciplinary divisions and boundaries, where mass entertainment industries are considered to be part of the domain of "media studies."

Alan Warde suggests that "the origins of the idea of culturalization" in the economy emerge "from reflections on consumption and its relationship to production" (2002: 186). In a cultural economy, consumption is not focused on the commodity as material object, nor on the ways in which objects are used and discarded. What is consumed are meanings and symbolic values which are not used up but which continue to circulate in ever increasing and expanding circuits of communication. In this sense, all cultural consumption is also always a simultaneous process of communication. As an economy, the cultural economy can be disaggregated into four processes: production, distribution, circulation, and consumption. As culture, the same four processes constitute a complete cycle of communication. The conceptualization of a cultural economy as a discursive object of analysis may be said to imply, necessarily, that it is also a process of communication. However, in empirical case studies, emphasis remains largely placed on how workers/producers incorporate economic ideas into their daily productive activities and, in the process, generate meanings and symbolic values. There has been little analysis in the emerging literature of the cultural economy of the activities of the consumer/receiver in decoding meanings and symbolic values.[5] This side of the cultural exchange still requires active research and theorization.

Media culture as a communication system has a unique feature: the receiver has no mechanism of immediate and direct response to the sender of information.

This one-way communication has been likened, by Rajagopal (2001: 5), to a "gift" without any obligation to reciprocity, leaving the receiver to believe that the reception is "free." It also frees the receiver to interpret, generate, and inscribe meanings and symbolic values upon "what" is communicated. However, as the "audience," receivers might perceive themselves as merely "receiving" meanings and symbolic values that inhere—i.e., are "encoded" by the producer—in the pop culture they consume. As the encoding and interpretive processes are inextricably intertwined, "negotiation" is the appropriate concept for this process of generating meanings and symbolic values.[6] Obviously, potentially new and different meanings and symbolic values are generated with each new audience or set of consumers. Each circuit of consumption/reception thus potentially adds a layer to the circulation of meaning and symbolic values. The negotiated meanings and symbolic values may be influential, even transformative of the subjectivity of the audience, thus further generating new meanings and symbolic values. Beyond the initial turn of communication where the medium is determined by the producer/broadcaster, the process of communication and circulation in subsequent circuits may take a different form, through a different medium with a different message with different consequences.[7] Finally, of course, each cycle of cultural consumption potentially generates a new cycle of financial benefits for the producer; for example, communication of positive meanings and symbolic values in post-reception commentaries and reviews are fundamental to the financial return producers receive. As a one-way communication from producer/broadcaster to multiple audiences, it is paramount to understand the reception processes and work of the audience in generating meanings and symbolic values.

A cultural economy necessarily operates "against the background of various kinds of ordering frame, from the swathe of regulations that order the conduct of competition to the mundane ordering of every economic life through various crucial infrastructures such as roads, pipes and cables" (Amin and Thrift 2004: xiv). As mentioned in the introduction, two conditions have enabled the emergence of a regional East Asian Pop Culture. First is the radical transformation of communication technologies—cables, satellite, and the Internet—which constitute the necessary infrastructure that facilitates the flow, circulation, and exhibition of pop culture. Second is the liberalization of media industries in the hitherto control-minded regimes in the region. However, liberalization does not mean a completely open-door policy. The governments of the region continue to regulate the flow of pop culture across their respective geo-political boundaries. Each government has its policies that promote pop culture export, financially and institutionally, not only for obvious economic reasons but also for its own political interest in culturally influencing audiences in the importing locations. Concurrently, each tries to control the inflow of foreign pop culture for reasons ranging from protecting its own media industry to insulating the "national" culture from "contamination" and political security and stability. These two concurrent processes of transnational flow and local reception and/or resistance are the result of a central contradiction in the economy of transnational pop culture; while the flow of pop culture is spatial and borderless, the local economy, in both production and consumption, is historical and national; the two logics inevitably rub up against each other (Ching 2000). The nation-state thus continues to have continuing and abiding economic and political investments in regulating transnational pop culture flows.

Production, which includes financing and all the technical skills such as writing, acting, singing, choreographing, dancing, filming and recording can, of course, be organized and executed within a single geographic location. However, with contemporary technology and the globalized economy, each of the necessary constituent activities of production can be disaggregated and thus executed at different locations, which means any combination of a co-production arrangement is possible. In contrast, the consumption/reception process is always grounded in a specific location. However, as Rajagopal points out, mass media as "an ongoing stream of communication shared by others engenders a sense of intimacy across social boundaries" (2001: 5) and, one should add, across national/spatial boundaries. New communication technologies enable consumers to transcend their grounded location to reach out to others across time and space to engage with consumers elsewhere, generating transnational audience communities.

In spite of the temporal and spatial flexibilities in production and consumption, the nations in East Asia can nevertheless be ranked in relation to each other according to their individual strengths in production, distribution, circulation, and consumption practices in order to establish a structure of their relative competitive positions in the transnational regional media market. A nation's relative position on these axes is primarily dependent on the historical development of its media industry; the more technically-developed the industry, reflected in the quality of its products, the greater the tendency for production and export to dominate over import and consumption. The relative position is secondarily affected by the size of the domestic market. While a small domestic market may tend to position the nation as a location that primarily imports and consumes, such as Singapore, domestic market size may be overridden by the history and technical quality of the domestic media industry, i.e., a nation with a small domestic market but technically high quality products is likely to be a production and export location, as in the case of Hong Kong and its Chinese-language film industry.[8] Conversely, China, with its huge market, is still primarily a location of import and consumption due to the weak production quality of its still nascent media industry. The relative positions of the nations in a regional pop culture economy constitute a structure that channels the boundary-crossing flows. As both a node in this structure and a regulatory regime, the nation/national is conceptually central to the analysis of regional pop culture. This structure will be explored in this and the next two chapters. The rest of the book will be dedicated to the reception/consumption processes of the regional transnational audience that activates the structure.

## The Structure of East Asian Pop Culture

Briefly, the structural configuration of the relative national positions in East Asian Pop Culture is as follows: Japan has the most established television industry with the highest quality of production. It is thus essentially a production site that leads the way in many aspects of pop culture production for other regional producers. For example, in spite of a formal ban since the end of the Second World War, Japanese cultural products continued to flow into Korea through different channels and Korean television stations were happy to appropriate ideas and formats from Japanese programs for their own productions. Importing increased rapidly after 1989, when the ban was lifted (Han 2000). By the end of the 1990s, as Japanese pop culture waned regionally, South Korea stepped into the niche and began to export its pop culture into the region, creating what is called the "Korean Wave." The Japanese and Korean pop cultures, singularly or together, would not have engendered a regional phenomenon were it not for the presence of the ethnic Chinese[9] population as consumers. This ethnic Chinese population has a long history of sharing pop culture in various Chinese languages that is produced, distributed, and circulated through a very well-established structure which we can discursively designate as Pop Culture China. Structurally, Japanese and Korean pop culture may be said to be grafted onto the historically established core of Pop Culture China, to constitute a transnational regional East Asian Pop Culture.

To complete the picture of the structure of the larger unit, a brief sketch of Pop Culture China is necessary here, but it will be examined in greater detail in the next chapter. Briefly, within Pop Culture China, Hong Kong has had a central position in the production and distribution of Chinese-language films, television programs, and pop music. It has been a Chinese-language film production hub since the 1930s, rising to become the dominant center in the 1950s. By the late 1970s, film production had declined while television had progressively moved to center stage both domestically and regionally. Hong Kong Cantonese pop music also gained popularity throughout Pop Culture China in the 1980s; even Minnan/Hokkien-speaking Taiwanese who do not understand Cantonese were singing Cantopop in karaoke bars. In the same decade, under the repressive, authoritarian Kuomintang regime, emerged what is now called the Taiwan New Wave cinema, which used Mandarin and was dominated by a handful of auteur filmmakers, such as Hou Hsiao-Hsien (侯孝贤) and the late Edward Yang (杨德昌).[10] This lasted for about a decade. During the Cold War period, communist China was largely excluded from the Chinese-language pop culture sphere. With the marketization of its economy and the commercialization of its media industry, China opened its doors to pop culture from the region. One of the greatest beneficiaries of this has been the Taiwan pop music industry. Ethnic Chinese musicians flowed into Taipei to record pop music in Mandarin to access the massive China market; Taipei emerged as the center for Mandarin pop music production and distribution and remains so today. Throughout this history, Singapore has always been predominantly a location of import and reception/consumption of pop culture from elsewhere in Pop Culture China, although most of the film producers in Hong Kong in the 1950s and 1960s were financed from Singapore, including the Shaw Brothers.

Structurally, the regional transnational flows of pop culture remain lopsided, with Japanese and Korean material flowing into Pop Culture China and, hitherto, very little flowing in the opposite direction. This is because the size of the total regional ethnic Chinese market makes dubbing and subtitling financially viable while the relatively small Japanese and Korean domestic markets would not be able to support the same processes on a routine basis. At best, occasional film or television is dubbed or subtitled. With their relatively well-established media industries, Hong Kong and Taiwan have emerged as locations for the dubbing and subtitling of Japanese and Korean television dramas for broadcasting at home and redistributing throughout Pop Culture China. Currently, the media industries in Singapore and mainland China remain relatively underdeveloped. Singapore, because of its small multiracial population, is unlikely to become a significant regional export player and will remain essentially an import and consumption location, as this is more cost-effective than self-production.[11] In contrast, China, with its huge domestic audience to support a competitive commercialized media industry, is likely to emerge as a major exporter of pop culture in the near future; evidence is already observable. Until then, with Taiwan and Hong Kong as intermediaries, Japanese and Korean pop culture is incorporated and integrated into the larger East Asian Pop Culture sphere.

## Production and Distribution

### Japan and Korea

According to Iwabuchi, "Japan is the only country, apart from the United States, where more than 95 per cent of TV programmes are produced domestically" (1994: 229). The highly developed television sector and the media industry's ability to finance expensive productions and stage expensive concerts and promotions at home have positioned the Japanese pop culture industry almost exclusively as an exporter. This has given rise to a ubiquitous impression that there is a "Japanization" of pop culture, from pop music to street fashion, throughout East Asia, in spite of the tentative nature of the Japanese pop culture industries when it comes to expanding into the rest of Asia (Iwabuchi 2002b: 85–120; Pang 2009:

122). This perceived ubiquity is clearly overdrawn when it comes to pop music and commercial films. Japanese commercial films have been all but non-existent in the region since at least the 1980s.

Pop music has a greater presence; however, its regional distribution and circulation, an index of popularity, is severely obstructed by the language barrier. Pop music cannot be dubbed. It can at best be replicated by completely substituting the original lyrics with the second language, a process commonly undertaken, for example, by Chinese singers with Western pop music. Japanese lyrics are nothing short of a string of "nonsense" sounds, incomprehensible and difficult to sing along with for an ethnic Chinese speaker without the requisite Japanese language competence. The regional sales figures of Japanese pop music are illustrative. Data from 2002 show that Hong Kong, Taiwan, Singapore, and China—in descending order of consumption—accounted for sixty-nine percent and South Korea for fourteen percent of the Japanese export; the eighty-three percent in total providing empirical evidence of an East Asian Pop Culture. However in Hong Kong, which accounts for up to thirty-seven percent of the total value of Japanese music exports to East and Southeast Asia, the sales figure was only eight percent of the annual total music record sales, and in Singapore Japanese music accounted for only three percent of the total music record sales (Otmazgin 2008a: 264–265). Obviously, in Pop Culture China, Chinese pop music still dominates. Attempts by Japanese pop musicians to deepen their popularity and increase their market shares in Pop Culture China markets would require them to sing in English, in duet with a Chinese singer, or more radically, to sing in Mandarin. They would also be advised to develop complex dance routines in live performances. Although there are undoubtedly pockets of avid fans of Japanese pop music, its numbers pale against the audience for Japanese television dramas regionally. A survey of Japanese pop culture (J-pop) among Thai youth demonstrates this: "28.3 percent of the students [surveyed] say they like J-Pop but 58.6 percent say they did not. Compared to manga and animation, these numbers show that J-Pop is not very popular among Thai students and has merely become a subculture" (Toyoshima 2008: 267).

The high quality of Japanese television is captured, in a rather essentialist manner, by an American commentator:

> The most positive aspect of the primacy of form and the perfection of role is the creation of excellent images. The Japanese concern with the visual, in combination with their advanced technology, ensures that Japanese television is often very pleasing to the eye. Sets are technically well designed and the photography is excellent . . . If television is used as a means of relaxation and escape, as opposed to education and enlightenment, it may be very enjoyable to lose oneself among the images without having to bother with the search for ideas. (Stronach 1989: 155)

Illustrative examples are Japanese television urban dramas, known as "trendy dramas" for obvious reasons. The storylines are generally about romance among young urban professionals. The visual pleasure comes largely from the fact that, on screen, the characters, major and minor, are very well dressed in designer clothes, live in cozy apartments, eat in expensive—usually Western—restaurants in the entertainment districts of the city and, above all, all the actors and actresses are beautiful men and women. According to the producer of the first successful drama, *Tokyo Love Story* (东京爱情故事 1991), when he was given the task as a producer, at age twenty-eight, Japanese television was filled with programs for middle-aged individuals and, understandably, he did not watch any of them. He asked himself, and people like him, what he/they would like to watch on television and came up with a simple list: beautiful people, beautiful clothes, good food, and good entertainment; the plot is secondary (Tōru 2004). Although the production cost per episode was phenomenally expensive, with about fifty percent going to pay the beautiful cast, in the euphoric days of the bubble economy, the local Japanese market was able to support the cost. No consideration was given to potential export markets. However, their popularity across East Asia, during the decade of the 1990s, was reflected not only in media attention but also in the academic analysis across the region they attracted (Iwabuchi 2004).[12] This was possibly a surprise to the Japanese producers and came as surplus profit when it happened.

Within the television drama genre, the quality of Japanese productions clearly sets the industry standard for producers elsewhere in East Asia. Perhaps the very high standard of production, and thus the high expectations of the Japanese audience, has contributed to the relative absence of imported pop culture products from elsewhere in East Asia into Japan. Whatever the reason, this impermeability to East Asian imports is not simply a question of the need for dubbing or translation because Japanese television stations regularly dub American programs. As mentioned above, Iwabuchi has argued that the absence of imports is ideological, namely, "Japan's refusal to accept that it shares the same temporality as other Asian nations" (Iwabuchi 2002b: 159).[13] Nevertheless, some cracks in the insularity appeared after the economic bubble burst. Japanese pop singers have partnered with ethnic Chinese singers in efforts to expand their market reach into the huge ethnic Chinese audience; for example, the collaboration between Mai Kuraki and Singapore/Taiwan singer Stefanie Sun Yanzi (孙燕姿), who sang a duet in English. In television, Korean dramas began to make inroads into the Japanese market and broke onto the small screen with the phenomenal success of *Winter Sonata* (*Gyeoul yeonga* 冬季恋歌) in 2003 (Mōri 2008).[14] Japan soon became one of the biggest regional importers of Korean television dramas, second only to China, where Korean dramas have displaced Taiwanese dramas as the primary import (Keane 2008: 151).

Exports of Japanese "trendy drama" began to wane by the late 1990s. The media space they occupied in Hong Kong, Taiwan, and Singapore was almost seamlessly refilled with Korean imports. As mentioned earlier, the Korean pop culture industry is most influenced by the standards of Japanese production. In spite of the formal ban on Japanese pop culture, even the government-owned Korean Broadcasting Station was guilty of illegal importing Japanese products (Han 2000: 14–15). In the words of one Korean cultural commentator: "We firmly lock and bar front doors but leave our back doors wide open. With our left hands we indignantly slap away any offers but we are busy snatching at any opportunities with our right. This has been our society's attitude toward popular Japanese culture during the last 30 years" (Do Jung Il quoted in Kim 2002: 1).[15] Thus, Japanese pop culture has been "copied," "partially integrated," "plagiarized," "mixed," and "reproduced" in Korean productions (Shim 2005: 247). Little wonder that Korean fans of Japanese pop music suggest, "When we listen to Korean songs it is easy to recognize similar or same parts from Japanese songs" (quoted in Kim 2002: 4). Kim further concludes that "in the case of TV animations and comics, most [Korean products] are adaptations of Japanese products so Japanese culture in Korea has already set its roots deep into the emotional structure of Koreans" (Kim 2002: 4). Similar observation of adaptation from Japanese products is made about Korean television dramas by Lee Dong-Hoo (2004). The formal ban was lifted in October 1998, with the Joint Declaration of the New 21st Century Korea–Japan Partnership. In 2002, the first Japanese and South Korean co-produced television drama, *Friends*—featuring a relationship between a Korean man and a Japanese woman—was broadcast in both nations simultaneously, marking both a pop culture and a "political" event in Korean–Japanese relations (Mōri 2008: 129).

Korean dramas quickly replaced Japanese "trendy dramas" in Hong Kong, Taiwan, Singapore, and China by the early 2000s, creating what is called the "Korean Wave." Shim argues that the relative ease of entry of Korean pop culture into the region was "facilitated" by the earlier popularity of Japanese pop culture "because of their similar aesthetic and cultural styles to the eyes of [regional] audience" (2005: 248). The expansion of Korean pop culture exports was the consequence of the Korean government's explicit policies in promoting pop culture as an export industry; policies supposedly developed after the government discovered that the successful Hollywood film, *Jurassic Park* (1993), "generated, with all its spin-off sales, foreign sales worth 1.5 million Hyundai cars," more than two years' worth of Hyundai's car exports (Shim 2002: 340). Indicative of the rapid expansion of Korean pop culture export, Korea's Ministry of Culture, Sports, and Tourism reported that Korean culture exports increased from US$12.7 million in 1999 to US$102 million in 2005 (Shim 2010: 124), and by 2007, it rose to an approximate US$1.5 billion, with Korean dramas constituting the largest proportion of export sales.[16]

This expansion was also partly a consequence of the changing conditions in the media industry in other parts of the region. Singapore is illustrative of this. In 2001, the local media monopoly that publishes all the major newspapers in all four official languages of the city-state—English, Mandarin, Malay, and Tamil, a south Indian language—ventured into commercial television under a new company called MediaWorks with two free-to-air stations, one in English (Channel I) and the other in Mandarin (Channel U). The English channel was an abject failure and the studio shut down within less than two years of its establishment. In contrast, Channel U was able to carve out a significant portion of the national audience from the already well-established Mandarin station, Channel 8, operated by the state-owned MediaCorp. It succeeded with a daily schedule that broadcast a combination of Korean dramas and local variety shows which use a format from Taiwan, which in turn is very similar to that used in Japan—high energy, rapid-fire banter from the team of program hosts, whose entire focus is on making fun of, or embarrassing, whoever appears as a guest on the show. The popularity of the Korean dramas pushed the established and dominant Channel 8 to import them as well, so that by late 2003, there was at least one Korean drama series on one Singaporean television station every night. The mutually-cannibalizing bidding war between 'the two stations for the same Korean dramas eventually led to a merger that saw MediaWorks integrated into MediaCorp.

One of the most remarkable regional successes of Korean television drama was the historical, costume serial *Jewel in the Palace* (*Dae Jang Geum* 2003). As a rule, the exported Korean dramas, like the Japanese television dramas before them, are contemporary, urban, and romantic. A small number of historical dramas were also exported to Taiwan and "managed to attract a small following due for the most part to the nostalgic emotions evoked in the Taiwanese viewers thinking that the Korean royal life portrayed in the drama [*Jang Huibin*, 1981] was a remnant of the lost 'traditions' of the Chinese culture" (Kim 2005: 188).[17] In the case of *Jewel*, the same sentiment might have been one of the elements that contributed to its success among the regional ethnic Chinese audience. In any case, "history"—the cultural and political connection between the Korean Choson dynasty period and the Chinese Ming dynasty—was merely a foil for a tale of court intrigue, with romance as a supporting theme. *Jewel* was first exported to Taiwan in 2004, dubbed and broadcast in Mandarin, and became the top drama program of the year. In 2005, it was dubbed into Cantonese and screened in Hong Kong on TVB, again to record-breaking ratings. The Hong Kong station made additional efforts to "indigenize" the Korean drama by providing brief explanations of the narrative before each episode and giving the Chinese language equivalent of the ingredients in culinary dishes and medical prescriptions that played a central role in the narrative. In 2005, the Taiwan dubbed and subtitled Mandarin version was re-exported to the Hunan Satellite TV Station in China and was broadcast nationally. Finally, it was also repeatedly broadcast in Singapore on both cable and free-to-air stations, completing the Pop Culture China circuit.

Korean movies made their debut in East Asia, as elsewhere, through the Hollywood-style blockbuster *Shiri* (1999), followed by *Joint Security Area* (*Gongdong Gyeongbi Guyeok* 2000). Both films translated the Cold War tension of North–South Korea into personalized relations. *Shiri* is a romance between secret agents from both sides of the divide, a female agent from the North being involved with a male counterpart from the South. *Joint Security Area* thematizes "illicit" friendship and camaraderie between North and South Korean soldiers who police the demilitarized zones. The Korean War theme was again successfully reprised in the box office hit *The Brotherhood of War* (*Taegukgi* 2004). A second category of Korean films that were popular in their time is what may be labeled "gangster comedies," such as *My Wife is a Gangster* (*Jopog Manura* 2001), in which criminals are humanized by their ineptness or goofiness in other aspects of their daily lives, which absolves them of all accusations, guilt, and punishment. This presence of Korean films has not been sustained; by the end of the decade only an occasional film would make it into the regional market. However, the successes in the first decade of the twenty-first century had spurred on the Korean film industry to actively promote, with the support of the government, a pan-Asian film industry as a strategy, of course, to promote Korean cinema itself. Of these efforts, one of the most important is the Pusan International Film Festival, launched in 1997. Its Pusan Asian Cinema Fund, among other festival awards, offers financial support for Asian filmmakers in the areas of script development, post-production, and documentary-making. Each year several awards are given in each category. Further, the Korean film industry took the initiative to establish the Asian Film Commission Network in 2004, with eighteen national commissions serving as members; a move that was welcomed by filmmakers in the region who see the future of filmmaking in East Asia in co-productions (Shim 2005: 250), a topic to be discussed later in this chapter.

## Hong Kong and Taiwan

In terms of production and export capacity, Hong Kong and Taiwan occupy dominant positions in the pan-ethnic Chinese segment of East Asian Pop Culture, as reflected in the ethnic Chinese entertainment industry being referred to as the *Gangtai* entertainment industry. During the height of the Cold War years, between the 1950s and 1970s, Hong Kong films and pop music had a constant presence in the Southeast Asian ethnic Chinese diaspora, particularly in Singapore and Malaysia. Hong Kong had been the major production site of Chinese movies from the 1950s to the late 1980s. The production rate slowed down considerably in the 1990s and by early 2000 there were no major production studios in Hong Kong and films were produced by independent filmmakers on low budgets (Teo 2008;

Curtin 2007: 68–84). Nevertheless, it remains the major production location for Chinese movies, increasingly in Mandarin, and its historical place as the premier Asian film production location continues to be widely acknowledged: "Hong Kong cinema is now a benchmark of achievement, a site of inspiration and cross-cultural borrowing, a model for emulation and a target of rivalry" (Morris 2005: 2).[18]

In contrast, Hong Kong's production of television drama programs has grown as a result of the major film producer, Shaw Brothers, switching to the small screen. According to Curtin (2003: 216–217), this was a very strategic move made by Shaw Brothers when it sensed that Hong Kong movies were on the decline because they were not addressing the concerns of emerging generations of locally-born citizens who were not interested in either the history or politics of mainland China or of the overseas Chinese diaspora. Television dramas that addressed local issues became hugely popular and have been "credited with sparking the revival of the commercial Chinese film industry and with fostering the growth of the Cantonese pop (Cantopop) music industry" (Curtin 2003: 217). The television dramas found a ready audience in Singapore; Chow Yun Fat (周润发) was first introduced to Singaporeans in the late 1970s on the television screen in the hugely popular drama, *Man in the Net* (网中人 1979).

In the 1980s, Cantopop ruled the airwaves of Chinese-language radio stations throughout the region; the Four Heavenly Kings (四大天王) of Jacky Cheung (张学友), Andy Lau (刘德华), Leon Lai (黎明), and Aaron Kwok (郭富城) were all the rage not only as singers but also as movie stars. However, Cantopop waned in the 1980s (Chu 2007). With the opening up of the huge China market and the impending and inevitable "incorporation" of Hong Kong as a Special Administrative Region of the People's Republic of China, all major Hong Kong pop music performers switched over to singing in Mandarin to catch the huge mainland market. For example, the Beijing native Faye Wong (王菲) had to sing in Cantonese early in her career in Hong Kong and reverted to singing in Mandarin with great success. This switch in language has enabled Taipei to emerge as a major recording location for Mandarin pop. On the other hand, Hong Kong production companies have been quick to capitalize on the huge market by making television series that are directed specifically at the mainland audience, and Hong Kong film-makers have increased the number of joint-productions they work on with China media companies (Ma 2006).

Taiwan had exported, in the 1980s, "traditional" family-themed costume television dramas about intrigue in huge extended families dictated by the Confucian principle of filial piety, often with the much maligned and oppressed daughter(s)-in-law eventually triumphing when her moral righteousness survives her long suffering.[19] However, since the success of the young adult romance drama *Meteor Garden* (流星花园), in 2000, it has also begun to export contemporary dramas. *Meteor Garden* was a trans-medium production by a Taiwanese producer re-scripting a Japanese *manga* story into a television drama. The drama, aimed at college students, introduced four completely unknown handsome young men of approximately the same height, collectively known as F4, to play the main characters. The drama was an instant success throughout East Asia. It was screened in Hong Kong and Singapore and subsequently in Korea in 2002. In China it was banned but the drama was watched on DVD.[20] Television success smoothed the way for F4's entry into pop music, transforming them into the hottest boy-band in the region, although their singing skills were noticeably limited. Every public appearance throughout the region drew huge crowds of screaming fans; for example, their appearance in a Shanghai shopping center had to be cut to ten minutes because of the crushing crowd, and their scheduled concert was canceled by the local government. Their success in East Asia has spawned other Taiwanese boy-bands and individual male singers who are heavily marketed in Pop Culture China. However, Taiwan never scored another regional hit drama after that. On the other hand, *Meteor Garden* as a story continued to be popular, leading subsequently to Japanese (*Hana Yori Dango*) and Korean (*Boys Over Flowers* or *Kkotboda Namja*) versions that were regionally distributed.

In pop music, as mentioned earlier, the opening up of the China market caused major ethnic Chinese singers to switch to singing in Mandarin, which in turn has enabled Taipei to emerge as the center for the Mandarin pop music industry. The entry and effect of Mandarin pop music in post-Cultural Revolution China has been dramatic. The withdrawal of state financial support for the arts as part of the marketization process "resulted in more traditional musical forms, such as Peking opera, being all but eradicated in open-market competition with Mandopop" (Moskowitz 2010: 21). The rise of Mandopop also gave rise to the prominence of Taiwanese Mandarin singers; among them Chang Hui-mei (张惠妹), a Taiwan aboriginal,[21] and Jay Chou (周杰伦), the hottest Mandarin-singing male vocalist of the 2000s, who can be credited with consolidating the radical break in Mandarin pop music from a predominance of romantic ballads by introducing rhythm and blues (R&B) and rap into mainstream Mandarin pop. Taiwan also features prominently as a place to train, record, and market music for all ethnic Chinese Mandarin singers from throughout Southeast Asia. For example, Malaysian and Singaporean ethnic Chinese singers who aspire to be in the Mandarin pop music world have to succeed in Taiwan. An example is Stefanie Sun Yanzi who won the Best Mandarin Female Vocalist at Taiwan's 2005 Golden Melody Awards and until the end of that decade was one of the most popular Mandopop singers.

## China and Singapore

Hitherto, China's presence as a production location for East Asian Pop Culture can be said to be marginal relative to its huge consumer market for imports from other East Asian locations. This is due in part to the underdevelopment of media industries under socialism. Furthermore, the extremely-quick piracy industry, which produces increasingly high quality products sold at a fraction of the cost of the original, has further discouraged investment. Commercialization of the state-owned media enterprises has not sufficiently improved the quality and style of their products for the more advanced consumers in the affluent East Asian locations to pick them up. In addition, there are two divergent, deeper "cultural" problems that constrain mainland Chinese pop culture in the export market.

First, China is tied to being the root-site of "traditional" Chinese culture. In this context, China media producers often translate historical events and literary classics of the historical or mythic past into films and/or television dramas. Famous historical/mythical epic novels, such as *The Water Margin* (水浒传) and *The Three Kingdoms* (三国演义), have been very well produced as long-running television dramas. Beyond the inherent richness of these narratives, such historical dramas clear censorship more readily (Keane 2008: 151). Such dramas have found ready markets in the region, especially in overseas ethnic Chinese markets, with Taiwan as the most important market (Keane 2008: 151). Like all historical dramas, they make relatively high demands on the audience to have some requisite knowledge of Chinese literature and history to fully appreciate them; consequently, their reception among non-ethnic Chinese and younger audiences is at best uncertain.

Second, pop culture from China, from rock music to television, films, and other visual art forms, is deeply inscribed and haunted by the history of communist revolution and by authoritarianism, both traditional and contemporary. The authoritarian theme and its constraining ideological effects are reflected in the works of internationally acclaimed director Zhang Yimou (张艺谋). Along with his critique of the oppressiveness of "Chinese tradition" in such films as *Raise the Red Lantern* (大红灯笼高高挂 1991) and his depiction of the rural poverty of contemporary China in films like *Not One Less* (一个都不能少 1999), he also made the monumental *Hero* (英雄 2002), which narrates a version of the failed assassination of the brutal Qin emperor, the first man to unify the fragmented territory into a centralized empire that was to become the basic territorial building block that, after further territorial annexation and consolidation over the next two thousand years, was to become present-day China. Zhang's movies, like those of other Chinese filmmakers, are unable to avoid political inscription and reading by domestic and foreign audiences. The reading by audiences in the West or Western-educated audiences in East Asia is very succinctly put by Chen Xiaoming:

> ... once his films enter the world film market, politics inevitably captures the spotlight. Hence, in the eyes of a Western beholder, Zhang Yimou's *Judou* [菊豆 1991] is interpreted as an innuendo against the gerontocracy, and *Raise the Red Lantern* (1992) is seen as a political

power struggle. Political readings of these Chinese films are not necessarily farfetched misreadings insofar as the cultural imaginary of Oriental culture has always already inculcated an invisible, but omnipresent, nexus of absolute power and totalitarianism, which overshadows Zhang Yimou's, and others', films. It does not matter whether such a power nexus refers to ancient feudalism or despotism, or to the "proletariat dictatorship" of modern China, for the cultural imaginary of Oriental culture is fundamentally timeless—the present is all but a reappearance of the past. Politics is thus a determinant situation in the cultural imaginary of China. (Chen 2000: 229)

Such complex political inscriptions are too taxing for mass pop culture audiences and the films are consequently generally relegated to the international art house and film festival circuits with their sophisticated audiences and are taken up for ideological and aesthetic analysis by academics working in film studies. Even his blockbuster *wuxia* (武侠) film, *Hero*, which grossed four billion yen in its Japanese release—the biggest ever for an Asian film in Japan—and ranked among the top five grossing foreign films in US cinema history, has been subjected to similar kinds of political debates.

In contemporary pop culture, the deep inscription of revolutionary politics and its discontents is perhaps most obvious in rock music from China where the lyrics are heavily laden with local politics (De Kloet 2000). Indeed, for Cui Jian (崔健), the most important rock musician during the Tiananmen period, "Rock is an ideology, not a set musical form" (quoted in Jones 1992: 115). Consequently, rock music from China is difficult for consumers who are not part of the local scene to understand. The result is that such artists are relegated to the margins as "alternative" music for a small body of aficionados, limiting their presence in Pop Culture China.

Likewise, Chinese television dramas suffer from a similar ideological straightjacket. Keane points out that "restrictions imposed by zealous officials on the thematic content of TV drama have led to a glut of dramas featuring good characters wronged by unscrupulous authorities, tragic characters molded from the clay of socialist realism. While some dramas have used partisan themes to excellent effect, such elements have reinforced perceptions of Mainland content as excessively ideological" (2008: 147). An illustrative example is one of the earliest highly popular melodramas, *Yearnings* (渴望, fifty episodes, 1990), which, according to Sheldon Lu, "marked the maturity of soap opera as a full-blown Chinese genre" (2001: 215). One of the scriptwriters was rather forthright and sarcastic about the drama's formula: "We tortured all these characters, making everyone suffer. We made sure all the good guys had a heart of gold, but we made them as unlucky as possible; and the bad guys are as bad as you can imagine—that's the sure way to a good drama" (quoted in Lu 2001: 205). Its success pleased Li Ruihuan, then boss of ideology and propaganda, who reportedly said after watching the show: "It tells us that an artistic work must entertain first, or it is useless to talk about educating people with it. The influence we exert must be subtle, imperceptible, and the people should be influenced without being conscious of it. In order to make socialist principles and moral virtues acceptable to the broad masses, we must learn to use the forms that the masses favour" (quoted in Lu 2001: 207–208).

Such ideology/pedagogy-heavy dramas became tiresome over time and eventually did not even attract China's domestic audience, let alone transnational ones. According to the director of China's Propaganda Department Arts Bureau, Li Baoshan, in 2003 "only 20 percent of television dramas in China experienced significant sales, that another 20 percent barely covered costs or made narrow profits, while 60 percent were unable to cover their costs of investments" (quoted in Keane 2008: 147). The effect, Keane observes, is "a dual impact: it impedes the confidence of the local industry and it opens the door for imports, whether these are consumed through broadcast channels or through video disk sales" (2008: 147). By early 2000, urban dramas of romance, imitating those from Japan, Korea, Taiwan, and Hong Kong, were being produced[22] and a few made it to Singapore in the weekend afternoon slot; for example, *Bourgeois Mansion* (白领公寓 2002). However, underfinancing has resulted in poor visual quality and mainland Chinese dramas are thus unable to live up to the viewing demands of the regional audience, who are by now used to a much higher standard of production. Overall, changes are afoot in China, which has an ambition to compete in the regional drama market, although much institutional reform in the television industry is needed.

With its very limited domestic multi-ethnic market, Singapore is quintessentially an import and consumption location. Although the population is overwhelmingly ethnic Chinese, Singapore has never had a Chinese-language film industry. Chinese cinema investors, Shaw Brothers, the Cathay Organization's Motion Pictures and General Investment Company (Chung 2009) and Kong Ngee (Wong 2006), were all financing and producing Chinese-language films in their studios in Hong Kong.[23] In the early 1990s, a small group of independent filmmakers emerged, notably including Eric Khoo and Jack Neo.[24] The government set up the Singapore Film Commission in 1995 to develop the local industry, with financial support for budding Singaporean filmmakers. The television corporation MediaCorp also set up Raintree Pictures in 1998, to produce local feature films and to invest in co-productions with regional partners. The latter is driven primarily by commercial considerations and secondarily by developing the Singapore film industry and related professions. At the beginning of the twenty-first century, there were still fewer than ten films produced each year.[25] From the very beginning in mid-1960s up to the present, the Singaporean television industry has depended on importing professionals from Hong Kong, who are, however, not ideologically free to develop the content. The local free-to-air television stations of the state-owned company, MediaCorp, produce dramas that are excessively concerned with local themes, heavily ideological and didactic, often in conjunction with government promotion of public policies and equally often sponsored by government agencies and government-linked commercial enterprises to dramatize industry-related concerns. Thus, as in China, these dramas have driven Singaporeans away from local dramas[26] and towards imported dramas from the rest of East Asia, ironically many imported by MediaCorp itself. To attempt to have a foothold in the East Asian Pop Culture market, since early 2000 Hong Kong television actors and actresses have been appearing in local Singaporean productions. There has never been a pop music industry, although some Singaporean Chinese-language singers have made it to Hong Kong and Taiwan over the years (Liew 2010). To gain a better sense of the obstacles that face the smallest player in the regional cultural economy, the case of Singapore as part of Pop Culture China and East Asian Pop Culture will be examined in greater detail in Chapter 4.

## Crossing National Boundaries

While the relative position of the constitutive nations in production and consumption is a meaningful way of analytically approaching the structure of East Asian Pop Culture, the framework nevertheless leaves out productions that cross national boundaries, as in cases of co-productions of films. Co-productions are more common in films because, unlike the markets for television drama and pop music which are highly regional, the film market is a global market. In the desire to gain ever larger audiences, co-produced films, with investors from within and beyond the East Asian region and "pan-ethnic Chinese" or "pan-Asian" cast, have been noticeable since early 2000. Among the successful productions must be the Hong Kong–China–Taiwan–US co-production *Crouching Tiger, Hidden Dragon* (卧虎藏龙 2000), directed by Taiwanese-American Ang Lee (李安) with a "pan-Chinese" cast in leading roles, including Hong Kong actor Chow Yun Fat, Taiwan actor Chang Chen (张震), mainland Chinese actress Zhang Ziyi (章子怡), and Malaysian-Chinese actress Michelle Yeoh (杨紫琼). This was quickly followed by Zhang Yimou's *Hero*, with Jet Li (李连杰), Tony Leung Chiu Wai (梁朝伟) and Maggie Cheung (张曼玉) from Hong Kong, and Zhang Ziyi and Chen Daoming (陈道明) from China. Expanding further into the region to include other East Asian cast members is Chinese director Chen Kaige's (陈凯歌) fantasy epic *The Promise* (无极 2005), which featured Japanese actor Hiroyuki Sanada (真田广之) and Korean actor Jang Dong-gun (张东建) in leading roles, alongside Nicholas Tse (谢霆锋) and Cecilia Cheung (张柏芝) from Hong Kong. Finally, stretching across the continent to South Asia is Jackie Chan's (成龙) *The Myth* (神话 2005), with Kim Hee-seon (金喜善) from Korea as the female lead and, in a supporting role, the Bollywood Indian actress Mallika Sherawat. Finally, from outside Hong Kong and China, the Korean movie *Musa* (*The Warrior* 武士 *Wushi* 2002) starred Zhang Ziyi in the lead female role. According to Teo (2008), Hong Kong producers undertook these inter-Asian productions largely in response to financial necessity because the much anticipated massive consumption capacity of China for Hong Kong films had hitherto not materialized. No doubt, the "pan-Chinese" and "pan-Asian" films are aimed at expanding transnational audience bases, hoping that the stars from different nations would attract the respective national audiences.

In each of the "pan-East Asian" efforts, the intertwined histories of the East Asian nations, histories of bitter memories of war and colonization, had to be suppressed in the film narrative. Consequently, most of these films, in spite of often being period costume dramas, are set in historically unspecified periods or in "mythic" lands, such as *The Myth* and *The Promise*. This also makes it easier to market the films globally. Yet, even when using such devices, the casting of Korean actor Jang Dong-gun as the slave to Japanese actor Hiroyuki Sanada could provide the discursive space for reading it as a metaphor of, and thus recalling, the history of colonization of Korea by Japan. Haunted by history, the Hollywood-made *Memoirs of a Geisha* (2005), featuring three ethnic Chinese actresses—Michelle Yeoh, Zhang Ziyi, and Gong Li (巩俐)—as geishas, was banned in China on the grounds that it might cause offence and public disturbance, especially in view of the low ebb in Japan–China international relations under Japanese Prime Minister Koizumi's term. Obviously, the pan-efforts have not been able to cross national boundaries without evoking the historical animosities within the region and without nationalist resistance. In spite of these historical and ideological obstacles, pan-Asian efforts are likely to continue their search for a formula for "success."

To date, pan-Asian cinematic collaborations have not achieved consistent box office success regionally. Indeed, regional reception often confounds the producers of such films. For example, the critical and box office successes of *Crouching Tiger, Hidden Dragon* in the West were in sharp contrast to its reception in East Asia, where it had lukewarm box office takings in China and Hong Kong, although it reportedly had a strong performance in box offices of Taiwan and Singapore (Landler 2001; Lu and Yeh 2005). On the other hand, Zhang Yimou's *Hero* achieved phenomenal success in China and in the regional market but was a relative failure in the West, managing to achieve only half of *Crouching Tiger*'s foreign takings (Kwok 2007). Chen Kaige's *The Promise* did poorly at both the regional and Hollywood box offices.[27] If pan-Asian cinema's financial success in the region is hampered by lingering historical hostilities between nation-states, its desire for a fruitful foray into the Hollywood market is equally incalculable given a seeming lack of formula for success so far.

The making of what is a pan-Asian cultural economy also extends to the construction of celebrities with transnational appeal. During the height of the J-pop wave in the 1990s, when Japanese idols were popular in many Asian countries, "many indigenous promoters and media organizations have collaborated with Japanese idol producers and promoters, facilitating a 'knowledge transfer' of Japanese-style idol production and marketing know-how to other Asian markets" (Aoyagi 2000: 319). An illustrious example of transnational pan-East Asian stardom is Takeshi Kaneshiro (金城武), who has a Japanese father and a Taiwanese mother, spent formative years in both countries and has worked in both locations as well as in Hong Kong. Looking at his performances across various mediums, Tsai (2005) argues that, combining his ability to speak multiple East Asian languages and cosmopolitan work experience, he has constructed a "neither here nor there" image that defies any easy classification of national identity within East Asia. It is perhaps such an image that has allowed Kaneshiro to become one of the most sought-after actors in pan-East Asian productions, starring in films including Zhang Yimou's *House of Flying Daggers* (十面埋伏 2004), Peter Chan's *Perhaps Love* (如果・爱 2005) and John Woo's *Red Cliff* (赤壁 2008) , all expensive blockbusters. Significantly, an identity as a pan-East Asian celebrity appears to impose severe limits on the ability of an actor to transcend the region, in spite of all the talk of media globalization. In this context, transnational Chinese stars' forays and achievements in Hollywood almost always lead to criticism of "inauthentic" performances or Orientalist exoticism meant to "seduce" the West, as Chu (2008) says of Zhang Ziyi's roles in *Memoirs* and *Rush Hour 2* (2001). Their presence in Hollywood appears to be almost always short-lived.

## Conclusion

The current structural arrangement of the production and export of East Asian Pop Culture can be summarized thus: Japan is the leader that sets the industry quality standard and is primarily a production and export location, though it does import a sizable amount of television drama from Korea, but no Chinese-language pop culture. Korea has made very conscious efforts to make its pop culture an export industry, especially after the 1997 Asian financial crisis. Hong Kong and Taiwan play central roles in the production of Chinese-language pop culture, with Hong Kong still playing a major role in films and television dramas, and Taiwan producing a high volume of Mandarin pop music. China and Singapore remain largely locations of import and consumption of East Asian Pop Culture. China, with its massive domestic market and an increasingly commercialized media industry, is making moves to break out of the ideological constraints imposed by the state to produce contemporary pop culture products that are able to compete in the regional market. Indeed, since early 2000, the state-owned television industry has signaled its intention to be a global player through the state-promoted policy of "going out." Meanwhile Singapore is trying to get into the regional business by using its investment power in co-productions, and has only a secondary interest in the development of its domestic media industry.

In the past two decades, there have been very impressive developments in pop culture production, distribution, circulation, and consumption in East Asia. With the possible exception of Japan, which has a domestic market large and wealthy enough to sustain its own pop culture industry, most pop culture is now produced for regional consumption. In Singapore in 2008–09, the free-to-air television station Channel U carried the tag line "Leading Asian Pop Culture" and featured movies and television dramas from across East Asia. Within East Asian Pop Culture, pop music is the least transnational in terms of volume of consumption and sales, television dramas are the most regionally-distributed and circulated product, and films from East Asian nations, particularly those from China's celebrity filmmakers understandably target the global market. This "totality" of an East Asian Pop Culture stands in juxtaposition to and competes vigorously with the presence of globalized American pop culture in every medium except cinema, where Hollywood dominates absolutely. The juxtaposition challenges easy and loose talk of American cultural hegemony and imperialism in the pop culture entertainment world.

Changes within East Asian Pop Culture are probably inevitable in the near future, with the rise of China's media industry, along with the rest of its economy. At the end of the first decade of the twenty-first century, the Korean pop culture industry continues to be the most aggressive in the East Asian market; in addition to the export of television dramas, Korean pop music producers are making inroads into the regional market by recruiting non-Koreans into their boy-and girl-bands. After the decade of the 1990s, when Japanese pop culture unmistakably dominated the small screens of East Asia, interest in the Japanese media industry appears to be waning, although its television dramas and pop singers have not disappeared completely from the regional market. The Japanese case perhaps foreshadows the trajectory of the so-called Korean Wave, which is showing signs of becoming a quiet but persistent flow into the rest of East Asia. This should be considered a huge gain in the regional market because, up to a decade ago, Korean pop culture was unheard of regionally. Regardless of what changes the future may hold, East Asian media-driven pop culture has become an integral part of the entertainment landscape in the everyday life of the regional population, raising the question of whether a pan-East Asian identity could be forged in the long term.

# 2

# Pop Culture China

The loosely-integrated East Asian pop culture economy is one of unequal flows and exchanges across national and cultural boundaries, with Japanese and Korean products exported to areas which have a predominantly ethnic Chinese population—China, Hong Kong, Taiwan, and Singapore. Although geographically in Southeast Asia, Singapore has always been an integral part of the Chinese-language pop culture industry due to its seventy-five percent majority ethnic Chinese population, who speak a multiplicity of Chinese languages or dialects. This transnational ethnic Chinese population constitutes the largest consumer market for Japanese and Korean pop culture exports; without it they would likely have remained local industries, with the exception of Japanese animation which has a very large market in the West, particularly in the US. The ethnic Chinese population has had a long history of exchanges in pop culture, dating back to the beginning of the twentieth century. In this sense, East Asian Pop Culture is built on the foundation of the historically well-established regional network of the Chinese-language cultural industries. Any analysis of East Asian Pop Culture requires knowledge of the history and organization of the ethnic Chinese pop culture network and the way it mediates the distribution and consumption of Japanese and Korean pop culture.

## Confucian Cultural China

In modern history, the globally-dispersed ethnic Chinese population outside China has always been vulnerable to an all-too-convenient process of being gathered under a collective name, the "Chinese" diaspora, or "overseas" Chinese community, suppressing but never erasing the histories of the different communities in different parts of the globe. Until the late nineteenth century, this overseas ethnic Chinese population may be properly referred to as a "diaspora" because the overwhelming majority of the population was indeed first-generation immigrants who considered themselves sojourners in foreign lands and continued to orient themselves to a "home" in China. Additionally, those born outside China might also be diasporic, if only by default, because they were denied citizenship in the countries of their birth and residence.[1] Under these circumstances, the politics of China was a constant factor that activated and divided this diasporic population into different camps, with different ideas about how to save China as a nation, how to lift the Chinese people out of the decaying dynastic, imperial regime and stifling traditions, and how to propel both people and nation into the modern world. For example, the Chinese diaspora in Southeast Asia was mobilized, at different times, to be united in opposition to the Japanese invasion of China, to be divided in allegiance to the Kuomintang and the Chinese Communist Party during the civil war, and to vicariously take pride in China's detonation of its first atomic bomb in the early 1950s. However, at the height of the Cold War, at the inaugural conference of the Non-Aligned Movement in Bandung, Indonesia in 1955, the then prime minister of the People's Republic, Zhou Enlai announced that ethnic Chinese outside China should obtain citizenship and develop allegiance to their respective countries of adoption. This effectively severed Chinese ethnicity from Chinese citizenship everywhere except Hong Kong, Macau, and Taiwan, which China claims as parts of its own territory. Nevertheless, this has not prevented occasional attempts to draw together the ethnic Chinese communities in the region to constitute a "greater," "cultural" China on the presumption of a shared "culture" that is presumed to be relatively stable and unchanging, i.e., essentialized, over time and space, among all ethnic Chinese.

One such attempt took place from the mid-1980s until 1997, a period of continuous rapid economic growth in Taiwan, Hong Kong, and Singapore, coupled with the economic opening-up of China. There was a euphoric atmosphere celebrating what appeared to be sustainable and miraculous capitalist economic growth in these predominantly ethnic Chinese economies. The presumed shared "Chineseness" was signified by the media labeling them "dragon" economies, referencing the dragon symbol of the Chinese imperial court. Enormous energies were invested in triumphal discourses of "pan-Chinese" economic successes, pan-Chinese culture, and pan-Chinese identity, often sponsored by the transnational Chinese business network and their enthusiastic intellectual promoters. Attempts at conceptualizing a greater cultural China included the convening of international conferences on topics ranging from Chinese business networks, to the character of Chinese family firms (Menkhoff and Gerke 2002), to ethnographies of the daily running of small family enterprises rationalized by the logic of Confucian family ideology (Yao 2002). At a more ambitious institutional level was the establishment of the Institute of East Asian Philosophies at the National University of Singapore, with the explicit aim of searching for the common philosophical and cultural roots of East Asian economic growth. Not surprisingly, its very first conference was focused on considering Confucianism as the equivalent of Protestant ethics as the basis of East Asian capitalism (Tu 1991a).

A major figure in the attempt to explain the rise of East Asian capitalism in Confucian terms has been the neo-Confucian philosopher Tu Weiming.[2] Rapid economic growth from the late 1960s until the early 1990s in the countries surrounding China provided Tu with the empirical evidence and discursive space to make two conceptual points. First, these countries arguably have a history of shared Confucian cultural heritage which originated in China, thus the people of these countries can be drawn together into a "cultural China." The inclusion of Japan and South Korea is critical because, although not ethnically Chinese, they are historico-culturally within the ambit of Confucianism. Indeed, the place of Confucian ideas in the everyday life of South Koreans remains observable today. Second, he surmises these surrounding countries "will come to set the economic and cultural agenda for the centre [China]" (Tu 1991: 12). These conceptual moves were articulated in his editorial introduction, entitled "Cultural China: The periphery as the center," to *The Living Tree: The Changing Meaning of Being Chinese Today*, a 1991 special issue of *Daedelus* (from the Annals of the American Academy of Arts and Science). For Tu, the desire behind the concept of "cultural China" is not only the displacement of China as the Chinese cultural center/core but more importantly, the possibility of resurrecting a reformed Confucianism that will unite the dispersed overseas Chinese communities, as well as Japan and Korea.

Even before the 1997 Asian financial crisis cast a pall on the economic euphoria and the idea of cultural China, skeptics abounded. Politically, the search for Confucian values had been read critically by detractors as ideological gloss over political authoritarianism in the less-than-democratic nations in the region. Economically, the actual might and reach of the economic power of the overseas Chinese communities had been a constant source of disagreement, given the obvious presence of multinational corporations in the newly-industrializing economies in the region. The "uniqueness" of the Chinese family firm had been exposed as, among other things, an institution founded on the exploitation of family labor, particularly of women and children (Yao 2002). Meanwhile, the Confucian thesis had morphed into the "Asian values" thesis, principally promoted by the Singapore government which had to downplay the Confucian thesis in order to accommodate the Malay and Indian communities in its multiethnic population (Chua 1995; Han 1999). With the 1997 Asian financial crisis, the faint-and half-hearted espousers of links between Confucian values and the rise of capitalism in Asia quickly scurried offstage. Only the staunchly, ideologically-committed have been willing to continue to fly the "Asian values" flag. Among them is Singapore's Lee Kuan Yew. Pestered by international journalists for his view on the so-called "Asian values" in the face of the economic crisis, he suggested:

> [There] has been a debasement of what I call Confucian value; I mean duty to friends and family. You're supposed to look after your family

and your extended family, and to be loyal and supportive of your friends. And you should do it from your private purse and not from the public treasury. Now when you have weak governments and corruption seeps in, then this private obligation is often fulfilled at the public expense, and that's wrong. (McCarthy 1998)

Lee is not without academic supporters in East Asia. The possibility of a reformed Confucianism for contemporary democratic politics continues to exercise the minds of many political and social scientists working in Asia (Tan 2004; Bell and Hahm 2003; Bell 2008).

The ideological and emotional desire for a Confucian cultural China lives off the assumption that Confucianism constitutes the foundational culture of everyday life for all ethnic Chinese in the world. Empirically, any cursory observation of Southeast Asia will suggest that this is a flimsy assumption. Take, for example, Singapore, where the learning of Mandarin is compulsory for all ethnic Chinese primary and secondary school students. In the late 1980s, in an attempt to shore up moral values against the supposedly corrupting cultural influences of Western liberalism, religious education of a type without God(s), was introduced as compulsory moral education in primary and secondary schools. Confucian ethics were offered as an option for ethnic Chinese students who professed no religion. Without any experts on Confucianism in the country, a first indication of the absence of Confucianism in daily life, the teaching materials were developed by a group of invited foreign experts, including Tu Weiming. The shallowness of Confucianism in the everyday life of Singaporeans was further exposed when most of the ethnic Chinese students opted for education in other religions. The evidence plainly suggested that any presumption of cultural "depth" in the grand Chinese philosophical traditions among ethnic Chinese Singaporeans was dubious. In the end, the moral education curriculum, including Confucian ethics, was quickly abandoned when local social scientists discovered that students were becoming more religious as a result of the lessons and this could potentially give rise to greater divisiveness among the multiracial and multi-religious population (Kuo, Quah, and Tong 1988).

Intellectual anxiety, criticism, and resistance to attempts to conceptualize a Confucian greater China have tended to be framed in terms of "Chinese chauvinism" rather than "Chinese nationalism" (Chun 1996; Ong 1999; Ang 2001), re-inscribing the recognition of difference between ethnicity and nation. This reiterates that, in the contemporary world, calling the ethnic Chinese population diasporic, which presupposes the presence of a home/nation, is highly problematic. Furthermore, it is now seldom a term of self-identity but more often than not is imposed on individuals by others for the latter's own self-interest[3] as the cultural definition of Chineseness has been unavoidably and increasingly marked by local politics.

## The Sinophone

A recent discursive critique and resistance to the idea of an essentialized cultural China comes in the concept of the "Sinophone": "a network of places of cultural production outside China and on the margins of China and Chineseness, where a historical process of heterogenizing and localizing of continued Chinese culture has been taking place for several centuries" (Shih 2007: 4). The ideological work that the Sinophone as a concept is meant to do is to frustrate the "flawless suturing . . . of either monolingual *putonghua* (Beijing standard), monological Chineseness, or a monolithic China and Chinese culture" by "foregrounding the values of difficulty, difference, and heterogeneity" (Shih 2007: 5) as "confirmation of the continuous existence of the Sinophone communities as significant sites of cultural production in a complex set of relations with such constructs as 'China,' 'Chinese' and 'Chineseness'" (Shih 2007: 4).

Critically, it should be noted that to a very significant extent, the supposed presumption of the "monolingual," "monological," and "monolithic" is an artifice of the English language. The singular terms of "Chinese" and "Chineseness" do not provide room for the "difficulty, difference, and heterogeneity" which every ethnic Chinese person knows and takes for granted. Such differences, heterogeneities, and difficulties manifest themselves in the everyday life of every sizable ethnic Chinese community, including urban populations in contemporary China, not only in terms of frequently and mutually incomprehensible languages but also in other large and small ways, right down to the variation of daily foods. In this sense no individual ethnic Chinese would ever presume "being Chinese" means a "singular/mono" anything and a self-proclamation of "being Chinese" is always a vague claim which is only substantiated contextually, depending on which, among the array of possible cultural elements, is called forth to substantiate the claim.

For example, when I am in Taiwan, I am often asked if I am a Minnan person (闽南人) as Minnan speakers are ubiquitous in Singapore. However, Minnan is a Mandarin term which is not commonly used by Singaporean speakers, who refer to themselves as Hokkien people (福建人), who speak Hokkien, the local dialect from Fujian (福建) province from whence their ancestors came. Furthermore, in Taiwan, the question would be asked in Mandarin and, if I answered in the affirmative, we could switch to using the Minnan/Hokkien language instead of continuing in Mandarin. My encounter in Hong Kong is equally complex, switching between Cantonese, Mandarin, and English in conversations with local ethnic Chinese Hong Kong citizens. Such common occurrences within ethnic Chinese communities, of course, constantly disrupt presumptions of any monologic. Additionally, in view of such language complexities, while "Francophone" refers to speakers of French and "Anglophone" refers to speakers of English, then to which Chinese language does the "Sino" in "Sinophone" refer?

On the idea of "Chineseness," Chun points out that identity is a "selective process in the mind of individual subject-actors grounded in local contexts of power and meaning" (1996: 130). Taking local context into consideration, until the signing, in 1984, of the agreement for its handover by the British to China, ethnic Chinese in Hong Kong had always assumed, rather unproblematically, that they were simply "Chinese." They were, of course, cognizant of the obvious differences in the cultures of everyday life in the rapaciously-capitalist Hong Kong and the then materially-deprived socialist China. These differences were conceptualized in terms of a "rural/urban" dichotomy rather than a difference of "identity"; the mainland Chinese were culturally "backward"—presented in Hong Kong films through a number of on-screen stereotypes such as "'Ah Chan" (new Chinese immigrants), "Big Circle Gangs" (gangsters from the mainland), and the later "Biaojie" (women officials from the Mainland) (Chu 2005: 317)—in contrast to the urbane Hong Kong Chinese (Ma 2000). Furthermore, it was frequently imagined that the capitalist culture of production and consumption of Hong Kong would eventually "triumph" culturally over socialist China, in spite of the hugely unequal demographic and geographical size, a kind of David and Goliath cultural battle. After 1984, the overwhelmingly local Cantonese population began to question their identity and the term "Hong Konger" first made its presence as a marker of self-identity for people from Hong Kong. Since the handover in 1997, the emphasis on difference has intensified, creating resistance to being absorbed by China. While some are happy to re-nationalize themselves (Ma 2000), others are resisting politically through demands for local autonomy and democracy. Cantonese has been chosen as the primary language of instruction in government-financed primary and secondary schools. The struggle to come to a satisfactory definition of themselves in cultural and political terms continues, with increasing numbers referring to themselves as "people from Hong Kong" (香港人).

In the cases of Taiwan and Singapore, "Chineseness" is now overlaid by the idea of the "nation," a jealous god that is unhappy with sharing its hold on its subjects. Until 1949, politically speaking, being ethnic Chinese might be said to be loosely coterminous with being a Chinese citizen. The defeat and retreat of the Kuomintang to Taiwan, which was named the Republic of China (ROC) introduced the first rupture between a cultural ethnic Chinese identity and citizenship, with both the People's Republic and the ROC claiming all ethnic Chinese as their own citizens. However, as mentioned above, in 1955, a second rupture was enacted; the Chinese government renounced its claim on overseas Chinese as citizens and encouraged them to take up citizenship in host countries, thus detaching Chinese ethnicity from Chinese citizenship. Since then, "nations," "nationalities," and "citizenships" have stood between an identification as being Chinese through ethnicity or nationality; "Chinese" has become an exclusive marker for citizens of China (中国人), whereas "Chinese" (华人) as ethnic-cultural marker can be of any nationality. Again, this is a distinction that the generic English term "Chinese" does not facilitate.

The persistence of China's territorial claim over Taiwan continues to occupy center stage in contemporary Taiwanese politics, generating political, cultural, and psychological pressures for both the government and citizens of that island. Anti-China sentiment is now a constitutive component of local political discourse. Undoubtedly, over the years the percentage of the ethnic Chinese population in Taiwan who agree with reunification with China is declining; if they cannot have political independence, they would still rather remain separate. The Minnan language is coming to be referred to as the "Taiwanese" language (台语), intentionally ignoring the fact that its origin lies in Fujian province in southern coastal China.[4] Families are beginning to tutor their children and insist that they speak "Taiwanese" at home. The trend of Taiwan citizens referring themselves as Taiwanese (台湾人) is increasing and is not restricted to those who desire political independence.

In the case of Singapore, the separation of Chinese ethnicity from Chinese nationality is complete. The ethnic Chinese constitute an overwhelming seventy-four percent of the national population, along with thirteen percent Malays and nine percent Indians. To claim this multiethnic population as citizens for itself, the Singapore state officially adopts multiculturalism as national policy and uses the term *Huaren* (华人) to denote its ethnic Chinese citizens (Chua 2009). This is a radical simplification of the complexities of language and identity among the ethnic Chinese population, which will be examined in the next chapter. The political developments in Hong Kong, Taiwan, and Singapore are but the most recent disruptions of any idea of a monolithic China for all ethnic Chinese. Within the contemporary context, following the practice of Singapore, "Huaren" can be adopted as a nation-neutral but ethnically-and-culturally-marked identity, reserving the term "Chinese" for those who are citizens of China and who could be of Han descent, or be from any of the officially-recognized "minority" nationalities. In this context, local sentiments have provided, and will continue to provide, the necessary ideological resources for constructions of difference between Huaren of different locations, rather than building on any idea of a shared "Chinese" culture.

## Pop Culture China and the De-centering of Chinese Identity

In contrast to the absence of a common grand philosophical discourse on Chinese culture and identity, there has been a long history of shared pop culture in various Chinese languages among the Huaren population in East Asia—China, Taiwan, Hong Kong, and Singapore—and beyond. Structurally central to this Chinese-language pop culture industry is the Shaw Brothers enterprise, whose legendary story is by now well-documented and only the briefest of sketches is necessary here (Curtin 2007; Fu 2008).[5] The four brothers started a movie-making studio in

Shanghai in the early 1920s. They moved the financing operation to Singapore at the end of the decade and from there established a string of movie houses throughout the Malay Peninsula. In the early 1930s, the movie studio was moved to Hong Kong, producing mainly Cantonese movies that fed into their movie houses in Southeast Asia. In the mid-1950s, the Hong Kong studios were reorganized and modernized into "the largest and best-equipped studio in the history of Chinese filmmaking and by launching Chinese language[s] cinema into an age of color and widescreen (Eastmancolor and Shawscape)" (Fu 2008: 5, original parenthesis). Throughout the 1950s and 1960s, Shaw Brothers was the largest Chinese-language filmmaker in the world. In the 1970s, Shaw Brothers gave up the movie-making business and shifted its attention to television entertainment, establishing TVB in Hong Kong. TVB soon became a major producer and exporter of television dramas for both the domestic audience and the global Huaren audience; the latter consuming them in video form. Since the 1990s, film production under independent producers has declined very significantly. Hong Kong remains a center for Chinese-language films, and it also continues to export locally-produced television dramas to Southeast Asia.

This pop culture traffic is facilitated by subtitling with a "common" written script that allows speakers of different regional Chinese languages or dialects to access the crisscrossing cultural material across the divides of distinct spoken languages. Here the subtitles that are placed to assist the hearing-impaired serve an additional, perhaps unintended, highly useful function. (The claim of a common written Chinese script needs qualification. Hong Kong writers, especially in the mass media, have long invented Cantonese characters that cannot be read in Mandarin. Alternatively, standard written characters are used to be read, contextually, with Cantonese sounds in order to be comprehensible; for example, *de xian* [得閒] reads smoothly in Cantonese as having free time, but awkwardly in Mandarin sounds. Experiments with this strategy are also taking place in Taiwan, where standard characters are meant to be read in Minnan sounds for Minnan meanings.) Intensified with new communication technologies, the cultural traffic among Huaren communities is thus intrinsically plural, not only in terms of language but also in terms of the cultural contexts at the locations of production and reception/consumption. The different cultural contexts create slippages in meanings and symbolic values encoded and decoded; as will be demonstrated in Chapter 4. Whether the border-crossing of Chinese-language pop culture into the geographically-dispersed Huaren populations can generate a sense of a transnational Huaren community remains largely unexamined. This chapter attempts to delineate some substantive and conceptual dimensions of this flow of Chinese-language pop culture across the Huaren population, a phenomenon discursively designated as Pop Culture China (Chua 2000).[6]

Within the Huaren-dominant locations in East Asia, the history of pop culture flows, exchanges, and reception/consumption began as far back as the 1930s, if not earlier, depending on the medium. The configuration of Pop Culture China is materially and symbolically without center; any search for a cultural center would be in vain. The dominant spoken language in the various locations of production and consumption differs: Cantonese in Hong Kong, Mandarin and Minnan/Hokkien in Taiwan, while in Singapore, all three languages were commonly used until the early 1970s when the use of "dialects" in the mass media was banned by government policy. This has effectively reduced the ability of younger Singaporeans to speak Hokkien and Cantonese; however, it has not erased these languages completely. Furthermore, the government has relaxed the ban in recent years and local movies now regularly carry a mixture of these languages.[7] The three locations illustrate that in an overseas Huaren community, Mandarin may be either the exclusive formal language of education—as in Singapore—or a supplementary language in schools—as in Hong Kong. The pop culture from different locations tends to reflect the dominance of the local spoken language because they are initially produced for the local audience and only exported to other Huaren communities when they prove successful locally.

In pop music, the languages primarily used are Mandarin, Cantonese, and Taiwanese/Minnan/Hokkien, depending on the native language of the singer and the location of the recording. However, these are not hard and fast elements, as a singer can switch back and forth between different Chinese languages depending on the pop music market. As noted in the last chapter, with the opening up of the China market, most popular Huaren singers, regardless of origin, have switched to recording in Mandarin. Songs are often produced in more than one Chinese language, for example, different versions of the same song might be produced in both Cantonese and Mandarin. Sometimes more than one Chinese language is used in a single song, especially in those from Taiwan and Southeast Asia and, increasingly, lines in English are added to the lyrics. This multilingual situation is equally pronounced in films, where the mixing of different Chinese languages within the same film has become increasingly common. For those who can read the written Chinese script, comprehension of the multilingual dialogue is facilitated by subtitles written in Chinese script. An example of mild mixing is the internationally acclaimed *Crouching Tiger, Hidden Dragon*, directed by Taiwanese Ang Lee in which Mandarin of different accents—as spoken by the actors from Malaysia, Hong Kong, Taiwan, and mainland China—were used, without a voice-over of standardized, official Mandarin.[8] A more complex example is the 2000 action movie, by director Tsui Hark (徐克), *Time and Tide* (順流逆流, *Shun Liu Ni Liu*), which used Spanish, Cantonese, Minnan/Hokkien (in the music), Minnan/Hokkien-accented Cantonese, and Mandarin of different accents. Finally, in Singapore, the official ban on the use of all Chinese languages except Mandarin in the mass media has been relaxed and many local films are now using different languages when appropriate for the sake of "authenticity." In short, Chinese-language films, especially those produced outside the mainland, use a much larger range of Chinese languages, including the languages of the countries in which the Huaren are citizens or new migrants.

Analytically, it is obvious that in Pop Culture China, Mandarin is not accorded the privileged center of being the "official" language of all Huaren living in different locations. Pop Culture China is "a decentered, multi-lingual, multi-nodal relatively well integrated cultural economy that operates under the presumed 'sameness' of a 'common' Chinese cultural heritage" (Tay 2009). Within this decentered arena, it would be conceptually and substantively premature to immediately attribute any kind of deep identity or cultural similarity to Huaren consumers of these multilingual Chinese cultural products. For example, it is certainly far-fetched to think that a group of Mandarin/Minnan-speaking young Taiwanese in a small karaoke room in Taipei will reflect seriously on their identity as "Chinese" when trying to sing one of the Cantonese songs by the China-born Mandarin singer, Faye Wong. It is, as they say, "just entertainment!" On the part of the producers of the cultural products, the mixing of Chinese languages, along with English, Japanese, or any other language, may be just a vehicle for expanding the potential market. Indeed, it is an inherent characteristic of pop culture consumption that the products constitute a passing fad for the overwhelming majority of its audience, with no deep investment in one's identity, except for a relatively small number of avid fans. This observation, drawn from another context, is generally true: "the show was being watched by several million people each week. Of those, a few thousand joined the listserv, and of those maybe [*sic*] two to three hundred participated regularly in the many fan activities. In our enthusiasm for the active fan we should not lose sight of the more mundane, even passive articulation with media that characterizes a great deal of media consumption" (Bird 2010: 91).

The sharing of a common written script, although with the above noted occasional local variations, renders the plurality of "Chineseness" highly interactive. This common written script engenders and enables spatial and national crisscrossing flows of constantly circulating practitioners, products, and consumption of Chinese-language pop culture among the globally-dispersed Huaren population, as comprehension across the language divides is facilitated by written subtitles. Hence, a soft-bedrock of shared "Chineseness," of a sense of "community" without a permanent cultural center and not necessarily amounting to a dominant identity for anyone in particular,[9] remains discursively imaginable and materially realizable. This discursive, imaginable, and realizable possibility is constantly being produced, made manifest, and visible through the loosely-coordinated economic and cultural social institutions whose activities collectively constitute the "Chinese entertainment cultural industry"; for example, producers of Chinese-language pop culture have already accounted for the entire regional audience market in their planning and financial considerations. Among these institutions are the entertainment pages of local Chinese-language(s) newspapers and magazines.

## Newspaper Print Space as Transnational Chinese Space

In his conceptualization of the "nation as an imaginary community," Benedict Anderson (1983) has given a prominent place to "print" as a vehicle that enables the forging of horizontal and egalitarian ties between individual and equal citizens. Within print media, daily newspapers are of specific importance. They provide the multitude of readers with a sense of "synchronicity" of inhabiting the "same" space and time that is essential to engendering a sense of identity derived from a presumption of being inhabitants of the "same" reading community, with any and every particular individual reader remaining unknown to any other. The space and content of the newspaper page enables the idea of community to be imagined and in a sense made manifest.

The pages of the daily national newspaper are representations, i.e., proxies, for the geographic, physical spaces contained within the nation's boundaries. The newspaper is in this sense an imaginary, textualized geography of the nation and its people. In principle, all the geographical spaces within the boundary must be represented on a routine basis—events from all locations should be reported daily without prejudice. The newspaper must therefore operate on a principle of "inclusion" of all the residents of all the spaces that are constitutive of the "community." To be inclusive and democratic, the pages of the daily newspaper are arguably blank spaces, in which different segments of people from the different locations within the community have the right to claim space. In principle, the empirical absence/ presence in the pages on a particular day is determined by the occurrence of events in a particular reported space rather than on the preferences or prejudices of the reporters and editors, who are supposedly objective in their decisions. In practice, not all locations and people within a nation can be reported on daily, simply because of the limitation of the page-space.

In the blank page-space, differences between locations are concurrently diminished and emphasized. They are emphasized by tagging the name of the place to an event reported. Simultaneously, differences must be "de-emphasized" in order to constitute the equality of all spaces and, by extension, the equality of all individual denizens within the geographically bounded community—no spatial location and no individual is formally more or less important than any other within this community boundary. At this level, all the places that are marked in any one day in the newspaper pages are taken together to signify the "inclusiveness" of all the specific locations as being equally and collectively constitutive of the community spatially. For the newspaper, these simultaneous processes are routine practices of journalism. They are what ethnomethodologists have noted as the "seen but unnoticed" character of newspaper reportage (Garfinkel, 1967).

In this chapter, I use the entertainment pages of a local Mandarin language newspaper which reports regularly on Chinese-language pop culture activities to demonstrate the material basis for the constitution of the boundaries of Pop Culture China as a "community." The March 3–8, 2010 entertainment pages of Singapore's national Chinese-language newspaper, *Lian He Zao Pao* (联合早报), will be used as a resource to demonstrate the various, relatively stable, if not invariant, features in the practical accomplishment of a sense of Pop Culture China.

## Pop Culture China as Practical Accomplishment

First, a human community must have physical boundaries with specific geographic spaces and places. To constitute the imaginary geography of Pop Culture China, the major locations in which Chinese-language pop culture is produced, distributed, and consumed must be present in the reportage to provide a sense of its geography. For an illustrative example, in the entertainment page of the March 4 edition of the *Lian He Zao Bao*, the following locations were reported on: Taiwan, Beijing, Shanghai, Sanya (三亚) (Hainan, China), Hong Kong, and Singapore; apart from Sanya, the appearance of the other locations is in fact quite typical of the daily entertainment pages in this national Chinese-language newspaper. The routine repetition of their co-presence on the same page reinforces the representation of these locations as "belonging together" as a relatively "coherent" geographic-spatial unit in the world. It also signifies these locations as the important nodes in this geographic-spatial unit.

Second, geographic spaces have to be inhabited by individuals and groups to become a human community; as such, the entertainment pages are peopled by pop culture personalities. For example, on the March 5 page, the lead story featured the lead actress Joanna Dong (董姿彦) and lead actor, Taiwanese Mo Tzu-yi (莫子仪) of a newly-released film by young Singaporean filmmaker Wee Li Lin (黄理菱), *Forever* (我爱你爱你爱你 2010). Dong is a Singaporean singer/actress relatively unknown in Pop Culture China as she has never ventured out of Singapore and sings predominantly American jazz. As this is a Singaporean national newspaper, it should be expected that prominent page-space be given to local artists; thus, in addition to this article, there were also prominent reports of local concerts by Tanya Chua (蔡健雅) on March 4 and JJ Lin (林俊杰) on March 7.

Another story on the same page covers Hong Kong star Aaron Kwok's two publicity appearances to promote two of his upcoming films; in Beijing, with Chinese actress Zhang Ziyi and in Hong Kong, with fellow cast members, for a romantic comedy. On March 7, there was a report of Faye Wong's five consecutive nights of performance in Hong Kong after eight years of absence from the stage. On the same page, a small item reported that the Chinese child actress Xu Jiao (徐娇), who appeared in Hong Kong filmmaker Stephen Chow's (周星驰) film *CJ 7* (2008), had enrolled in a school in Taipei, where she was currently shooting a new film. Each of these personalities is often tagged by his/her place of origin. This is particularly necessary for new and emergent entertainers, who may not be sufficiently known to readers for such information to be omitted. However, in instances such as Aaron Kwok, Zhang Ziyi, and Faye Wong, who are well-established and widely known celebrities—a phenomenon to be discussed in the next section—the place of origin can be, and often is, omitted in reports because it is presumed to be "common" knowledge among readers. In the deletion of their place of origin, the particular entertainment celebrity comes to simply belong to the Pop Culture China community itself, without qualification.[10]

Third, the inhabitants, i.e., the entertainers, in and of Pop Culture China must not be static but must be mobile, traversing the geographical spaces and places which together constitute the bounded space of the community. Thus, performances of an artist from one location in another are frequently reported events; for example, in the Aaron Kwok article, it was reported that before his appearance in Beijing he had been in Hong Kong to promote another film. The Taipei-based Singaporean singer Stefanie Sun Yanzi was reported, on March 3, to have announced her return to the music world in Beijing, after four years of absence from recording and performing. Every event in the entertainment world can potentially be turned into a vehicle to present its inhabitant-performers as a community. Thus the announcement of Sun's return was used as an occasion to roll out the other Taiwan-based, big name male and female Mandopop singers—boy-band MayDay (五月天), Jolin Tsai (蔡依林), Jay Chou, David Tao (陶喆), Elva Hsiao (萧亚轩) and Taiwanese television variety show host Zhang Xiaoyan (张小燕) were all reported to have sent congratulations and messages of encouragement.

Events in the calendar of Pop Culture China are even better vehicles to present the gathering of the inhabitant-performers who are constantly on the move, instantiating the community.[11] An example is the annual Golden Melody Awards in Taiwan. Reports from before, during and after the event covered the "gathering" of stars who came from different corners of Pop Culture China to one location to compete for the awards—not only were the winners worthy of write-ups, but the losers were also worthy of mention, particularly their "magnanimity" or their "bitterness" in losing. The 2010 Award was held on June 26. Taiwan aboriginal singer, Chang Hui-mei was the big winner, receiving the Best Female Singer, Best Song, and Best Album of the Year awards. Before the event, a report on June 21, suggested that Chang Hui-mei was hoping to be successful in winning the Best Female Singer award with her new album, after having recently failed in a love affair. On the other hand, Singapore singer Tanya Chua felt no pressure in the competition, after having won the title twice before (in 2005 and 2007). In the post-award gossip, on June 28, it was reported that David Tao, who was absent from the ceremony but had won the Best Male Singer Award, was in Singapore where he had been found in the company of a "hot babe" and did not even know he had won because he was too drunk. Meanwhile, the male Singaporean singer JJ Lin cried into his beer and champagne for his failure to win anything.

Events outside the terrain dominated by Huaren populations also serve to bring the Pop Culture China community into relief among other communities of entertainers. An excellent example was the report from the annual Cannes International Film Festival on the entertainment page of *Lian He Zao Pao* on May 22, 2004: a photograph of the actors and actresses in Wong Kar Wai's (王家卫) then much-anticipated new film, *2046*, included Zhang Ziyi and Gong Li from China, Tony Leung and Carina Lau (刘嘉玲) from Hong Kong and Takeshi Kaneshiro, the Taiwan-born, Tokyo-based Japanese actor.[12] Another photograph brought together Andy Lau from Hong Kong, Zhang Yimou, the famous fifth-generation director from China, Zhang Ziyi from China, and Takeshi Kaneshiro from Taiwan, for Zhang's *wuxia* film, *House of the Flying Daggers*. The gathering of all these inhabitants of the community on the same page, in words and pictures, is a "visualization" of the synchronicity and inclusiveness of the community in celebration, thus affirming the very discursive object of Pop Culture China.

Finally, the inhabitant-performers are often presented 'interactively.' The report discussed above of Sun's return to performance and recording shows that she is among her friends and fellow Taiwan-based Mandopop singers. In the Aaron Kwok article, it was mentioned that when he was working in Taiwan, he had never collaborated with the lead actress René Liu (刘若英) who starred in a new romantic comedy film that was currently in production. However, when he saw her at a mutual friend's wedding, "I thought she was a sexy woman" and had since then been looking forward to working with her on a film. These reported personal connections signify the presence of a "community" in which the inhabitants are familiar, if not friends, with each other; the newspaper's term for this community is "circle" (*quan* 圈).

The above list of features found in the newspaper page-space, is part of the construction and visual "representation/realization" of Pop Culture China as a "community," though it is obviously not an exhaustive list. However, to the extent that without them a visualized realization of the imagined community would be unlikely to succeed, they may be considered a minimal list of essential features. In this sense, they are essential but normally unnoticed textual structuring strategies that "realize" the implicit claim of a newspaper as the printed proxy or representation of the community which it both constructs and serves simultaneously.

# Celebrities

In the construction and visual realization of Pop Culture China, it is the entertainers who are constantly featured in the page-space of the entertainment pages. In addition to news about cultural products—new entrants to the scene, new films, new television shows, new music album releases and concert tours—the trials and tribulations of the entertainers are regular features in these pages. "News" on and about the entertainers concerns "personal" events that are conventionally labeled as "gossip," such as public misdemeanors like drunkenness or speeding, "secrets" from their pre-celebrity days, "unholy" liaisons, marriages, divorces, and other entangled sexual relations. For example, in the above report on March 5, Zhang Ziyi was reported to have said that during the period of filming with Kwok, she was in a very "low" state, facing a lot of pressure and yet, could not share it with family and friends as she was unwilling to burden them. On the March 5 page, there was also a very lengthy story about the relationship between Ella Chen (陈嘉桦), a member of the very popular three member girl-band, S.H.E., and her current boyfriend, a Malaysian who works for a cosmetic agency. The narrative started favorably but ended with gossip about his flirtatious ways with women and a list of her past failed relationships with a string of men. On March 6, there was a report about the shooting location in Taiwan of Taiwan-American filmmaker, Ang Lee's new film, an adaptation of the multi-award winning novel, *Life of Pi* (Martel 2001). A supplementary article, carried within what was supposedly a review of a new book on the life and films of Lee, narrated an incident when the generally-calm director lost his temper, let out a loud scream and kicked a door as he rushed out of a room during the closing days of shooting for his box-office success *Eat Drink Man Woman* (*Yin Shi Nan Nu* 饮食男女). The film was made in 1994!

These reports in the daily newspaper are both a reflection of the current popularity of the celebrities themselves and of the contribution of the entertainment pages to their popularity. This was part of the media process of manufacturing entertainers as celebrities, defined here as those "who, through specific personal achievements—their doings, rather than their ways of life—gaining an appearance in the news and concomitantly considerable albeit fleeting public attention" (Langer quoted in Turner, Bonner, and Marshall 2000: 11). They conform closely to two established observations about the media construction of celebrities. First, as Turner, Bonner and Marshall point out, "[a]mong the defining attributes of the signifying system which produces celebrity is the dissolving of the boundary between public and private lives" (2000: 12). Second, this blurring of difference is executed with an interest, arising from skepticism towards the media hype and commercial marketing, to "uncover" the "real" self of the celebrity in question. The suspicion and the interest to tear away the media veil have been formulated as "the 'oppositional resentment' of the popular audience" (Turner, Bonner, and Marshall,

2000: 13). The entertainment pages thus routinely and concurrently valorize Chinese-language entertainers as icons—or, to be consistent with the language used in Chinese-language media, as "idols"—in some reports while in other reports "expose" their anti-social, deviant, or otherwise iconoclastic behavior, as if to cut them down to size. Finally, the significance of celebrities in engendering a sense of community among pop culture audience/consumers has been succinctly stated by Wark (quoted in Turner, Bonner, and Marshall 2000: 14): "We may not like the same celebrities, we may not like them at all, but it is the existence of a population of celebrities, about whom to disagree, that makes it possible to constitute a sense of belonging ... to something beyond the particular culture with which each of us might identify."

## Incorporating Korean and Japanese Pop Culture

As argued in Chapter 1, Japanese pop culture in the early 1990s and, subsequently Korean pop culture in the late 1990s have been grafted onto the historically-deeper Pop Culture China distribution structure. This is not surprisingly reflected in the entertainment pages under examination. On March 3, there was a report on the misbehavior of Japanese boy-band, Kishida, who donned Nazi uniforms for an MTV performance in Japan, causing protest from the Simon Wiesenthal Center for being insensitive and hurting Jewish sentiments. The band immediately apologized in several languages and promised never to use the same uniform again in future appearances. On March 4, there was a report of another boy-band, SMAP, secretly shooting a mobile phone commercial over a four-day period at the newly opened casino resort, Marina Bay Sands, in Singapore.

Just below the Kishida story was a similar story of "costume malfunction" reported about Korean actress, Lee Da-hae (李多海) who, during her attendance of the Seoul Arts and Culture Awards, had a white piece of lining showing under her bright yellow dress as she walked onto the red carpet. This led to mischievous speculation that it was a sanitary pad or used toilet paper, causing her to lament her embarrassment and hurt for being an instant laughing stock in the limelight. On March 7, there was a short report on the forthcoming marriage between Korean actor Jeong Jun-ho (郑俊浩) and actress Lee Ha-jung (李河静) laced with gossip that she was two months' pregnant—perhaps because they had known each other for only three months and had recently purchased a home together in a neighborhood filled with other Korean stars. Finally, on March 8, it was reported that two members of the currently "hot" boy-band, Super Junior, Choi Si-won (崔始源) and Lee Dong-hae (李东海), had agreed to shoot a thirteen-part television drama with Taiwanese actress Ivy Chen (陈意涵), entitled *Extravagant Challenge* (华丽 的挑战), adapted from a Japanese manga, and financed by a Taiwanese television station (八大), to be shot in Taiwan. The contracting of two members of one of the hottest Korean boy-bands as lead actors in a drama by the Taiwanese television station obviously reflects the popularity of the band in Pop Culture China and it is clearly also an instance of a transnational collaboration aimed at the pan-East Asian market. Related to the band, it was reported one of the members of its splinter group, Super Junior-M, which sings in Mandarin to capture Taiwanese and China audiences, was hurt when a rock was thrown at him during a concert, causing speculation on the Internet that it was an act of revenge from the already-departed Super Junior Chinese member, Han Geng (韩庚), as he had left under the very acrimonious condition of suing the talent company over his thirteen-year contract.

Most of these reports are gossip by nature, which may be of interest to Singaporean fans of East Asian Pop Culture in general or, respectively, of Japanese or Korean pop culture specifically. Indeed, the Singaporean PhD student in geography at the National University of Singapore who assisted me, on the spur of the moment, to decipher the Chinese scripted names of the Korean actors and actresses in the reports had no difficulties in instantly identifying the Korean stars and the occasion of the "costume malfunction" of Lee Da-hae. She also had knowledge of the drama series in which the two members of Super Junior are involved. However, her knowledge was gained from Internet sources, as she watches Korean television dramas before they are available on commercial television stations.

Another cursory but telling detail that indicates "incorporation" of the Japanese and Korean singers and actors into the imaginary space of Pop Culture China is visually presented in the entertainment pages in the relative size of photographs that accompany the reports. As a Singaporean national newspaper, understandably, the Singapore singers such as Stefanie Sun, JJ Lin and Tanya Chua were given a large amount of space. Sun's story took a little more than a quarter of a page, half of which was a large photograph; Lin's and Chua's local concerts were both given half a page, half of which was a photograph in each case. Of the rest of the reported items, Taiwan and Hong Kong celebrities, such as Ella of S.H.E. and Faye Wong, were given more photographic space than Japanese and Korean celebrities, with the exception of the photograph of SMAP, which needed to be large enough to accommodate all five members. The relative sizes are arguably indicative of the centrality of Pop Culture China in the local newspaper's construction of East Asian Pop Culture.

To reinforce the claim that Korean and Japanese pop culture are incorporated into Pop Culture China, as demonstrated in the analysis of the Singapore Chinese script newspaper, a quick perusal of the online version of one newspaper from each of Taiwan, Hong Kong, and Japan for two weeks (February 21–28 and March 8–15) was conducted. As space does not permit full analysis, summary observations are provided here. In Taiwan, the daily entertainment pages of *Lian He Bao* (United Daily News 联合报), dedicate most coverage to local stars and promotional activities of local pop culture. However, Hong Kong and Singapore singers of Mandopop were featured quite prominently. The more familiar Chinese artists, like Zhang Ziyi, were also reported on, but in shorter snippets. In addition, Korean boy-band Super Junior-M's visit to Taipei and Japanese singer-actor Takuya Kimura's (木村拓哉) upcoming blockbuster film were featured. One sees here the presence of celebrities from all parts of Pop Culture China, especially Mandarin pop musicians reflecting Taiwan's position as the center for Mandopop music production. There is also the incorporation of Korean and Japanese pop musicians pertaining to their visits to Taiwan.

In Hong Kong's *Ming Pao* (明报), the entertainment pages' coverage was mainly on Hong Kong celebrities and socialites; widespread coverage was dedicated to Hong Kong actress Isabella Leong's (梁洛施) breakup with Richard Li (李泽楷), a tycoon in his own right, after she bore him three sons out of wedlock. During the two weeks of analysis of the paper, while some mainland Chinese artists received headline features, there was not a single feature of a Taiwanese or Singaporean artist. In the week of February 21–28, a member from the Japanese female singing group, AKB48, was featured twice because she was doing promotional work in Hong Kong. Korean artists were featured sporadically. Here the absence of Taiwanese and Singaporean artists may or may not be the norm. Their presence or absence on any particular day or week would likely depend on whether they were undertaking activities pertaining to the Hong Kong entertainment scene. However, as neither Taiwan nor Singapore are major producers of Chinese language films and Hong Kong is quite self-sufficient in Cantonese television drama production, the absence of Taiwanese and Singaporean artists in Hong Kong papers is not surprising. China, on the other hand, has become a survival pipeline for the Hong Kong film industry and one can therefore expect China to feature regularly in the entertainment pages of Hong Kong newspapers.

In the case of *Asahi Shimbun* (朝日新闻) from Japan, the newspaper did not have dedicated entertainment pages; short write-ups of Japanese television dramas were provided in the Arts and Lifestyle section. There was no coverage of any other pop culture news.

A search of the English edition of two Korean dailies on the Internet yielded the following results. In *JoongAng Daily* (中央日报), from March 2–11, apart from news about Korean celebrities, there were two items from Japan; an announcement that Girls' Generation was to tour Japan in May 2011, and news that another girl-band, Kara, had released a DVD that topped the charts in sales in Japan for the week of February 23.[13] In *Chosun Ilbo* (朝鲜日报), from March 4–11, only the Girls' Generation forthcoming tour of Japan was reported.[14] In both the Japanese and Korean cases, it is obvious that Pop Culture China is not of interest to local newspapers or their audiences, reflecting the absence of imports of Chinese-language pop culture into both nations. Any reception/consumption of such imports is at best a niche market.

## Reading Chinese Entertainment News

Pop Culture China as an imagined "community" is not complete without the audience/consumers of the pop culture products. Although the readers of the entertainment pages are external to the text, their real presence is assumed in the idea of the newspaper as a vehicle of communication. Beyond serving as part of the advertising and marketing effort for pop culture products, the entertainment pages featuring the textualized entertainers bind the readers not only to the entertainers but also to each other; in this sense the pages help to "hold" the entertainers and the readers together. This reader population is not a monolithic, consciously organized mass "community." They range from readers who only skim the entertainment pages to fans of specific celebrities who would cut out features on their idols and preserve the cuttings in their collections of memorabilia. Regardless of the degree of intensity of involvement with the pop culture scene or specific artists, readers are persistently drawn into the territories and lives of Pop Culture China entertainer-citizens who are reported on in the newspaper pages.

Each reader may be isolated from other readers without an awareness of each other's presence and interests. Unlike avid fans who actively seek out various fan communities, more often than not, only a weak sense of a "community" of readers would manifest, and only "occasionally," in both senses of "on an occasion" and "infrequently," among readers of newspapers, for example, when information in the entertainment pages emerges as a topic of conversation in chance gatherings between friends and/or strangers. Such information serves as conversational "currency" that circulates within the reader-community, however fleetingly. Given the occasional character of this "community," one should not attribute too much depth to the "Chineseness" of the Huaren consumers of the multilingual Chinese pop culture. The "shallowness" of identity is partly reinforced by the very character of pop culture and its consumption: celebrities and popular music, films and television dramas come and go in quick succession and audience/consumers' interests pass equally swiftly, without any deep investment in what is favored at any one moment. In these circumstances, being culturally "Chinese" and being part of the "globally-dispersed-Huaren-community" is a rather ephemeral identity, and by no means an exclusive one, within the constellation of possible identities for each of the consumers in the Chinese-language(s) popular cultural industry.

## Conclusion

This chapter argues that the conceptualization of the "overseas" Huaren population as a "diasporic" community which references China and is united by a sense of "Chineseness" based on traditional belief systems and institutions, such as Confucianism, is highly problematic. This is because knowledge of the belief systems and institutions in "traditional" Confucian culture has been declining in each successive local-born population throughout the global geographic dispersion of the Huaren population. In contrast, the Huaren population continues to be connected by flows and exchanges of pop culture in multiple Chinese languages, where comprehension across language divides is facilitated by a shared written script, with occasional local variations. This dense traffic of cultural production, circulation, and consumption holds within it the potential for the emergence of an imaginable "pan-Huaren community," which can be made manifest through different channels, modes, and media of communication and, may therefore be discursively designated Pop Culture China. This "imagined" and "imaginable" community can be made manifest indirectly through the entertainment pages of Chinese-language newspapers, which can demonstrably be treated analytically as the proxy for the spatial boundaries of Pop Culture China. The imaginary geography of Pop Culture China in these pages is signified particularly by the major cities, acting as sign-posts that mark the spatial territory, and its entertainer-inhabitants, whose lives and activities are reported daily. To the extent that these predominantly-Huaren locations and communities are importing and consuming pop culture from Japan and Korea, the imaginary geography will also include production centers and celebrities from these two countries as well. At this expanded level, the pages may be proxy for a larger East Asian Pop Culture, where the centrality of Pop Culture China is unmistakable. The other inhabitants of Pop Culture China are the readers/audience/consumers of the entertainment pages and the related cultural products that are outside these pages. On occasions when information gleaned from reading the pages serves as the cultural currency in conversation among co-present participants, the potential for community is instantiated. However, such occasional and occasioned "community" should not be invested with any presumption of lasting, long-term identity among the conversationalists, whose interests in the latest pop culture material and celebrities are likely to be passing fancies.

# 3

# Taiwan's Present/Singapore's Past Mediated by the Hokkien Language

This chapter is in the strict sense a digression from or a parenthesis to the discussion of East Asian Pop Culture in that it examines an issue in Pop Culture China that was raised in Chapter 2, in order to round out that discussion of Pop Culture China. As mentioned, the intrinsically plural cultural traffic among Huaren communities in terms of the different languages and the different cultural contexts in the locations of production and reception/consumption creates slippages in meanings and symbolic values encoded at production and decoded at reception, with negotiated outcomes. Indeed, producers in Pop Culture China are well aware of this situation. Michael Curtin's interview with Michael Woo, a Hong Kong producer who has moved to Singapore to work for MediaCorp, deserves to be quoted at length as it demonstrates this awareness producers have about operating across the Pop Culture China markets:

> He [Michael Woo, a Hong Kong producer working in Singapore for MediaCorp] lets out a mischievous laugh and then notes that, by comparison, layers of cultural difference make it difficult to produce contemporary series that resonate with Chinese audiences in several markets. For example, in Hong Kong, "you have a lot of criminal cases," he explains. "You have M-16 or AK-47 or whatever in the street— ga-ga-ga-ga-ga-gah—just like a movie," he says, spraying the air with imaginary machine gun fire, "but it's the real thing. Here [Singapore] you can't see that. Triad societies in Hong Kong, Taiwan—although we don't say it, we know (they are a) common phenomenon. Here, we can't say we don't have them, but it's minimal. Corruption. Here, we don't say we don't have it, but it's minimal. I know this for a fact." Consequently, Singaporean viewers don't tend to show the same enthusiasm as audiences in Hong Kong and Taiwan show for triad dramas. Indeed, local film exhibitors make a similar observation, noting that Singaporean audiences tend to like romances and comedies, but even with these genres, tastes diverge, says Woo, and again it has to do with the social experience of the audiences. Woo points to the successful

Beijing author Wang Shuo, whose many novels have been adapted by TV producers in the PRC. With the roiling changes of mainland society as his backdrop, Wang is renowned for weaving social commentary into his romances. "As an industry worker, I appreciate his stories," remarks Woo, "but the common audience (in Singapore), they don't appreciate it, because they don't come from that culture. They don't understand that the change from a closed economic system to an open market economy can cause a change of mindset that can create conflicts in a love story, and maybe the Taiwanese don't understand this either. It's a type of contemporary culture, but you have to be part of it. It doesn't matter if you speak Chinese and you are Chinese, you still might not understand it." (Curtin 2007: 182–183)

For reasons to do with their different migration histories from China, the majority of the Taiwan population and the majority of Singaporean Huaren were hewn from the same present-day southern Chinese province of Fujian, speaking the local Minnan language.[1] Their migration from China to Taiwan took place in the seventeenth century (Chen 1980), while the mass migration to Singapore began in the early nineteenth century and continued until just after the Second World War. Both the province and the language are known as Hokkien in the local pronunciation.[2] However, while the language continues to be known as Hokkien in Southeast Asian Huaren communities, it has come to be elevated to the "national" language in Taiwan, where it is now commonly referred to as Taiwanese (*taiyu* 台语). Nevertheless, a Hokkien-speaking person from Southeast Asia will have little problem, other than different local accents, conversing with a Taiwanese Minnan person. Obviously, Taiwan and Singapore have very different histories, contemporary political and cultural contexts and attitudes towards China. These different conditions with a common language provide an opportunity to examine the micropolitics and slippages in meaning and symbolic order when a Hokkien-language movie crosses national-political-cultural borders from Taiwan to Singapore.

## Hokkien Films: A Synopsis

This analysis will be conducted through two films, one from each location, and the reception of the Taiwanese film in Singapore. The Singaporean film, *Money No Enough*, the "Singlish" translation of the Mandarin title *Qian bu gou yong* (钱不够用), is the highest box office returning film in local film history. The Taiwanese film *Tai ping tian guo* (太平天国), known in English as *Buddha Bless America*, was screened to a full house during the 1998 Singapore International Film Festival. Both are, in the main, Hokkien films, with Mandarin and English making their appropriate appearances through the respective characters in the films.[3]

The narrative of *Money* is straightforwardly about the trials and eventual financial success of three men who are good friends; one has been educated in Mandarin (in Singapore, colloquially known as "Chinese"-educated, in contrast to being "English"-educated) and the other two are with little, if any, formal education, that is, they are illiterate, hence monolingual Hokkien speakers, with some facility in Mandarin picked up from the streets or during their primary school days, before failing or dropping out.[4] Like eighty-five percent of contemporary Singaporeans, they live in public housing estates. At the beginning of the film, the Mandarin speaker has a white-collar job, gambles and makes gains on the stock market, and confidently buys a large number of consumer durables, such as a monstrous television set and a car, all on monthly installment payments. As the film unfolds, he loses his job to a younger man who has been educated overseas in English, his stock holdings crash, vendors repossess all the hire-purchase goods and his wife leaves taking with her their only child. His attempts to secure a new job fail one after another, for want of an English education and other "certified" skills—in Singaporean parlance, he has "no paper qualification." He is left with an empty flat; fortunately for him the public housing authority, unlike private financial institutions, does not repossess flats on account of the financial difficulties of lessees.

Meanwhile, one of his two friends, who is a building renovation contractor, is cheated of his working capital, forcing him to borrow money from a loan shark. Predictably, he cannot pay the high interest on the loan and is reduced to being a fugitive from debt collectors, whose only means of recovering unpaid loans is violence. The third and least able man works as a lowly "waiter" at the local *kopi-tiam* (coffee shop) and, in spite of his advanced years, still lives with his mother. His sole ambition is to get a girlfriend. At their most destitute, the three friends pool their meager financial means to set up a car wash business after hearing about a friend's success in this trade. One thing leads to another and they become successful in that business, which extends to owning outright a dealership for car-care products. With this success, the educated one is reunited with his family and the other two simply continue to spend lavishly on women in karaoke lounges.

The Taiwanese film, *Buddha*, centers on the events that rupture and eventually transform the moral basis of life in a farming village when it is commandeered for military exercises by the US Army stationed in Taiwan. Throughout the entire episode, the villagers' disposition is one of incomprehension. The adults do not understand the point of the exercises and must watch on as their tilled land is destroyed by tanks and bombs. Their attempt at protest is thrown into disarray by the warning shots fired by the US soldiers. The only person who stands up against the destruction is a village widow who owns a cabbage patch. Determined to protect the vegetables, she camps out at her patch and each time they come past, she literally stands in the way of the traffic of tanks and other military vehicles. The American military, out of frustrated incomprehension, divert their tanks away from her patch. The other villagers, herded into the village school building and kept away from their daily routine of work, spend their days idling, gambling, and drinking. The children, let off from attending school, do not realize the danger of the mock battlefield and run around freely amongst the soldiers, tanks, and guns. This reduction to idleness leads to the corruption of the villagers. The adults, seduced by an outside Taiwanese agent who promises to buy the loot, steal everything from the military, from canned goods to army uniforms, and even items that they do not know what to do with, such as a box of condoms. The children hang out at the army camp for goodies from the soldiers, peer into the bar where there are prostitutes who have been brought in from the city, see disco dancing and hear rock and roll music for the first time, and fight over bullet and bomb casings, which they sell for cash.

A central narrative thread is built around an unemployed village teacher, apparently the only literate person in the village. He is fascinated by everything about the United States; its politics, its wealth and particularly its science and technology, "knowledge" of which he obtains from newspapers. His younger brother has returned from the city after having lost an unspecified number of fingers in an industrial accident at his previous factory employment. The severed fingers were soaked in some liquid and kept in glass jar, and the unemployed teacher believes they could be sewn back in place someday. The arrival of the US military is just the opportunity they have been waiting for. So, one evening, the young man shows up at the entrance to the bar with his jarful of fingers and tries to get the US soldiers to look at his hand and fingers. A soldier and a prostitute who meet him at the door think that the fingers are props for begging and stuff some US dollars into his hand, to his consternation. The same happens when his "knowledgeable" brother accompanies him to the military camp; however, this time, the older brother feels insulted, screams that they are not beggars and throws the money back at the US soldier, to the latter's puzzlement.

The moral corruption of the villagers reaches its highest point when the wife of the unemployed village teacher begins to despise her husband's refrain from stealing from the US military, reading his moral integrity as cowardice. In anger, he takes off with his brother to steal the "biggest" loot the village will ever see. As night falls, they pull two huge black metal boxes into the village on a cart, to the great admiration of all. The villagers open the boxes after much difficulty, only to discover two dead American soldiers, one black and one white. Admiration turns instantly into admonition of the brothers for bringing bad luck to the village. Bowls of rice and incense are immediately prepared to propitiate the spirits of the two dead soldiers. The possibility of burying the corpses in the village is rejected by the villagers for fear that their spirits would not make it back to the US and would thus visit the villagers in the future. Thus, without any assistance from the others, the two brothers tow the coffins to the side of a road to let them be picked up by the military, which was by then shutting down its exercises and leaving the village. As the film draws towards its close, the village slowly returns to its previous way of life.

## The Positioning of Hokkien

In *Money*, throughout the film, the dialogue between the three main characters and in most of their social encounters is in Hokkien. English makes brief appearances on two occasions. First, when the Mandarin-speaking main character is fired from his job he speaks in English and second, after becoming successful, he has to use English in his dealings with the manager of the car-care products company and during his public relations appearance in front of the mass media. Mandarin is used in conversations at the coffee shop among the main characters and with their friends. The hierarchies of social, cultural and economic power between the three languages vary inversely with the predominance of the languages in the film. The small amount of English-language dialogue emphatically enhances its privileged, indeed hegemonic, position in the working life of Singaporeans. Its dominance in Singaporean economic life is revealed when the Mandarin-speaking main character loses his job and is unable to find another for want of competence in English. The significance of a facility with Mandarin is less explicit and becomes apparent only after it is juxtaposed against Hokkien in the film, as follows.

The political position and representation of Hokkien manifests immediately in the very genre of the film: a slapstick comedy in which the audience's laughter is largely drawn from the antics of the on-screen characters. Significantly in *Money* laughter is also drawn from puns made in the Hokkien language.[5] An example is the repeated scene in which one of the regular female customers of the coffee shop orders her usual *nai cha* (奶茶), Mandarin for "tea with milk." The waiter character consistently shouts out the order to the counter, as is common practice in such neighborhood coffee shops in Singapore. In this instance his shouting is more for the enjoyment of everyone present, including the film audience, of course: "This lady wants *teh nee*," which in Hokkien could slide from "This lady would like tea with milk" to "This lady wants her breasts squeezed." In Hokkien "milk" and "breast" are the same word, while a slight shift in tone renders the sound for "tea" into the sound for "squeeze." In addition to the puns, the "pathetic" character of Hokkien speakers is also portrayed in the scene featuring the funeral of the coffee shop waiter's mother; his shameless sisters begin to quarrel about the funeral costs through their crocodile tears and false wailings in hilarious, laughable Hokkien dialogue. Finally, Hokkien as the language of the low life is driven home by the swearing and cursing of the gangsters who are the henchmen of the loan shark. Throughout the film the use of Hokkien is intentionally crude, uncouth and bawdy; that is, intentionally "low class."

A similar positioning of Hokkien as the language of the lowest social class—the marginally employed, the unemployed and the unemployable—can be found in most Singapore-produced films released in the 1990s. In the film *Mee Pok Man* (*The Noodle Vendor*, 1995), the winner of multiple international film festival awards, the noodle vendor lives on the furthest edge of the underbelly of Singapore, surrounded by Hokkien-speaking pimps and prostitutes and is himself without voice. Similarly in the film *Eating Air* (1999), another favorite on the international film festival circuit, the English title is perhaps an intentional mistranslation of the Hokkien, *chia hong* (*chi feng* 吃风 in Mandarin), which signifies the youth in the film as "living on air." The literal translation would be "eating wind," metaphorically meaning "enjoying leisure," with a particular connotation of road travel when one can feel the wind on the face. In the case of this film, the main characters, whose names are Ah Boy and Ah Gu (Cow, *niu* 牛 in Mandarin), are riding motorcycles through empty city streets. In this film Hokkien-speaking youth spend their days getting up late, staying out of their homes all night and riding around on flashy motorcycles or hanging out in electronic games arcades; a life of leisure for themselves and a life of uselessness in the eyes of others. They are as much irrelevant to as alienated from Singapore society.

It should be noted that in contrast with this stigmatizing positioning of Hokkien speakers as low life, there have also been popular cultural attempts to "romanticize" them in the generic character of what is locally called the *Ah Beng* and his female counterpart, *Ah Lian*. These are caricatures of the Singlish-speaking Singaporeans who are "adorably" laughable to the middle-class, English-educated writers and audience for whom switching code from "the Queen's English" to Singlish is a marker of "authentic" Singaporean identity. The most successful construction of a pair of such characters on-screen is found in the very popular television family sitcom, *Phua Chu Kang*, which features the comedy of everyday life in the family of a poorly-educated building renovation contractor (who else?), similar to the character in *Money*. Not surprisingly, the show's popularity is based on the "silliness" of the *Phua* and his *Lian* wife Rosie, even as they triumph repeatedly over their university-educated but lacking-in-common-sense architect brother and his West-loving and pretentious wife.[6] This middle-class romanticizing of the adorable and guileless is often rudely disrupted in real life by the behavior of the supposedly "real" *Ah Bengs*. For example, when a young lawyer who was watching a movie with his girlfriend told a group of young men to stop talking on their mobile phones during the show, he was beaten up by the four youths. Two columnists writing in English immediately reminded their readers of the "reality" of the *Ah Bengs*' fists (Tan 2000 and Long 2000).

In a country where forty years of continuous economic growth has engendered a substantial middle class and where an individual's social and economic status is dependent on academic and professional achievements, monolingual Hokkien speakers are in reality individuals who have been left behind by Singapore's rapid economic and cultural developments. The representation of Hokkien as a low-class language that is neither used nor suitable for a civil community in *Money* and other films may thus be justified as an exercise in artistic "social realism," in *cinema veritae*. The socially "real" serves as the ideological alibi for negative stigmatization.

Similarly, *Buddha Bless America* is also a Hokkien film in which American English and Mandarin are used by the appropriate characters on screen. However, in contrast to *Money*, in which all the characters in the film are able to conduct low-level communication in all three languages, in *Buddha*, the incomprehension of the villagers about all that has befallen them is intensified by the mutually-incomprehensible languages of the villagers' Hokkien, the heavily northern-accented Mandarin of the Mainland-migrant (外省人) military men and the English of the US Army personnel. The villagers, young and old, cannot make themselves understood because they do not speak American English. The Taiwanese military personnel, a representation of the Kuomintang army which retreated from mainland China in 1947, who act/intervene as translators/go-betweens between the villagers and the US army, are non-Hokkien-speaking, inept in American English and their heavily northern-accented Mandarin is incomprehensible to the villagers. Finally, American English is completely strange to all the villagers. The impossibility of crossing the language barriers is the root cause of all the misunderstandings between the three different parties and the consequences are often as humorous as they are lamentable.

This mutual incomprehension is an interesting structuring of the politics between the speakers of the three languages; it allows all three to be placed on the same plane, without apparently privileging any one over the others in spite of the obvious differences in political power/force. Mutual incomprehension enables the powerless villages (via the director's ideological positioning) to subvert the intentions of the powerful US military machine; for example, the incomprehensible Hokkien protestations of the middle-aged village woman in the face of the tanks and soldiers (perhaps a humorous version of the unknown man in front of the tank that rolled into Tiananmen in 1989?) forced the military machine to divert its progress and not only spared the life of the woman but also saved her lowly cabbage patch. The bewilderment and frustration of the US soldiers in this confrontation is quite humorously portrayed in the film. In another instance, the US military personnel, upon discovery that the villagers have been stealing their supplies, chase the villagers to their schoolhouse but find no evidence after ransacking the makeshift rooms in the building. The US military officer's statement of apology to the villagers is (mis)translated by the Mandarin-speaking military officer into a thorough scolding of the villagers for disgracing the Taiwan nation and a declaration that future infractions will be punishable by military court. The US military officer has no idea at all of what has happened to his apology, nor more importantly, the feelings his mistranslated "speech" have generated among the villagers towards US military and US–Taiwan relations, when US soldiers are supposed to be friends of Taiwan in Cold War rhetoric. It is not clear to the audience whether the Mandarin-speaking officer's mistranslation is intentional or for lack of understanding of the US officer's speech. Finally, the US soldiers' exclamation of "Hey you!" to villagers is misused by the villagers to swear at each other. In all these instances, mutual incomprehension of the three languages acts, without any on-screen characters' apparent subjective intentions, to frustrate the powerful US and Taiwan military officers and simultaneously provides the avenue for the villagers' resistance to the former power and oppression they had been subjected to.

## Hokkien: The Suppressed Language

The different political positioning of Hokkien, the common language of both the majority of Huaren in Singapore and the majority of Taiwanese, is the consequence of the respective political histories and trajectories of the three languages—Hokkien, Mandarin and English—in the two countries. A convenient starting point for mapping the trajectory of the politics of languages in Taiwan is the 1947 defeat of the Kuomintang (KMT) by the Chinese Communist Party in mainland China. Retreating to the island of Taiwan, the KMT established itself as a government-in-exile in this "province" of China; insisting on Taiwan as a province was necessary to institutionalize the discursive political space for the KMT's expressed ambition to "re-conquer" the Mainland (反攻大陆). From the local Taiwanese point of view, however, the retreating KMT was an invading and colonizing force from the mainland Chinese provinces. Hence, Taiwan residents who are either members or descendants of members of the retreating KMT are still known/labeled as "people from outside provinces" (外省人).

Upon arrival in Taiwan, the KMT set out to continue the legacy of the 1911 Republican Revolution, which overthrew the Qing dynasty and ended imperialism in China. It "felt compelled to define national identity [for Taiwan] in terms of race, language and history" and also "to invoke, resuscitate and reinvent tradition for the purpose of legitimising its own vision of modern society" (Chun 1995: 51). Its idea of the nation was, of course, a "Chinese" nation. Citing the works of Gellner (1983) and Benedict Andersen (1983), Chun suggests that, as in all nation-state building projects, a central prerequisite is universal literacy for the realization of a "national" culture through a "common colloquial language" (1995: 50); the KMT's choice was, of course, Mandarin for the realization of "Chinese" culture in Taiwan. Thus Mandarin became the language of government and public administration, of state-supported education and of "national" representation in general, i.e., the "national" language (*guoyu* 国语). As contemporary politics for Taiwanese independence shows, the imposition of Mandarin may have been successful, as it is now a common language, especially among the educated and especially in the north of the island. However, its attempt at transforming Taiwan into a Chinese "nation" is becoming increasingly alienating to the people of Taiwan.

For Hokkien-speaking Taiwanese, the imposition of Mandarin was an act of repressive political violence against both the language and its speakers. Against this history of repressive colonization, the Hokkien language is an emotive rallying beacon around which anti-KMT sentiments can be organized and harnessed. Rhetorically elevated to the "ethno-national" language of Taiwanese people, it has become a political resource that can confer upon its speakers the status of Taiwanese nationalists and can be deployed in opposition to not only Mandarin but also the KMT and its Chinese nationalism. Not surprisingly, as contemporary Taiwan pulls politically and ideologically further and further away from China, in spite of the latter's territorial claim on the island as part of the Chinese state, Hokkien is now commonly known as *taiyu* (台语, the Taiwanese language). Indeed, the most vehement of Taiwanese nationalists will speak no language other than Hokkien in Taiwan, although those who aspire to state power have to compromise and speak both Mandarin and Hokkien in public. The readiness of invoking Hokkien as the Taiwanese language in the new nationalism clearly demonstrates that at the level of everyday life and within domestic spaces Hokkien has never been under any threat of total erasure, especially given its demographic dominance.[7] Instead, it has accommodated Mandarin and both languages have achieved common usage among the current residents in Taiwan who switch between and mix the codes of the two languages in their daily transactions, including in political speeches and mass media broadcasts.

In addition to these two languages, one also needs to consider the place of English in Taiwan, which was introduced and is still associated with US military presence on the island. The US continues to be a staunch supporter of Taiwan's resistance to being coercively absorbed by China, regardless of the fact of the winding down but not complete erasure of Cold War hostilities. Reflecting the global economic interest that befits a newly industrialized economy, English is taught in secondary schools. However, the language does not feature significantly in Taiwanese everyday life. With the exception of those who studied in tertiary institutions in Britain or the US, even university students who can read English competently are reluctant to speak, let alone write, in the language.[8] The contemporary situation in Taiwan is thus one of equal predominance of Hokkien and Mandarin, reflected in the common use of mixed codes in daily life, with English as a kind of specialized knowledge for those with reasons to know it well, but it is largely incomprehensible to the majority of the population.

The fate of Hokkien in Singapore has also been politically determined by the state, which is dominated by the single party of the People's Action Party (PAP), which has ruled since 1959 without any interruption. Historically, a total of thirteen Chinese "dialects"[9] were officially listed in the 1957 census of the British colonial government (Purushotam, 1998: 32),[10] with Hokkien spoken by the majority. In the absence of any British colonial effort, the larger groups within the immigrant community set up schools in their respective languages. However, in the early decades of the twentieth century, in response to the modernist movement in China, the language of instruction of Chinese schools in Singapore, and in some other parts of Southeast Asia, switched to Mandarin. Nevertheless, the different Huaren languages continued to be used widely in daily transactions, not only among Huaren but between them and the other racial groups in the region, such as Indians and Malays. The importance of Hokkien, in particular, was driven home to the then would-be first prime minister of Singapore, Lee Kuan Yew, in the early years of political mobilization towards independence from British colonial rule. According to Lee,

> When I made my first speech in Hokkien in 1961 during the Hong Lim by-elections, the children in China Street hooted with derision and contempt. I was unintelligible. I was talking gibberish. They laughed and jeered at me. I was in no mood for laughter. I could not give up. I just had to make myself understood. (Quoted in Purushotam, 1998: 53–54)

However, as the above analysis of *Money* shows, Hokkien has clearly lost its political position and been marginalized. Its displacement from centrality in the everyday life of Huaren in Singapore involves a complex politics of languages in the national formation of a multiracial post-colonial Singapore.

Immediately after the Second World War, Britain began to prepare Malaya, of which Singapore was a part, for political independence. When the Federation of Malaya was granted independence in 1957, Singapore was retained by the British Colonial Office. While this was clearly unacceptable to the emergent Singaporean political leaders of all political leanings, they nevertheless also found it difficult to imagine Singapore as an independent island nation. The uncertainty was "resolved" when, in the face of a possible alleged "communist" electoral victory on the island, the Malayan government initiated the formation of Malaysia, incorporating Malaya, Singapore, Sabah and Sarawak, the two small British territories on the Indonesian island of Borneo. Malaysia became an independent nation in 1963. However, within just two years, Singapore would leave and became the independent island nation that had been inconceivable; *realpolitik* had triumphed over political imagination.

Throughout this period, the political positioning of the different languages of the resident population was a constant source of concern in the imagining of a new nation. Desire to be part of Malaya and later, the reality of becoming part of Malaysia had led to the adoption of Malay as the "national" language. Before that, in 1956, the first elected assembly agreed to adopt Mandarin as the language of Chinese education, making official what was already the common practice in Chinese schools, regardless of the languages spoken at home. With separation from Malaysia, and a demographic dominance of more than seventy percent, the suggestion of adopting Mandarin as the "national" language of Singapore was mooted by various segments of the Huaren community. In spite of its dependence on Huaren electoral support, the newly-independent government resisted this suggestion because of the perceived hostile geopolitical environment in Southeast Asia, which would not have accepted the establishment of a "Chinese" state with equanimity. A system of four official languages was instituted: Mandarin, Malay, Tamil (a south Indian language spoken by the majority of resident Indians) and English, which was adopted as the language of government, public administration and commerce.

English thus became even more entrenched in an independent Singapore which, without any natural resources, would have to make its way in the global economy where facility with English would be a necessity. Economic realism among the people was evident in the continuous expansion of enrollment in English-language schools at the expense of those in the other three languages (Purushotam, 1998: 65). To allay the apprehension of the different racial groups the government introduced a bilingual policy, in which all students were compelled to take English in their respective ethnic-medium schools. This bilingual education policy further evolved from an education system in which different schools operated with different primary languages of instruction, to the present national system in which English is the primary medium of instruction, while every student has to take their respective "mother-tongue" language as a second language. The dominance of English is thus complete, disadvantaging all who are not fluent in it, regardless of their fluency in other official languages. Mandarin, along with other second languages, has thus been displaced. Over the years, the learning of Mandarin has increasingly come to be treated as an inconvenience, if not an obstacle, by some Chinese students and their parents, with the government continually accommodating these complaints by weakening the requirement of second language learning in schools. Teaching and learning Mandarin in school continues to be a very emotive issue in Singapore; one which the ruling party is unable to ignore politically.[11]

Ironically, difficulties with instituting the learning of Mandarin in schools caused a further displacement, indeed suppression, of other Chinese languages. In 1978, a study by the Ministry of Education discovered that the bilingual education system was not working among Chinese students because their competence in both English and Mandarin remained seriously deficient after completion of primary education, creating great wastage of monetary and human resources. As the students were still overwhelmingly speaking different Chinese languages at home, Mandarin was a new language to master; in practice, Chinese students were coping with three languages. It was argued that learning Mandarin in school would be greatly facilitated if it were also spoken at home. The government, with the support of Huaren civil organizations, initiated the "Speak Mandarin" campaign in 1979, which has been ongoing—each year one month is dedicated as the Speak Mandarin Month, during which the city is bombarded with posters and other forms of public messages to speak Mandarin. Furthermore, the use of other Chinese languages, already officially marginalized as dialects, was banned from all public broadcast media; all imported programs—Cantonese from Hong Kong and Hokkien from Taiwan—have since been dubbed into Mandarin.[12] After more than twenty years of promotion of Mandarin, Hokkien has become a language spoken by the young who did not make the grade in the highly-competitive bilingual education system and by the old who had never received formal education; both groups constitute the lowest-educated working class. The language hierarchy in contemporary Singapore is, in descending order, English, Mandarin and Hokkien, as depicted and reflected in the film *Money*.

State formation in Singapore and Taiwan, respectively, displays two different trajectories in the political displacement of Hokkien by Mandarin as the language of the "Chinese." In Taiwan the displacement has not been very successful and Hokkien is being revived in the name of Taiwan nationalism against China; witness the ubiquitous use of Hokkien idioms and popular songs as campaign slogans and theme songs during political elections. Tying the language to a Taiwan-nation, as opposed to a Chinese-nation, guarantees its continuing relevance in Taiwan. In contrast, Hokkien is a dying language in Singapore. Singapore Huaren who are below twenty-five years of age are either completely incapable of using Hokkien or possess a rudimentary knowledge of the language at best, reduced to only an ability to "understand" when spoken to but unable to maintain a conversation, except for occasional words or phrases for emphatic expression. At home, young children are increasingly unable to converse with grandparents who are exclusively Hokkien-speaking, and in the public sphere, the aged are being coerced into speaking Mandarin rather than the young learning Hokkien, reversing any Confucian notion of venerating elders.

## Reception of Hokkien Films in Singapore

The very differently fated trajectories of the Hokkien language are reflected in its political positioning in films produced in Taiwan and Singapore, as the analysis above shows. Consequently, as Hokkien films cross national boundaries, from Taiwan to Singapore and vice versa, one would expect the reception of these films to be significantly determined by the respective audience's local political history and contemporary cultural configuration. For this occasion, I will restrict myself to the reception/reading of Taiwanese films in Singapore.[13]

After a period of about twenty years, during which not a single film was made in Singapore, movie-making appears to be emerging again since the early 1990s. One common element of 1990s films is the depiction of the underbelly of Singapore's economic success story. They feature the marginal, the poor, the working class and the alienated Singaporean, individually or in groups. Among the box office successes are those films that use predominantly Hokkien in the on-screen dialogue, of these the most successful is the film *Money No Enough*, with box office sales of about six million Singaporean dollars, edging out the box office takings of the Hollywood blockbuster, *Titanic* (1997). *Money* attracted large audiences into the cineplexes in public housing estates, in part because the film depicts and reflects the daily life of the lesser-educated, lower-middle income earners who are the majority of public housing estate residents.

It was one of the very first occasions, since the banning of "dialects" in broadcast media in 1979, that Hokkien speakers got to see themselves represented on the big screen. Indeed, many were openly amazed that the made-in-Singapore Hokkien film was allowed to screen in movie houses. By bringing Hokkien to the big screen, the film staged a "return of the repressed" that brought pleasure to all Hokkien speakers, regardless of levels of language competence; viewing pleasure was intensified because it was done in the suppressed language, their language. Ironically, this pleasure was also largely at their own expense because the on-screen Hokkien speakers were caricatures of "crude," "illiterate" characters who were generally the butt of slapstick antics and jokes in the film. This doubled pleasure of liberation and self-parody brought the Hokkien-speaking spectators out in droves to see *Money*; adult children brought their elderly parents who seldom walk into a movie house, because films are usually in English or Mandarin. This doubled pleasure also constitutes a frame through which Singaporean audiences watch Hokkien films. It can be shown to be at work in Singaporeans' viewing of Hokkien films imported from Taiwan as well.[14]

In the film *Buddha Bless America*, what comes through to the Singapore audience is a "comedy" of errors that arises out of both the mutual incomprehension of the three languages—Hokkien, northern-accented Mandarin and American English—and also the "ignorance" of the monolingual, Hokkien-speaking villagers, who are, in colloquial Singaporean, likened to "tortoises from the hills" (*suah koo*; *shan gui* 山龟 in Mandarin). Thus, the widow who successfully diverts the US tanks and soldiers is hilarious for her screaming and stubbornness that wins out; the soaking of the severed fingers is laughable because of the villagers' lack of scientific knowledge; the dragging home of the refrigerated metal coffins is funny for the ignorance it displays; the subsequent attempt to propitiate the spirits of the US soldiers is laughable for its superstition; and the adoption by the boys of "Hey you!" as "swear" words is laughable to anyone who understands English, which is most Singaporeans except the uneducated elderly. These are all imaginable ways for the illiterate, monolingual Hokkien speakers, who inhabit the margins of a highly competitive, highly skilled and highly professionalized urban economy that is well integrated into global capitalism, to behave.

Undoubtedly, there will be Taiwanese people who will see the "comedy" in these scenes. However, the scenes are more likely to be seen as "tragi-comic," with greater empathy for the multiple ways in which the moral life of the village is invaded and trampled upon by the US–Kuomintang military machinery, within the complex politics of contemporary Taiwanese nationalism and the Kuomintang "Chinese" nation. The way in which this politics is manifest, namely the juxtaposition of the mutual incomprehensibility of the three languages, is likely to be lost on the Singaporean audience. Furthermore, the highly urban perceptual horizon of Singaporeans has no purchase on life in a rural community. The very stable political condition, laced with rhetorical anti-Western sentiment, itself a refracted contemporary expression of a colonialism that is externalized, provides Singaporeans with no access to the sentiments of the Hokkien villagers concerning their internal colonization by the Kuomintang mainlanders and their US allies.

Yet ironically, in a country in which the educated and successful speak only English and Mandarin in all social transactions and increasingly also at home, the marginalization and suppression of Hokkien and its speakers are processes of internal colonization that are even more violent than they have been in Taiwan. Where it is possible in Taiwan to raise Hokkien from the status of a language of political protest and subversion to the status of the language of ethno-nationalism, Hokkien speakers in Singapore are condemned to a slow but certain silencing and eventual disappearance. The erasure of their histories in the collective memory of the Singapore nation because their past and participation in local history can no longer be communicated fully becomes more certain as each successive generation becomes less and less competent in the Hokkien language, to the vanishing point of total incompetence. The occasional return of the repressed through an occasional Hokkien film,[15] which draws in big crowds, marks the language's demise all the more tragically, as fewer and fewer Singaporeans are able to understand the films, beyond the comic scenes, for want of linguistic competence, no matter where the film is produced.

## Conclusion

The intrinsically plural cultural traffic among Huaren communities in terms of languages and cultural contexts between geo-political locations creates slippages in meanings and symbolic values encoded at production and decoded at reception, with negotiated outcomes. The shared presence of Hokkien as the language of the Huaren majority in Singapore and Taiwan provides a privileged opportunity to analyze these potential slippages. The difference in the current position of

Hokkien in each nation tells us much about the cultural politics in the respective histories and future trajectories in the state formation of these two polities. To the extent that it is possible to still call the Hokkien-speaking Taiwanese, "Chinese," then the differences in the fate of the language in Singapore and Taiwan are themselves a manifestation of the different and respective ways of "doing" Chineseness, symbolically and materially, giving the lie to claims of a monolithic and monological "cultural China" as a viable construction of the overseas Chinese communities worldwide. This chapter also embarks on a direction for comparative cultural analysis of locations in which Huaren are either the majority or a relatively homogenous population, shifting the focus from the conventional comparative studies in economy and/or politics in these late industrializing societies.

# 4

# Placing Singapore in East Asian Pop Culture

To return to East Asian Pop Culture, as pointed out in previous chapters, Singapore is essentially a location of reception/consumption of pop culture not only from East Asia but also from other regions of the world. This is largely as a consequence of its small and ethnically heterogeneous population, which is unlike that of other East Asian Pop Culture locations where the populations are highly homogenous and thus support a "national"-language pop culture.[1] The small audience population is fragmented firstly in terms of language. In a country with four official languages—English, Mandarin, Malay, and Tamil—each language group potentially constitutes a separate media audience, however, in practice most Singaporeans are bilingual and therefore could be in more than one language audience.[2]

Secondly, Huaren and Indian audiences are further fragmented by intra-ethnic language differences. Within the population of approximately three million Huaren, the dominant languages used to be Hokkien (福建语), Teochew (潮州语) and Cantonese (粤语). These languages have been suppressed by the government policy of exclusive use of Mandarin in all broadcast media, an issue taken up later in this chapter.[3] However, the suppressed languages continue to survive in everyday transactions, particularly among the working-class Huaren and those above fifty years of age, who were denied public education during the colonial period. Snippets of these languages are also often used by younger people, including students, as a conscious, pleasurable "resistance" to the official "speak Mandarin" policy. Among Indians, Tamil, Hindi and Bengali may be the most common languages, along with other smaller language groups, although only Tamil is recognized by the government as an official language.

Finally, onto these complexities of Asian languages has to be added the dominance of English in contemporary Singapore. As a post-British colonial location the Singapore government, at the point of political self-government, decided to capitalize on the global economic advantages of English and adopted it as the language of education, government and public administration, and commerce.[4] Thus, English has become the everyday language of all locally-educated Singaporeans.

English-language media is able to reach the national aggregate of all English-language speakers across the three Asian ethnicities. The highly-fragmented and complex language situation obviously has serious implications for the local media industry.

On the production side, since the mid-1980s, the Singapore government has been espousing a desire to develop "cultural industries" as one wing of the national export economy. However, several rather ambitious plans did not materialize: plans for a significant size television studio in the western part of the island were never realized, and the Tang Dynasty City, putatively a replica of the old Chinese city of Chang'an that was built as a theme park and studio for Chinese-language movies and costing one hundred million Singaporean dollars in 1992, closed its doors in 1997, heavily in debt and by 2011 faced demolition by the landlord, the state-owned Jurong Town Corporation. An attempt to develop a joint-venture with an Italian film company to build a movie studio also came to naught. As it currently stands, television programs in all four languages continue to be produced routinely by the one television corporation, MediaCorp, which is increasing its outsourcing for material produced by local production houses. There is no significant record company in any of the languages. Only a very small number of films are produced annually, and those are by two small but notable film companies, Raintree Pictures, owned by MediaCorp, and Zhao Wei Films, helmed by the independent filmmaker Eric Khoo.

New developments, however, can be found in new digital media. The Economic Development Board (EDB), the key institution which brings in foreign investment to targeted industrial sectors, has a creative industries division dedicated to developing collaboration with foreign enterprises for the production of cultural commodities. Its focus is on developing technical production capability, especially in film and television production, in order to establish Singapore as a technical production site rather than developing local content,[5] a strategy chastised by another local creative industry player for making Singapore a production sweat-shop. On the pop culture front, the push is for the development of animation and computer gaming. The outstanding success story here is the EDB, leveraging on Singapore's good communication technology infrastructure and financial co-investment capacity, in partnership with the biggest home-grown entertainment technology provider, Creative Technology, attracting Lucasfilm into a joint venture, in 2004, to set up Lucasfilm Singapore as a co-production site for the *Star Wars* animation series and related themes for online games for the global market. Again, the emphasis here is on technical production, and its multiplier effects in business opportunities, such as increasing the skills of other media-related businesses like advertising and the computer gaming industry. However, this desired effect does not seem to be panning out, as local companies who experienced early success began to fail by late 2010 (Tham 2010). It is of little surprise, therefore, that the government's initiative has had little impact on Singapore's place in East Asian Pop Culture.

The failures of the earlier plans to develop television and film studios and the relatively miniscule size of the local media industry indicates clearly that Singapore, in contrast to Hong Kong, may be a meeting point for global businesses, but this does not include the confluence of media and pop culture players. Singapore might be a hub for certain global industries, such as finance and logistics, but it is definitely not a "media capital" (Curtin 2003). The government's expressed desire to be a regional "media hub" can only be achieved through "hothouse" strategies, rather than organic growth. With its very significant investment capacity, managed under its sovereign wealth funds Temasek and Government Investment Corporations, the Singapore government is able to invest heavily, from scratch, in industries which it has selected as potential growth points for the national economy. Such hothouse strategies have achieved some measure of success, as seen in the case of digital media, partly spearheaded by the joint venture with Lucasfilms. In terms of its declared ambition to be a "regional hub," the region does not extend beyond Southeast Asia, where its economic dominance leaves it without real challenges from the neighboring countries; here, there is the relative success of the twenty-four hour regional news channel, Channel News Asia (Yue 2006).

On the consumption side, the largest potential audience bases are, obviously, for English and Mandarin programs. Logically, English-language programs are potentially the larger of the two audience bases because firstly, they have a multi-ethnic audience as most Singaporeans are educated in public schools where English is the primary language and their ethnic language is taught as a second language. Secondly, in an education system that favors English, the English proficiency of locally-educated Huaren tends to be greater than their mastery of Mandarin. Empirically, English-language pop culture from the US is consumed enthusiastically by Singaporeans of all races. Like everywhere else throughout East Asia, cinemas are dominated by Hollywood films. American pop music is the staple on English-language radio stations as are American television programs for Channel 5, the English-language free-to-air television channel. Against the high quality of US products, local films, pop music, and television dramas in English compare poorly and thus attract a very small audience.[6]

However, against logical expectation, local television dramas in Mandarin have consistently garnered the highest ratings from their very first introduction in the early 1980s. For the first drama in 1982, "viewership was about 600,000 nightly, which compared favorably even with imported English movies such as *Poltergeist* (406,000 viewers)"; subsequently, the "number of serials with an average viewership of more than one million increased from one in 1990/1991 to four in 1991/1992" (Tan and Soh 1994: 83). However, with the massive arrival of dramas imported from the rest of East Asia on both free-to-air and cable channels, coupled with the lack of development in the quality of local productions, viewership has declined significantly (Lin 2010) and local productions increasingly struggle to hold their own. In pop music, the Mandarin music station 93.3 FM (醉心频道) consistently has the highest annual audience rating nationally, beating many English-language pop music stations. Established in 1990, 93.3 has done the most to promote Mandarin pop music in Singapore, organizing meet-the-star sessions and the Golden Melody Awards. Consequently, it has the support of Mandarin pop singers who contribute one-liner promotional broadcasts for the station. The apparent anomaly of Mandarin programs having the largest audience can be explained by the high proportion of working-class and older people in the Mandarin audience, who have a weak or marginal command of the English language. Consequently, the Huaren as mass audience tend to gravitate towards Mandarin pop culture; in the 2010 national census, fifty percent of Singaporeans continue to use Mandarin or another Chinese language at home.

The Huaren mass audience accounts for Singapore's position in East Asian Pop Culture. On the production side, Singapore is a marginal location in the overall structure of East Asian Pop Culture, and its media industry players have to seek different opportunities, paths and modes of "inserting" themselves into the more accessible Pop Culture China, ranging from individual Singaporean artists finding a career in production centers such as Taiwan and Hong Kong, to co-production arrangements between Singapore media companies with other East Asian partners. On the consumption side, Singapore is a location to which pop culture from all points of East Asia flows freely, consequently making a large proportion of the Singaporean audience a quintessentially transnational audience of imported East Asian Pop Culture. This asymmetrical combination of marginal production and primary consumption advantageously positions Singapore as a good vantage point from which to observe and analyze some of the industrial and reception processes at work within East Asian Pop Culture in one of its constitutive locations. The discussion will begin with the film industry, which has the least significant regional role to play in East Asian Pop Culture, followed by pop music and, finally, television dramas.

## The Singapore Film Industry

From the 1960s, for three decades, Singapore had no film industry to speak of. From the mid-1990s onwards, a trickle of between five and eight feature films have been produced each year, largely by independent producers and directors, many of whom are only able to do one feature film every few years, if they are able to get beyond their first production (Millet 2006). Production picked up from 2007 with fifteen films that year and seventeen the year following; whether this will be sustained is uncertain. The increased production rate is partly a consequence of government financial assistance. The Singapore Film Commission was established in 1998 and incorporated into the Media Development Authority (MDA) in 2003, with the mission of providing financial support for production and training to improve and expand Singapore's talent base among filmmakers. Apart from financing short films, the Commission was prepared to co-invest up to one million Singaporean dollars in the production of feature films, "to be repaid with revenue from the movie after its commercial release" and also to co-produce with foreign producers with the aim of improving local production standards and reaching an audience beyond the small domestic market (Millet 2006: 100). Since 2005, the MDA has been active in promoting Singaporean films internationally, with administrative support and infrastructure for Singaporean filmmakers to showcase their work in international film festivals, including an entire week of screenings in 2009 at the Singapore Pavilion at the Cannes International Film Festival. In the East Asian context, the MDA has also been spearheading efforts to develop cooperation with Chinese and Korean film producers.

Currently the only major film production studio in Singapore is Raintree Pictures, established in 1998 as a subsidiary of the government-owned media enterprise, MediaCorp. It began initially with the aim of producing local movies "to complement its TV production operations" (Curtin 2007: 185), i.e., to enable television actors to extend their career into movies so as to retain them in Singapore. In its domestic film ventures, it has scored some box office successes, particularly with the early films of local television actor-turned-filmmaker, Jack Neo. *I Not Stupid* (2002) and *I Not Stupid Too* (2006) are two of the highest-grossing local movies, behind Jack Neo's very first, independently-funded movie, *Money No Enough* (1998) and, in 2007, *881* by the much younger independent filmmaker, Royston Tan. However, "founded with an eye towards profitability," Daniel Yun—then the managing director of Raintree Pictures—"tried to leverage his [limited] resources through a series of strategic partnerships" (Curtin 2007: 188), largely with Hong Kong producers. The early co-productions were also vehicles for improving the production quality and skills of local talents, while introducing Singaporean actors into the regional market. Driven by the profit motive, Raintree soon strayed from this nationalist mission and now is often just a movie investment enterprise in search of box office returns (Millet 2006: 103–104). Joint ventures are primarily with Hong Kong producers in "Chinese" films, with casts and shooting locations from across Pop Culture China. A co-production with Thai-based filmmakers, the Pang brothers, of Applause Pictures, scored a box office success with the horror film *The Eye* (见鬼 2002). Other investment box office successes include *Infernal Affairs II* (无间道II 2003), the second part of a trilogy, and *Painted Skin* (画皮 2008), the first "horror" film to be released in China after decades of the genre being banned under communist ideology on the arts. In these instances, neither Singaporean actors nor locations feature at all.

Within the domestic film industry only one filmmaker, Jack Neo, has been consistently successful in the domestic box office. His debut film, *Money No Enough*, in 1998 is still the highest grossing movie in the history of Singapore's industry. Between 2002 and 2007 Raintree Pictures funded a movie a year with Jack Neo. All these movies either made money or recovered their production costs. Without doubt, Neo has contributed to the development of Chinese-language films in Singapore. His most popular films critically examine the aspirations and struggles of lower income strata Singaporeans in their struggles to eventual, triumphal financial success. As the main characters in these films are from the lower income strata, the most appropriate or authentic languages for dialogue among the on-screen characters are Hokkien and Mandarin, with occasional English phases, often intentionally mispronounced for comic effects. Up until the late 1960s in Singapore, many Chinese languages—Hokkien, Cantonese, Teochew, Hakka, and more—were living languages among the Huaren, with Mandarin as the language of education in Chinese-language schools and spoken only by those who had formal Chinese education. In the early 1970s, based on a very serious misconception that speakers of different Chinese languages were unable to communicate with each other, the largely English-language-educated leaders of the government banned all Chinese languages (labeled "dialects") but Mandarin from all broadcast media, which in turn was based on yet another mistaken assumption that Mandarin would unify the multi-tongued local Huaren population. With this policy in place for the past thirty years, the ability of Huaren in Singapore to speak multiple Chinese languages has greatly diminished. Most under thirty are now unable to speak any Chinese language except the Mandarin they had to learn as a compulsory ethnic "mother tongue" in primary and secondary schools. However, the "dialects" have not disappeared, they continue to be the home language for less-educated families; thus, they continue to have a quiet existence under the official Mandarin language.

The other Chinese languages, among which is Hokkien, have become and remain languages of the economically, socially, and culturally marginalized. Hokkien is therefore the ideal vehicle for depicting the lives of lower income Singaporeans amidst an affluent national economy that is now of First World income and living standards. Neo's films speak to the Singaporean masses about their daily life and resonate with the local audience. Watching his films in the neighborhood cinemas in the public housing estates, where all but the highest ten percent of wage-earners in Singapore live, has an added pleasure: middle-aged and older people, especially women, who seldom go to the movies, come in small groups and discuss animatedly the "moral" dilemmas in the film throughout the entire duration of its screening. It is not dissimilar to watching television and talking back to the characters on screen in the privacy of one's home. Beyond this domestic audience, Neo's films have a modicum of success with audiences in the region, particularly in Malaysia, which shares many cultural similarities with

Singapore. His film *I Not Stupid* is about the very stressful life of a group of low achieving primary school students from different family backgrounds and was particularly successful in Hong Kong as a film about the importance of education because it resonates with the competitive education situation there. This reception is in contrast to that of the local Singaporean audience who read Neo's film as a critique of the Singapore government's education policies. With its predominant use of Hokkien/Minnan mixed with Mandarin and English, the film also had a receptive audience in Taiwan.

The box office success of predominantly Hokkien films has also pried open the space for other filmmakers to use Chinese languages, thus expanding the degree of freedom in filmmaking in Singapore. The most recent example is a Raintree Pictures film by local filmmaker Kelvin Tong. *It's A Great Great World* (大世界 2011) is set in the Singapore of the 1950s and 1960s, and narrates the lives of some of the workers in a Shaw Brothers amusement park from which the film takes its title. Appropriately for that historical period, when polyglot Chinese-language speakers were the norm, the on-screen dialogue is multilingual Chinese—Hokkien, Cantonese, Teochew, Hainanese and Mandarin. On the personal front, Neo's commercial successes have enabled him to set up his own production company, Neo Studios, in 2007, cutting the financial apron strings that tied him to Raintree Pictures. Under this umbrella, Neo has been able to produce films in the same slap-stick comedy genre that are made with a stable of actors who have been part of his career, although now formulaic comedies are beginning to tire and box office takings are declining steadily.

Beyond the domestic market, ironically, Singaporean directors and films appear to have greater success in English; art house films have had particular success on the international festival circuit. Each year since 2004, a Singaporean film has been selected either for showcase or competition in the Cannes International Film Festival. The most successful has been independent filmmaker, Eric Khoo; three of his four films so far have been shown at Cannes: *12 Storeys* (1997), *Be With Me* (2004), shown during the Directors' Fortnight and *My Magic* (2008) selected for the main competition. *Be With Me* was disqualified from competing in the Best Foreign Language Film category at the American Academy Awards in 2005 on the grounds that it contained "too much English" (Chan 2008). This is of course ironic because one of the features that makes Khoo's film a "Singaporean" film is the use of various Huaren languages (Marchetti 2005). In sharp contrast with Jack Neo's films which end happily with upward mobility and financial success for working-class individuals, Khoo takes aim at the underbelly of a nation which is touted around the world as a triumphal story of capitalist economic development, rising from underdevelopment to become one of the wealthiest countries globally. Arguably, it is this very overt "critique" of the Singapore success story that is what is attractive about Khoo's film on the international festival circuit. [7]

## Singaporean Mandarin Singers in Pop Culture China

As Liew suggests, since the political and economic closure of China that led to the emergence of *Gangtai* entertainment within Huaren communities, Singapore and Malaysia have provided "raw recruits" for Pop Culture China (2010: 183). Although the numbers are not large, those who succeed can become quite prominent; for example, Michelle Yeoh, the Malaysian actress who flourished in Hong Kong and subsequently Hollywood, and Tsai Ming Liang (蔡明亮), a prominent Malaysian art house filmmaker in Taiwan. In general, however, in the last twenty years, actors from Singapore and elsewhere in Southeast Asia have not fared well in Hong Kong. Several Singaporeans who were doing well in the domestic television scene returned to local stations after making no headway in trying to expand their careers into movies and television in Hong Kong.[8] The Singaporean artists who are the most successful and well integrated into Pop Culture China are undoubtedly the Mandarin pop singers. To gain access to this regional audience, a Singaporean singer has to leave home, either for a period of time or for specific projects elsewhere in Pop Culture China; the destination has shifted from Hong Kong in the 1980s to Taipei beginning in the early 1990s and will potentially shift again, this time to China, in the near future.

SJ is a good example. Like many children from middle class families, she had taken piano lessons when she was in primary school, but not after that. Throughout her teen years, including those as an undergraduate at the National University of Singapore, she participated in singing competitions. In her first year at university, she won a talent contest on campus. It was then that she was "discovered" by a Chinese-language music producer. She did not want to give up her university education and stayed on until she completed her undergraduate degree. Meanwhile, she continued to write melodies, while another person wrote the lyrics. Together with the producer, the three established a music company. She has a preference for singing in English and still hopes to be able to do so professionally in the future, but was realistic enough to accept that she stood a better chance, at the beginning of her career, by singing in Mandarin for an East Asian audience. This also meant a change in her musical style, from rock music to ballads.[9]

By mid-2004, more than three years after the partnership was established, they were ready to release her first album. However, instead of looking for a record company in Singapore, she received a contract for an album with a major Taiwanese record company. Significantly, SJ, the lyricist and the producer completed all the writing of the music in Singapore. The songs for the album were all recorded in a Singapore studio; Singapore has all the technical facilities and professionals for sound recording. Indeed, many Taiwanese artists travel to Singapore to record with specific Singaporean producers because of the latter's technical skills. The master for the album of ten songs, nine of which were written by SJ herself, had already been recorded in Singapore. Only the actual pressing of the disk was done in Taiwan. In September of that year, SJ left Singapore for Taipei to prepare for the launch of her very first album.

The reason for this is very simple: there is no record company in Singapore willing to invest in the huge publicity costs needed to promote the album and, hopefully, create a "star." Several record companies were established in Singapore in the early 1990s but most have folded; currently there is only one local company, Ocean Butterfly, and one subsidiary of the multinational Bertlesmann-Sony, Hype. This is largely because of how small the consumer market in Singapore is. That English is the lingua franca limits the sales of Mandarin pop music to a significantly smaller audience/consumer than its Huaren population of more than two million would suggest. For Mandarin music, record sales of ten thousand copies would be considered a massive success in Singapore, compared to sales in the hundreds of thousands in Taiwan. Given this economy of scale, the Taiwan record company, H.I.M., which has the very popular three-person female band S.H.E. within its stable, was willing to invest in a new talent.

For at least two months after her arrival in Taiwan, SJ spent her time immersed in the Taiwanese environment, honing her Mandarin language skills (she did not speak Minnan/Taiwanese), getting used to the youth culture and receiving training in grooming and public relations before the album was released. Once the album debuted, she was kept busy around the clock, performing in high schools and colleges and making appearances in shopping districts and malls; she could do up to three mini-performances a day, crisscrossing the island from one city to another. (If sales of an album are good, this frantic kind of schedule of activities would last about two months; if an album does not take off, then it could be as short as one month.) After the launch in Taiwan, she returned to Singapore to promote the album. SJ's first album did sufficiently well in 2005 and was followed by a second, but too much was invested in publicity for this second album, leaving her uncertain of her future as a pop singer.

The path taken by SJ was pioneered by the hugely successful Stefanie Sun. Sun trained in a very small music school in Singapore and was penning songs for other singers during her undergraduate days at the Nanyang Technological University.[10] Upon graduation she arrived in Taipei in 2000 and became an instant success. She stayed on top of the game for the next ten years, winning competitive awards throughout Pop Culture China, selling more than ten million albums and reaching national icon status in Singapore, her homeland. Since then there have been other successful singers—including Tanya Chua, JJ Lin and Ah Du (阿杜)—and song writers such as Liang Wen Fu (梁文福) and Lee Wei Song (李伟松). However, for every success story there is an unknown number of those whose aspirations have been crushed in very short time, such as SJ, and others who did not even get to first base and remain nameless.

As mentioned in previous chapters, the path to Taiwan was a result of the shift in Chinese-language pop music from Cantonese pop to Mandarin pop upon the opening of the China market to commercial pop music. In the early years of the market opening until the early 1990s, "the entire Chinese Putonghua [Mandarin] pop song market was almost swept away by Cantopop" (Fung 2007: 432). Cantopop stars such as the late Anita Mui Yim-Fong (who died in 2003) reigned, while Beijing native Faye Wong had to "hide her mainland Chinese identity as a migrant to Hong Kong by singing in Cantonese with her Beijing accent deliberately suppressed" (Fung 2007: 430). However, by the mid-1990s, as Chinese consumers began to demand music in Mandarin, the national language of mainland China, Taiwan pop music in Mandarin became mainstream and displaced Cantopop. By the late 1990s Taiwan Mandarin pop dominated not only in China but throughout Pop Culture China, and Taipei became the location that makes or breaks the career of all aspirants in Mandarin pop music, as illustrated by the Singaporean singers and song writers.

## Television

The small consumer market, coupled with state regulations on ownership within the media industry, has resulted in the monopolization of the media industry. The print media has been monopolized by the Singapore Press Holdings (SPH), which publishes all the local newspapers and most of the popular magazines. The broadcast media was monopolized by government-owned radio and television stations, Radio and Television Singapore (RTS), from its inception in the early 1960s; the two media were subsequently separated and the television company was named Television Corporation of Singapore (TCS), which was renamed MediaCorp in 2001. As mentioned in Chapter 1, in that same year, the newspaper monopoly Singapore Press Holdings entered the television business through their company MediaWorks, with two free-to-air stations. The English-language channel failed almost immediately but the Mandarin Channel U was able to sustain itself through the importation of East Asian, particularly Korean, television dramas. Nevertheless, in the end, it was financially compelled to merge with MediaCorp in 2004, which means MediaCorp now controls six free-to-air stations. Two of these are dedicated to Mandarin programs; Channel 8 and Channel U both screen a mix of local productions and imported East Asian programs. However, in the several years leading up to 2011, Channel U, with the tag line "带动亚洲流行" ("Leading Asian Pop"), has placed greater emphasis on screening imported East Asian television programs. An occasional art house film from East Asia is screened on the "art" station, Okto. All imported East Asian programs are dubbed into Mandarin and often have English and Malay subtitles.[11]

The prime time slots on Channel 8 are scheduled for locally produced dramas, variety shows and other local interest programs. Variety shows have increasingly adopted the format of those made in Taiwan, which in turn has borrowed from Japan—zany, fast-talking hosts and hostesses whose entire aim is to make fun of, and embarrass, the participants on the show, in front of the studio audience. There are two one-hour locally produced dramas serials on every weekday evening, at seven and nine, before the national news. These serials generally center on family drama, much like most of the serials from Taiwan, Hong Kong and Korea; Japanese trendy dramas tend to build their stories around young, urban professionals who are living on their own and have thus dispensed with their family. The contents, however, remain decidedly local, with themes that are often about current government social policies. Until recently, these drama programs consistently retained the highest audience ratings among Singaporeans. Imported programs are screened after the news at ten, which would be considered the late night program slots. In contrast, apart from the nightly news, Channel U has been increasingly dedicated to the screening of imported dramas.

Significantly, MediaCorp putatively produces up to one thousand hours of drama per year. With the exception of a small export to China, little of this is exported to the rest of East Asia, in spite of being in the same genre of family drama. Distributors in Singapore suggest that this is largely because their qualities—scripting, acting, costumes and locations—are inferior to those of Hong Kong, Taiwan and Korea. The low production quality of Singaporean programs is largely due to low budgets, especially relative to those in Japan which set the aesthetic standard for the whole of East Asia: "[t]he Japanese concern with the visual, in combination with their advanced technology, ensures that Japanese television is often very pleasing to the eye" (Stronach 1989: 155).

The weakness of the scripts, however, is not simply a technical nor financial matter, but is also cultural. Under the paternalistic and watchful eye of the long-governing People's Action Party, the daily life of Singaporeans has a "homogenous" quality; with eighty-five percent of the population living in homogenously designed, high-rise, public housing buildings, the routines of everyone is relatively homogenized. Although there are extremes in incomes and standards of living, social and economic inequalities are not paraded by the rich in public. There is no society page in the daily newspapers. Glitzy parties of the rich are only photographed and reported in small, exclusive circulation magazines that are often distributed for free to selected households, establishments or high income residential districts. The local culture is decidedly one of middle class homogeneity. This is an image which is ideologically preferred by the government, which promotes it with the assistance of the mass media. The local media is prohibited from reporting alternative lifestyles, such as that of gays and lesbians. Locally produced films are also prohibited from imaging violence frontally; for example, a shooting cannot be filmed and represented directly. Instead it has to be "sanitized;" a shot can be fired in one frame, followed by the collapse of the antagonist's body in another frame. Even in news items, visual images of violence are limited to "representational" images, such as blood stains on the ground rather than the body that had been injured or otherwise violated. Without edginess of any kind, the drama serials are bland to non-Singaporeans but appeal to locals, perhaps because it is a mirror for Singaporeans themselves, and especially since these serials are quick to incorporate government policies into their scripts.

However, in the interest of securing portions of the regional market, television channels have initiated various modes of collaboration with Hong Kong and Taiwan artists and production companies. One such mode is to invite Hong Kong actors and actresses to star in programs produced in Singaporean studios, with Singaporeans playing support roles. The more notable among such programs are *Living with Lydia* (2001–2004, 52 episodes) with the late Lydia Shum (沈殿霞) and *Oh! Carol* (2002, 13 episodes) with Carol Cheng (郑裕玲). Significantly, both programs are in English and both Hong Kong actresses acted exclusively in English for the first time in their career. Both programs lasted two seasons as weekly comedies. In other instances, Hong Kong stars are placed into local Mandarin dramas; for example, the 2002–2003 courtroom drama *Innocently Guilty* (法内有情), starring the Hong Kong actress, Anita Yuen (袁咏仪).

The reverse mode of placing Singaporean actors as co-stars in dramas produced in Hong Kong, Taiwan or China is also undertaken. For example, Singaporean actress Kym Ng (钟琴), appeared in a joint production, between Channel U and Taiwanese production company, Sanlih E-Television, of a teenage drama entitled *Westside Story* (西街少年 2003), referencing Taipei's teenage shopping area *Ximending* (West Gate Square). The drama featured the members of the all-male singer-cum-actor group, 5566, who were hot at the time, with Kym playing the mother of the lead character. In all these collaborations, Singaporean actors and actresses tend to play supporting roles in the programs, as if they were apprentices to the other Huaren stars, vicariously sharing some of the popularity of the latter. It is also a means of introducing Singaporean artists into Pop Culture China.[12] These collaborative efforts appear to have waned and become less frequent since the end of the 2000s.

## Imported Pop Culture

As mentioned above, Channel 8 and Channel U, the two Mandarin channels, rely on importing a mix of variety shows, movies and dramas from the rest of East Asia to fill up their programming time. Programs that are not originally in Mandarin are dubbed into Mandarin. Significantly, in terms of films, those from Hong Kong dominate while Taiwanese, Korean and Japanese films are not regular features.

However, some of the popular Korean and Japanese films, especially the art house films, have been featured on the free-to-air arts channel, Okto, of MediaCorp. In imported dramas, Hong Kong has had a constant presence since the beginning of television broadcasting in the early 1960s. The now global star from Hong Kong, Chow Yun Fat, was first introduced to Singaporeans on the small screen in the 1979 Cantonese drama about new immigrants from mainland China to Hong Kong, *Man in the Net*.

Before merging with the state-owned MediaCorp in 2004, Channel U tried to maintain a fifty-fifty program mix of in-house productions and imports. As a strategy to garner an audience base from scratch, Channel U introduced Korean dramas, which had already begun to make inroads into Taiwanese and Hong Kong television space but remained neglected by MediaCorp. Channel U had acquired a store of the earlier Korean dramas and released these from the very outset of its broadcast. After familiarizing the Singaporean audience with earlier dramas, it released the hugely popular, *Autumn in My Heart* (*Gaeul donghwa* 秋天的童话, 2000), the first in the *Endless Love* four-part series which included *Winter Sonata, A Scent of Summer* (*Yoereum hyanggi* 夏日香气, 2003) and *Spring Waltz* (*Bomui walcheu* 春天华尔兹, 2006). The strategy worked well, enabling the new Channel U to capture and establish an audience base quickly, causing the established MediaCorp to compete to purchase Korean dramas for Channel 8. This mutually cannibalizing competition that was to the advantage of Korean drama producers ended with the merger of the two companies. After the merger, Korean dramas have continued to have a highly visible presence in Channel U programming, as they became an integral part of the daily programming of the station.

By early 2000, dramas and other variety programs from all parts of East Asia had become staples and integral parts of the daily programming on Singaporean free-to-air Mandarin television stations. While imported drama series from different East Asian locations share broadly equal screening time and space on Singapore's Mandarin-language channels, imported variety shows tend to be dominated by Taiwanese programs. These programs, following the Japanese format, are characterized by a rapid-fire team of hosts, whose sole objective is to make fun of the members of the studio audience who willingly participate in the games on the show.[13] The level of tolerance of participating audience members for slapstick antics and other forms of embarrassment is staggering to anyone unfamiliar with this format. Taiwanese instead of Japanese programs are imported primarily because they are already in Mandarin and thus do not incur additional dubbing costs. Significantly, locally-produced Mandarin variety programs have increasingly taken on many of the "zany" characteristics of the Taiwanese and Japanese programs.

The importation of East Asian television programs intensified from 2000 onwards, when Singapore Telemedia, another state-owned corporation, established StarHub TV as the sole provider of pay cable television, with 152 channels. Then, in 2007, the state-owned Singapore telephone company, SingTel, established mio TV as another cable television provider with fifty channels. Under StarHub TV, there are three Korean channels that screen a variety of programs, including drama; two Japan channels, NHK and JET TV (JET also screens Taiwanese programs) and, twenty Chinese, Taiwanese and Hong Kong channels, with VV 1 and 2, TVB 8, TVB Xing He and TVB Classic screening exclusively Hong Kong dramas; MTV China and Channel V which screen music videos and related programs, Star Chinese 1 and 2, and Celestial Movies and Celestial Classic Movies which screen Chinese-language films. The rest are a mix of programs. Thus the now dropped tag line of "Leading [East] Asian Pop," used by free-to-air Mandarin-language Channel U, in reality belies the fact that Singapore has been and continues to be invaded by the wave, rather than leading it. Furthermore, locally produced dramas, which often embed very explicit reference to government social policies, are thus relevant and didactic, and are potentially "tiresome" to Singaporean audiences. Faced with the competition of programs imported from Hong Kong, Taiwan, Korea and Japan on both free-to-air and cable stations, local dramas have been losing ground to the superior qualities of the imported ones.

Without any local record industry, Singaporean radio stations are almost completely dependent on imported pop music; the best of Singaporean Mandarin pop singers release their albums in Taiwan. Thus, the most popular Mandarin music station, 93.3 FM, plays music from the whole of East Asia, especially Mandarin pop, with dedicated hours each week for Japanese and Korean pop music; each has a small but very dedicated audience. The predominance of Mandopop is reflected in the station's use of Huaren singers from Pop Culture China to reiterate on radio the station's tag line—每时每刻有音乐 ("Every moment there is music")—in Mandarin, throughout the day, incorporating them into the local pop music scene. These singers have become increasingly incorporated into local entertainment events; for example, many attend the annual Golden Melody Awards, organized by MediaCorp. Huaren performers from Pop Culture China also regularly make guest appearances in annual fund-raising variety shows for local charities. In some instances, two variety shows are held, one exclusively with local Singaporean artists and the other with all the invited performers; the two shows compete in raising donations from the Singaporean audience. Singaporean Huaren pop culture may be said to have seamlessly incorporated Pop Culture China into its own site and space.

## Transnational Audience

To complete the examination of Singapore as a space of reception/consumption of East Asian Pop Culture, it is now necessary to shift focus and look at the processes of reception in practice in Singapore. While the production process of pop culture—from financing, to filming or recording, to post-production—can be disaggregated and organized transnationally, and pop culture can flow across porous national boundaries and cultural spaces, reception/consumption is, in contrast, thoroughly grounded in specific geographical locations. Consumers are embedded within particular physical and cultural spaces, within which specific viewing pleasures and meanings are generated. Of course, the "local" cultural space is not hermetically sealed but is rather a porous contact zone that actively engages, appropriates and absorbs cultural elements and fragments from all contact points. Without such openness and interactions, there would be no such discursive object as East Asian Popular Culture.

Conceptually, there are at least three possible audience positions for the reception of pop culture programs. First and least complicated is an audience watching a locally produced program. Audience identification with the themes and characters may be said to come "naturally"—the phenomenological "natural attitude of everyday life"—and references can be readily made to individuals, activities and events that one either knows or is familiar with that are similar to those on screen. The audience may be said to "know" the screen representations of events, issues and characters from the "inside." There is an excess of knowledge that can be drawn upon to judge the "accuracy" and "truth" of the program content and "critical reflections" can be based upon this knowledge. In this sense, the program may be used as a "critical" mirror to one's own life and community, a common practice of reviewers and critics. For example, Kim Soyoung's (2003) analysis of the eclipse of "Korean women" in blockbuster films, such as *Joint Security Area* (2000), as indicative of a generalized shrinking of the "women's sphere" and the elevation of male-bonding in post 1997 financial crisis Korea.

Second, the audience could be a diasporic subject watching or listening to a piece of pop culture that thematically references the homeland; the program may be made by homeland or foreign producers. Here, the audience position and relation to the content is both geographically and analytically once removed; nevertheless, one still possesses the same knowingness as the audience at home.[14] Depending on the physical distance and length of time away from home, reception and judgment are likely to be more hesitant. An additional "nationalist" element may arise if the program is foreign-produced; the diasporic audience may evoke "accuracy" of representation as the basis for protesting that the foreign producer is politically motivated to misrepresent or affirm the representation as a reasonable critique of conditions in the "homeland;" the "accuracy" of representation is obviously highly dependent on the eyes of the beholder. Detailed analysis of the diasporic subject position in East Asian Pop Culture is also a common focus in media studies, for example, Shim's (2007) analysis of the reception and effects of Korean television dramas on Korean women living in Singapore, or Sun's (2002) insightful analysis of the various television programs focusing on new China immigrants in foreign lands.[15]

Third is when an audience is watching an imported program. This viewing position brings into relief the conceptual and substantive issues concerning differences between the cultures in the locations of production and reception. The program has been uprooted from its "home" culture and relocated transnationally into the cultural context of the receiving audience, who will bring the latter context to bear on the content and read accordingly. Strictly, only in this third audience position may a pop culture product be said to have crossed a "cultural" boundary, beyond the mere fact of having been exported/imported into a different location as an economic activity. This is the situation of a "transnational" audience. With the emergence of an East Asian Pop Culture, the transnational reception of pop culture within the region has been subjected to comparative analysis from different East Asian locations, as in the case of the Korean Wave (Chua and Iwabuchi 2008) and the earlier Japanese trendy drama (Iwabuchi 2002).

Each of these three positions involves a different investment of self-identification by the audience, who need to relate in some way to the on-screen characters, themes and music. Each of these positions is, of course, a field of analysis in its own right, illuminating different aspects of audience-ship. For an East Asian Pop Culture, the central analytic focus is on how products crisscross cultural boundaries regionally to reach transnational audiences. The analytic starting point would, therefore, have to be that of an audience watching imported pop culture, the position of a transnational audience. This will be the perspective taken in the following discussion of the Singaporean audience of East Asian Pop Culture. Before proceeding, one methodological point needs to be made.

Different pop culture genres make different demands on an audience's commitment in terms of time and attention; each thus imposes different methodological constraints on audience research. A piece of pop music requires no more than a few minutes of the audience's time and a film usually no more than a couple of hours. In contrast, television drama demands an audience's sustained viewing at regular intervals, from once a day to once every week; many other activities need to be sacrificed or at least displaced in order to catch each episode, or efforts have to be made to record the episode if missing it cannot be helped, and then time has to be found to watch the episode before the next instalment is screened. These demands amount to an active participation with what is on-screen, which draws the audience into a virtual but intimate relationship with the characters in the drama. In all three genres, audience interest is further sustained by the routine write-ups in local newspapers and entertainment magazines, and by conversations with friends. However, the serial structure of television drama provides opportunities to dissect the latest episode and speculate about upcoming developments, thus extending audience interest beyond a single song or a single film. Not surprisingly, audience reception studies tend to be focused on television programs rather than pop music or cinema. The same will be true in this instance.

## When East Asian Drama Comes to Singapore: Routes of Travel

Since the late 1970s, by official policy in Singapore, all imported television pro-grams and films from East Asia, including those in other Chinese languages such as Cantonese or Minnan, are dubbed into Mandarin, the exclusive language for broadcast media. For those who are not competent in Mandarin, English subtitles are frequently provided to enable the program to reach the educated population, but it excludes those who are not literate in English or Mandarin.[16] The duo-sound technology in television, which allows one to watch Korean and Japanese pro-grams in their original languages, with added Mandarin subtitles is, significantly, not available for Chinese-language programs. This language restriction is limited to free-to-air channels; one Hokkien and one Cantonese channel each are available on StarHub cable television.

Dubbing into Mandarin programs in other Chinese languages creates a strange effect on the Singaporean reception of films and television programs from elsewhere in Pop Culture China because often two Chinese languages appear simultaneously, one in the on-screen dialogue, the other in subtitles. As pointed out previously, comprehension across Chinese-language divisions is facilitated by the use of a common written script, with occasional local variations, in sub-titles. For example, watching the Hong Kong film *72 Tenants* (72 家租客 2010) in Singapore, the dialogue in Mandarin did not match the subtitles, which was clearer if read in Cantonese. Questions concerning which was the original lan-guage of the film arose. It is likely that the film originally had Cantonese dialogue and Cantonese subtitles, making it potentially comprehensible for the Mainland audience residing in Hong Kong and those across the border in southern China. Upon arrival in Singapore, the Cantonese dialogue was dubbed into Mandarin but the original Cantonese subtitles remained unchanged. Alternatively, the dialogue could have been in Mandarin originally, to tap into the larger China market, with the subtitles in Cantonese for the local Hong Kong audience, and upon arrival in Singapore, nothing was changed. Similar two-language situations occur on dubbed television dramas imported from Hong Kong; however, here it seems fairly appar-ent that the original Cantonese subtitles were left unchanged.

On a different occasion, I was watching a Korean gangster comedy in which, similarly, the dialogue was in Mandarin and the subtitles in Cantonese. Here, the migratory path of this Korean film is potentially very mysterious. The film was likely first subtitled in Cantonese in Hong Kong, but there was no clue as to whether it was dubbed in the same language. It is likely to have been subsequently exported from Hong Kong to Singapore, where it was dubbed in Mandarin, with the Cantonese subtitles left untouched. If so, the film traveled from Korea to Hong Kong and was then re-exported to Singapore. Or could it have been dubbed in Mandarin and subtitled in Cantonese in Hong Kong in the first place, in order to capture both the Mandarin and Cantonese speaking audiences in Hong Kong and across the border in southern China, since there is a significant, and increasing, population of Mandarin-only speaking Chinese migrants in Hong Kong? And was the film then re-exported to Singapore, where no additional dubbing was done? Finally, could it have been imported to Singapore first and dubbed in Mandarin as required by government policy, but subtitled in Cantonese in preparation for re-export to Hong Kong? The circulation path of this particular film, as in many other instances, remains an interesting empirical question in Singapore and, perhaps, throughout Pop Culture China. This remains an empirical question for comparative studies.

## Pleasure of the Foreign

Obviously, the "foreignness" of imported programs is a major part of the viewing pleasure for a locally grounded audience. Many East Asian media researchers have pointed out that the "foreign" on screen allows a local audience to project their desires and aspirations (Ko 2005); for example, the onscreen modern consumerist culture of Japan and Korea is a desired future aspired to by audiences in less economically developed locations, such as Vietnam (Thomas 2004). The most immediately foreign difference is, of course, language; however, this is usually technically managed through dubbing or subtitles, which serve to "domesticate" the foreign; there will be more on this domestication effect in the next chapter. Other markers of foreignness are, however, generally retained.

First, background music, particularly the theme songs of dramas, is generally left untouched. However, this can be an unreliable marker of the production location. Often, music foreign to the production location is used; for example, Taiwan dramas often come with background music sung in Japanese in the interest of "exoticizing" local dramas for local audiences and/or for exporting them to foreign locations. English-language theme songs are also common in East Asian television dramas. This complicates one's ability to locate the drama's "origin."

Second, scenery on screen is one of the most stable markers of foreignness. Scenery transports a physically grounded audience into a foreign space and place; it is a mode of visual tourism. Avid fans of a foreign television drama often become so enamored by the scenery that the shooting locations become "must visit" places for the fans-turned-tourists and, upon arrival, they feel completely familiar with the environment and experience a sense of déjà vu. At the peak of their popularity, Singaporean tour promoters regularly organized tours for fans to the filming locations of "trendy dramas" in Tokyo; they did the same for television dramas in Korea.[17] Unsurprisingly, capitalizing on the success of Korean television dramas in East Asia, the Korean tourism industry continues to freely promote filming sites of popular dramas as tourist attractions. In this way, on-screen sights have become real tourist sites.

Third, traditional costumes and ethnic foods are also convenient markers of foreignness; as in real life, both traditional costumes and ethnic foods are inscribed on the female characters who embody the nation/national culture. These items are always used to great effect in historical dramas. A very good example is the case of the regionally hugely popular Korean drama, *Dae Jang Geum* (2003), which could be said to have paved the way for the exporting of Korean historical dramas, which until then had been mainly urban-based romance and family dramas.

A particular marker of foreignness that is peculiar to Singaporeans extends and combines scenery and costume: not traditional costumes, but contemporary fashion. A marker of foreignness to specifically Singaporean audiences is the changing scenery of the four seasons in temperate Northeast Asia—Japan, Korea and China. Seasons are completely foreign to Singaporeans who live in permanently hot, tropical weather. Autumn, with its changing colors of the trees, and winter, with its cold and snow, are quintessentially romantic—enhancing the romantic themes of many urban dramas—for Singaporeans. Along with the cool and cold weather of autumn and winter is the associated fashion. The consistently hot, humid, tropical climate is the bane of the fashionable because it denies them seasonal changes. The fashionable Singaporean is thus jealous of the layers upon layers of warm clothes that enable the making of fashion statements; (s)he is denied the layering effects of fashion.

In spite of the attractiveness of the "foreign" and the pleasure audiences derive from viewing it, pleasurable identification with the "foreign" on screen is only part of the viewing practices of an audience. Conversely, "foreignness" can also be incomprehensible and can offend and alienate a local audience, leading to a perceived distance from, disinterest in and rejection of the foreign. Therefore, other on-screen elements that enable the audience to positively identify with the program are necessary. For now, it is noted that the relatively similar modern urban conditions and the relatively strong emphasis on the importance of the family in East Asian societies function as significant anchors that Singaporean audiences can use to ground their identification with the world portrayed.

## Urban Stories

As a modern city-state with no rural hinterland, contemporary Singaporeans in general have little or no contact with things and sentiments rural.[18] In contrast to the idea of the "uniqueness" and "boundedness" of a traditional culture, the contemporary "urban" of global capitalism increasingly lacks cultural and spatial specificity; it is anywhere, anyplace and anyone. The "urban" penetrates and passes through porous spatial boundaries through this "sameness," which is highly visual and immediate, encoded in corporate architecture, shopping malls with display windows of global brands, mass rapid transit infrastructure, high rise residential towers, and museums, galleries, restaurants and bars in rejuvenated "heritage" districts. This sameness is only poorly masked by cities representing themselves through iconic buildings designed by global, celebrity designer-architects. This sameness also permeates the socio-cultural conditions of the contemporary urban, facilitating cultural border-crossing, including the flows of pop culture. Such is the condition of contemporary Singapore, city-state. The rapid capitalist economic development of Singapore, from the mid-1960s to the mid-1990s, replicates that of Japan, Korea, Taiwan and Hong Kong.

The entire East Asian region is one shining example of the benefits of the globalization of capitalism and its local effect, namely the rapid expansion of the urban middle class. This is reflected in the television dramas that crisscross the region. The visual images on screen of urban middle class lifestyles transcend the relativities of real incomes in different East Asian locations; each urban middle class stratum, embedded in its own economic context, can achieve a comparable level of lifestyle consumption. In this sense, urban middle class East Asians can be given interchangeable bodies on screen, despite geographical dispersion. Young professionals throughout East Asia, including Singapore, are able to identify with their screen representations in a "clear, direct, and seemingly transparent" manner, through the "immediate and efficacious" mass media (Chow 1995: 10). To put it more categorically, urban dramas are imaginable, realistic and foster identification among those who are willing to be interpolated into the screen, temporarily suspending their national/ethnic identities.

Intensification of urbanization across the region has resulted in a competitive capitalist ethos that emphasizes individualism in achievements and consumption. However, unlike American urban dramas—such as *Friends* and *Sex and the City*—in which the family has all but disappeared, in East Asian urban television dramas the family and its influence still has a presence, alternating between being an obstacle to and/or a refuge from life in the city. This presence varies across the region and is reflected in respective television dramas. In a survey of regional dramas, Kang and Soo (2009) found that, at one end of the spectrum, references to the family have largely disappeared in Japanese "trendy" drama. At the other, it continues to be very prominently present and strong versions of Confucian filial piety are often scripted into Korean urban dramas. Hong Kong and Taiwanese dramas also have prominent family themes, but family members are as likely to be engaged in life and death feuds, making the extended family a living hell, as they are to be a loving and caring haven from the cruel city. To risk a generalization, in East Asian television dramas Confucian family ideology continues to serve as a foil for the urban middle class, which is increasingly inscribed with the competitive individualism dictated by global capitalism.

Besides the "sameness" of urban middle class culture, the physiognomy of East Asians also facilitates identification with each other. Following the Japanese lead, East Asian Pop Culture, particularly in pop music and television dramas, consciously cultivates a genre of "beautiful" youth—boyish leading men with long, brown-tinted hair that is full and fluffed up, who are earnest, if not innocent—a mode of "beautiful masculinity," for example, Korean Bae Yong-joon (Maliangkay 2010; Jung 2011)[19] and Taiwanese Jerry Yan. The female leads are beautiful and self-confident, with fashionable but non-revealing clothes, showing very little explicit sexuality. The packaging is so similar across East Asian television dramas that an indoor shot in a modern office setting from a Korean drama looks very much like similar shots in productions from Taiwan or Japan or, increasingly, from Hong Kong; the indoor shots of domestic spaces are often differentiated by items of traditional décor. Only the trained eyes of aficionados who can recognize particular actors and actresses are able to distinguish one country's product from that of another. The similarity of physiognomy and packaging facilitates visual and discursive space for the projection of an idea of "Asianness," displacing nationalities.

All the above features of East Asian television dramas—urban middle class consumerism, family and physiognomy—dovetail with the socio-cultural features of the Singaporean audience. Unsurprisingly, as a rule, popular imported dramas from Japan and Korea are almost all urban dramas, such as romance dramas of young, single professionals, either living on their own or with their families of origin, or romances among young couples with mismatched family backgrounds, or family dramas built around business competition between feuding families. The trials and tribulations of urban living are, to varying degrees, familiar to Singaporeans, making the urban stories accessible. They can readily identify with the themes, characters and social phenomena on screen as representations of the "urban" that are familiar, if not similar to their own situation. This enables a Singaporean audience, if they so desire, to allow themselves to identify with these representations. Actual viewing practices of watching "foreign" programs are an intermittent process of identification with and distancing from the narratives and activities on screen; a process analyzed in greater detail in the next chapter.

## Conclusion

This chapter examines the conditions of production in Singapore's pop culture industry, noting especially its relative insignificance due to both the smallness of its domestic market and absence of the necessary financial, cultural, personnel and industrial elements that are essential for the making of a media capital such as Hong Kong. The government and industry players have made some attempts to overcome Singapore's relatively marginal position by "hothousing" some parts of the pop culture industry, especially in digital media and through co-productions with other regional players. This chapter also examined some of the particularities of the entry into the market and reception of imported East Asian Pop Culture by the Singaporean audience as a transnational audience. Of course, each localized audience of respective, constituent regional locations will have their own set of particularistic characteristics grounded in and derived from their respective everyday life. However, it is conceivable that, given their common urban middle class capitalist consumer modernity, East Asian Pop Culture audiences across the region may share certain practices and experiences by virtue of their similar social, economic and urban cultural dispositions.

# 5

# The Structure of Identification and Distancing in Watching East Asian Television Drama

The routine flows of television drama series across national, cultural and linguistic boundaries in East Asia have been characterized "as a self-aware but non-consensual force field articulated by the region's mixed postcolonial experiences, negotiation with globalization, and interacting media cultures" (Tsai 2005: 102). Within this non-consensual force field are the highly uneven flows of Japanese and Korean products entering Pop Culture China and a trickle at best of the reverse flow of Chinese languages products into Korea and Japan, particularly the latter.[1] In part as a consequence of lower production qualities, Chinese languages productions in every location have been losing their domestic audience to imported Korean and Japanese dramas for the past two decades.

As mentioned in Chapter 1, of the three genres of transnational East Asian Pop Culture—music, films and television dramas—drama has the most pronounced and tractable impact on the cultural practices of the audience. As pointed out in an earlier chapter, this is because serial drama demands regular viewing by the audience. Many activities need to be displaced, even sacrificed, in order to catch the regularly scheduled episodes. If one misses an episode, efforts then have to be made to view it before the next instalment is screened. The result is an active engagement, with each episode drawing the audience further into a virtual but intimate relationship with the characters in the drama. It is thus unsurprising that media audience reception research generally focuses on television audiences.

It is by now commonplace to suggest that the meaning of a media text is not simply the apprehending of the writer/producer's intended meaning by the reader/audience. Nevertheless, that the writer/producer does intend and encode a certain meaning remains the case; furthermore, this encoded meaning may be said to be the "dominant" or "preferred" meaning of the text.[2] This dominant meaning frames the space of identification with the characters in the text, as selected by the writer/producer, for the reader/audience. It creates the reception space and position—a subject position—for its reader/audience. If the audience accedes, consciously or otherwise, to the dominant meaning and subject position offered by the text, one would be identifying with its preferred character(s); conversely, when one resists the dominant meaning and subject position offered, one distances oneself from the same character(s).

It should be noted that the text is not consumed only as an entire unit, as a coherent whole, but also in a fragmentary manner. In addition to an overall sense of the whole, different components of the text may be treated differently by the same audience. Consistent with this fragmentary consumption, reception of a text involves intermittent moments of identification and distancing from the dominant meaning during real time reading/watching. This, combined with the fact that audiences bring to bear their own context within which to interpret the text, and come to the text from different angles to actively develop preferred meanings of their own, means they may end up accepting, modifying, resisting or otherwise disrupting the dominant meaning.[3] Consequently, given that decoding is part of the reception process, acceptance of the dominant meaning and assigned space and position is never guaranteed. The meaning derived by a reader/audience is thus unavoidably a negotiated outcome (Rajagopal 2001: 10).[4]

When analysing audience reception of imported programs, i.e., the reception practices of a transnational audience, one fundamental dimension needs to be added to the general reception process, namely, the foreignness of the drama to the audience. In practice, foreignness is part of the audience's viewing pleasure. Conceptually, the audience's awareness that the program is foreign complicates the normal identification/distancing process. This awareness raises hurdles to identification and makes distancing relatively easy. Significantly, existing research on audience reception has paid scant attention to the foreign elements of imported programs. This is surprising, considering the global domination of US television programs which are technically foreign in all locations but the US. Yet, this foreignness is seldom problematized, perhaps because it has been absorbed into the increasingly undifferentiated sign of the "global" media and/or under the loosely formulated idea of "cultural imperialism," implying minimally a "cultural contamination" of the local and maximally, an unreflexive acceptance of the US-determined dominant meanings for the media text (Chua 2000). As this chapter addresses the question "How does a Huaren audience, as a transnational audience, read/watch an imported Korean/Japanese television drama series?" foreignness needs to be foregrounded analytically.

## Dubbing as Domestication

Korean and Japanese dramas are normally dubbed and/or subtitled in Pop Culture China in different Chinese languages depending on where they enter Pop Culture China—Cantonese in Hong Kong, Mandarin dialogue and complex Chinese script in subtitles in Taiwan, Mandarin and simplified Chinese scripts in Singapore and China—making the imported products accessible to the Huaren audience.[5] With duo-sound technology in television, a Huaren audience can watch Korean and Japanese programs in the original languages with Chinese language subtitles if they so choose. Some of the complexities that arise from this language situation have already been discussed in Chapters 3 and 4. Now, let us return to the question of dubbing and its effect on the audience.

Dubbing is the translation of the on-screen dialogue from its original or "source" language to one that is common within the local or "target" audience. For example, a Korean program will be dubbed into Cantonese for the Hong Kong audience. Technically, dubbing is not simply the replacement of the words in one language with the equivalent words in another. Before dubbing can take place, a translation of the given script has to be undertaken; this is followed by the "synchronization of the translated dialogue so that it matches the actors' mouth movements and the other images as closely as possible" (Martinez, 2004: 4). Constrained by the need to synchronize lip movements (lip-sync), particularly in close-up shots of the characters on screen, the translator "must move away from literal conceptions of translation and build up confidence in his or her abilities to put forward alternatives that move away from the source text to focus on the function of the text and on the viewer" (Chaume 2004: 35); in short, some changes to the original dialogue that suit the cultural context of the target viewer are unavoidable, indeed necessary. "Visual synchrony" between the translated words and the lip movements is the most important aspect in creating "the impression that the actors on screen are pronouncing the translated word," in creating the belief that it is a "local" program (ibid).[6] Where synchronization fails, the program loses a significant part of its realism.

Beyond the issue of synchrony, there are political and cultural problems that need to be dealt with in dubbing. In the translation process, terms, expressions and contextual references in the source language may have no equivalent in the target language. Faced with such a problem, translation is generally oriented to the cultural context of the target audience and changed accordingly; in the translation/dubbing profession, "an acceptable translation is that which is oriented toward the norms of the target language and culture" (Agost 2004: 71). At its most extreme, "fidelity" to the original is so relaxed that target "oral colloquial language" is used "to provide the viewers what they are used to" rather than sticking to the greater demands of written norms (Agost 2004: 68–69). Cultural elements of the target audience are thus introduced into the dubbed text. However, with attention to synchronization, insertions from the culture of the target audience are largely visually "unseen" by the audience. Taken together, the aggregated effect of the dubbing process is ultimately one through which "a particular target culture that, for historical, social and political or economic reasons, seeks to domesticate a foreign product and to make both the translator and the translation invisible" (Chaume 2004: 39).

When Korean and Japanese television dramas are dubbed into a Chinese language, local colloquial expressions are conventionally adopted, intensifying the orientation of the program to the cultural context of the target language. This is, for example, very apparent in the dubbing of the very popular Korean period drama series, *Jewel in the Palace* into Cantonese in Hong Kong and into Mandarin in Taiwan.[7] The drama chronicles the rise of a palace cook who subsequently became the first female doctor to the emperor in the Korean imperial court in the sixteenth century. The popularity of *Jewel* was something of a breakthrough (Leung 2008); the drama was covered very extensively by print media in China, Hong Kong and Taiwan (Kim 2009). Although Korea produces a very substantial number of historical, costume drama series, until *Jewel*, very few had been exported successfully as such dramas are best appreciated if the audience has some requisite knowledge of the history in question. In *Jewel*, there is actually very little Korean historical content. History merely serves as a frame for a story of court intrigue, a moral tale of good versus bad, narrated consistently in close-up focus on the main characters; no demand is made of the audience to know anything about sixteenth century Korea. It is a story of personal growth, petty intrigue, greed versus righteousness and romance, dressed in period costumes.[8]

The translation/dubbing of *Jewel* was further supported by several elements. First, consistent with actual practice during the sixteenth century, written documents within the television drama, from reports in the imperial court to personal letters, were often written in actual Chinese ideograms or calligraphic Korean script, which is similar to Chinese writing. To further domesticate the series, the Hong Kong television station intervened directly by providing additional "explanation," in a Cantonese voice-over, giving the Chinese equivalents to the Korean recipes and medicinal items featured on screen. Finally, the relatively similar physiognomy of East Asians is generally already a factor that facilitates domestication of each other's films and dramas. Other processes of domestication were also at work outside the television broadcast. As the dubbed versions were "produced with a Chinese-speaking audience in mind, all other aspects of the packaging [of the DVDs] of such serials were also 'sinicised,' including the plot synopsis and title" (Yin and Liew 2005: 221).

In combination, the localizing practices made *Jewel* easily consumable throughout Pop Culture China. All the processes involved in dubbing did more than translate the dialogue at the language level, they also transformed the series into a "local" program; translation/dubbing thus also creates a "transmutation" of the program. Watching a dubbed program is thus equivalent to watching a locally produced program; audiences are drawn into the consumption of the familiar, which facilitates real-time identification with the characters on screen. The most extreme domestication process is, perhaps, the reported use of Korean dramas as material for the teaching of Mandarin in Singapore. One of the teachers in a junior college reported: "We cut *Winter Sonata* into various video clips, and students are supposed to expand the story line using their own words [in Mandarin]" (quoted in Yin and Liew 2005: 222). To generalize, the relative ease of identification facilitated by translation/dubbing undoubtedly contributes very significantly to the popularity of television dramas that circulate within East Asia.

## Foreignness Preserved: Clothes and Urban Icons

While the target audience of an imported drama enjoy the reception made easy by dubbing, they are nevertheless also attracted to its foreignness and difference— the exoticism of the foreign, the "not us"—as an important component of their viewing pleasure. This foreignness is, of course, preserved in the visual dimension of the television drama, particularly through costumes and images of foreign locations. Ethnic costumes are a common signifier of culture and, therefore, a very convenient vehicle for signalling difference between groups; tradition is often inscribed on the female body through ethnic costumes. It is, therefore, unremarkable to single out ethnic costumes as an element that preserves the foreignness in a television drama series, as in the case of *Jewel*.

However, as suggested, historical period dramas with traditional costumes are not easily exportable. The regionally successful dramas tend to be of the urban, contemporary romance genre, where the characters on screen don international fashions; thus eliminating the single-most convenient carrier of foreignness. In an urban drama, if one turns off the sound or watches it dubbed, the relatively similar physiognomy of East Asians renders it difficult for an audience, who is unfamiliar and unable to identify the actors and actresses on screen, to discern from an indoor close-up shot of the faces on screen, the country of origin of the drama. Under such conditions, the foreignness for the consumer/audience comes through the iconic images of the outdoors that metonymically represent the city/cities in which the drama is set. Foreignness is literally a source of viewing pleasure when it is presented visually on screen, instead of discursively in dialogue. The Tokyo Tower, the needle-tower in Shanghai, the Hong Kong ferry and, more generically, consumer and leisure sites such as Jeju Island in Korea, the shopping district in Tokyo Bay and, even more generically, street scenes where the neon signs are in the local language, have all been transformed by their appearance in television dramas into strategically marketed tourist sites for the respective drama's fans. This transformation of places that are seen on television into tourist sites—sights to sites—is evidence of the viewing pleasure derived from the foreign; the exoticness of watching the foreign materializes in the exotic gaze of the tourist.

Taking the dubbing processes and the visual-foreignness together, it is apparent that the transnational reception of imported media products, including television dramas, involves a combination of the processes of identification and difference/

distancing in which these processes either occur simultaneously or in a series of inter-mittent moments of one or the other. Empirically, this identification/distancing is replicated in the reception practices of the transnational audience for imported pop culture, including East Asian Pop Culture. Methodologically, we should be able to utilize empirical observations from different locations to construct a composite of the figure of the transnational audience and his/her reception practices.

## Real-time Identification and Difference

Audience (inter)reactions with the characters and activities on screen are immedi-ate and direct during actual viewing time. Audiences have been known to rework such identification with what is represented on screen into their everyday life; the active discussion, among television drama fans, of characters and activities on screen vis-à-vis their daily life is a commonly observed phenomenon among researchers (Ang 2001). Leung provides an example from the context of the Hong Kong audience of Japanese drama:

> Many times in life I encountered obstacles, or often I feel frustrated at not being able to utilize my capabilities, hence I do identify with the male led in *Long Vacation* [Japanese television drama]. But I find one thing quite reassuring in the drama. When Kimura Takuya summoned the determination to win the piano contest and eventually won it, it seemed that his "vacation" had ended. I hope my "vacation" will end like his.[9] (2004: 94)

Another example comes from a Singaporean audience member:

> Such things can happen anywhere in this world. It's just that it is filmed in Japan and the characters are Japanese. But when you are talking about love, sex, and marriage, it happens anywhere in the world where someone, out of a situation, has sex with someone else on a fateful night and then thinks about it and, you know, wonders, "Why did I do it?" (MacLachlan and Chua 2004: 147)

In both instances the structure of the sentiment of identification from dif-ferent audience members embedded in different locations is broadly similar: "I can understand the character and why she acts the way she does. It can happen to anyone, including me. I would do the same if I were in her position"; in which "anyone" implies simply being "human."

An alternative mode of identification can be seen in a comparative study of Hong Kong and Singaporean audiences of Korean dramas. Lin and Tong found that both audiences said: they liked the very realistic and sophisticated portrayals of what they called "Asian" ways of expressing various kinds of relations and emo-tional attachments among the characters. One of the relationships they appreciated most is the deep connection among family members, and the virtues of filial piety that characters possessed. Many of them said they were drawn by the "family warmth," "strong sense of family," and "traditional family virtues" depicted in the dramas. For example, a Hong Kong informant, July (age 30, social worker) said that Korean culture is "very close to Chinese culture" (2008: 98–99).

The feeling of the viewer that he/she is able to "identify with the character and his/her actions because we are [East] Asians," suggests a sense of "cultural proximity" within the regional audience. The basis of the Hong Kong and Singapore Huaren audience for identification with what is Korean on screen is allegedly Confucianism as the shared culture of East Asia. This corresponds with some Korean commentators' understanding of why Korean dramas are popular in East Asia (Lee 2008: 181). In Singapore, this basis of identification is further reinforced by the official promotion of the family institution and values as the fundamental building blocks of society through the reductionist rhetoric of Confucian ethics. Parenthetically, one needs to raise the question: for these Hong Kong and Singapore Huaren audiences, is "being Asian" the same as "being Chinese"?

Identification on an abstract level with "being human" and "being Asian" displaces the factual foreignness of the Korean or Japanese dramas for the Huaren audience. However, it does not erase the factual foreignness and its difference. Difference lies always just under the surface of identification.

As soon as the characters and actions on screen are in opposition to the audience's sentiments, foreignness/difference surfaces immediately and is used by the audience to distance itself from what is happening on screen. For example, a Singaporean audience of married women apparently has a tendency to resist Japanese dramatic representations of sexual relations:

> [The Japanese] want to be first in everything. Their technology is first and this may affect them. They want to be advanced in everything ... And unconsciously, it may influence their thinking, their attitude towards sex, their values. (MacLachlan and Chua 2004: 164)

The difference between the "Japanese they" and "Singaporean us" is emphatic and unmistakable in this expression, even though the "Singaporean us" is not explicitly mentioned. Another Singaporean example:

> I have a wish. I wish these Japanese dramas would not encourage our youths to accept those one-night love relationships so easily, sleep with each other and that's it. This is very unacceptable.[10] (MacLachlan and Chua 2004: 165)

Here foreignness/difference is evoked by the audience member in order to distance herself from what is on screen. Foreignness/difference provoked a sense of displeasure with and critique of the culture of the location of production, Japan/Japaneseness.

Examining the intermittent identification/distancing practices of audiences, we see that identification is predicated on "abstract" categories of "human" and "Asian" that allow a presumption of similarities. Conversely, the specificities of the "culture" of the production location represented on screen in imported dramas are evoked by the same audience to create "difference" as the basis of distancing themselves. Audiences can and do switch between the two at will. Such intermittent practice appears to apply also to audience identification with individual actors, as Jung (2011) found in the case of female Japanese fans of Bae Yong-joon who demonstrate a similar tendency of identifying with his "soft" masculinity while distancing themselves from his later muscular image and his role as a cunning and sexually depraved character in the film *Untold Scandal* (2003). This intermittent switching rather than consistent identification sustained throughout the reading/watching of an imported television drama suggests that the conventional assumption that "cultural proximity" is the basis of identification with and pleasure in watching foreign programs needs greater elaboration and specification. It also has implications for the formation of a stable identity for the audience vis-à-vis the television programs.

## Capitalist Modernity: Distance and Desire

Beyond the actual watching of a drama at the individual level, Iwabuchi (2008) has shown that there is also a "national" level of the "like us/unlike us" response, i.e., a combined identification and distancing at work. Here the use of foreignness/difference is critical. This can be evoked as a critique of the audience's own culture in two ways. First, the more conventional instance is more implicitly than explicitly expressed. This is when the audience treats the drama as a fantasy, which is in fact the common attitude of the overwhelming majority of the television drama audience. If, for the audience, fantasy is substantively an "escape" from the reality of everyday life, then, beneath this sense of escape is, of course, a critique of that everyday life that makes the escape necessary.

Second, a particularistic reiteration of this "fantasy/escape" mode in East Asian Pop Culture can be found in Iwabuchi's (2002a; 2002b) suggestion that Japanese audiences feel a sense of "nostalgia" when they watch dramas from elsewhere in East Asia. In the less developed parts of Asia, the Japanese "find purity, energy and dreams" (2002a: 550). Nostalgia, in the intentional misrecognition of the past as an "ideal," is also simultaneously a critique and an expression of dissatisfaction with the present; the Japanese audience's sense of nostalgia in looking at the "vitality" of the rest of Asia, which is less economically developed, is also a critique of their over-consumerist present society. According to Jung, it is this "nostalgia" that explains the attraction middle-aged Japanese women's feel toward the main character in *Winter Sonata* and, by extension, to the actor Bae Yong-joon himself (Jung 2011). This is captured in one fan's statement: "We used to have that kind of man in Japan. But now it's hard to find that kind of character (virtue) from young Japanese men" (quoted in Jung 2011: 62). Self-critique would also explain why some of these middle-aged Japanese women in the audience take it upon them-selves to change not only their own but also larger societal attitudes towards Korea and Koreans, particularly those Koreans who live in Japan and have hitherto been largely marginalized and discriminated against by Japanese society (Mōri 2008; Iwabuchi 2008).

Conceptually, and ironically, it is these two uses of difference which dove-tail into each other that dictate the way East Asian Pop Culture is read in differ-ent regional locations. In analyzing how other parts of Asia are presented in the Japanese media and in interviews with Japanese audiences of East Asian Pop Culture, Iwabuchi found that the mainstream Japanese audience has a tendency to "appreciate" the media-mediated cultural representation—as "visualization of society" (Hartley 1996: 210)—of other parts of Asia with a sense of "nostalgia," a sense of "loss" of its own past, especially in the post-bubble economy period when the Japanese economy was stuck in the doldrums: "as we [Japanese] walked around Hong Kong and Bangkok, we found the energy of the people to be overwhelming. It was the same kind of raw vigour that Japan had once during the high economic growth era." (A report in a weekly magazine, quoted in Iwabuchi 2004: 155)

For example, with specific reference to the representation of Vietnam in the popular Japanese television drama *Doku* (1996), Iwabuchi further argues that for Japanese audiences, "[b]ecause they are still not quite modern, Vietnamese are energetic and can afford dreams of a bright future; hence, they are expected to unilaterally afford Japanese people spiritual nourishment" (2004: 156). In this instance, Japan's past is being inscribed by the Japanese onto Vietnam's present; in post-bubble economy Japan, Japanese people no longer "dream of a bright future," thus, the present Vietnamese struggle for development is both "nostalgic" and "inspirational" for the Japanese; as Iwabuchi puts it, "'our' [Japanese] past and memory are found in 'their' [the rest of Asia's] present" (2002a: 549). This Japanese attitude of placing itself ahead of the rest of Asia is of long standing. Since the nine-teenth century, Japan has persistently seen itself as "being in Asia but not part of Asia" because it is ahead of the rest of Asia.[11] This places contemporaneous "other" Asian locations in a culturally and historically "backward" position vis-à-vis Japan, a cultural-historical temporality defined by levels of development in terms of capi-talist modernity, which denies others in Asia as coeval equals.[12]

Ironically, this inscription appears to dovetail with Vietnamese youth's self-projection of their future. For Vietnamese youth, the urban lifestyle they see fea-tured in East Asian dramas "signifies prosperity and sophistication and engenders longing, a longing for a richer consumer world, for technical expertise and creativ-ity, and for societies that foster these elements" (Thomas 2004: 186).[13] For them, "modernity" is reduced to and signified by an expansion of mass consumerism;

the "coalescence of popular culture with modernity and mass consumption in Vietnam has released a storm of desire for products and consumer cultures of East Asia" (Iwabuchi et al. 2004: 7). Similarly, young Taiwanese fans of Japanese television dramas suggest similar desires. According to Ko, these fans latch on to the well-crafted representation of the contemporary urban landscape as an index of "realism" in Japanese television dramas:

> Japanese idol dramas provide a *real imaginary*, and the imagery is manifested beautifully into a spectacle of modernity. Therefore, the metropolitan Tokyo is re-presented as the locus where the individuals pursue freedom, love, and careers; the imagery of "Tokyo" is a *visual place* that mediates between reality and dreams. These dreams have not yet been realized in Taipei, but are already presented on screen ... not the Tokyo in Japan, but the "Tokyo" on screen.[14] (2004: 123, original italics)

Significantly, Iwabuchi argues, there are exceptions in the Japanese audiences of pop culture from elsewhere in East Asia who do not place the rest of the region in an undifferentiated "nostalgic-past" of Japan. For example, Japanese fans of Hong Kong pop culture consider themselves to be "a community of taste," as Hong Kong pop culture is not readily available and is not part of the mainstream in Japanese entertainment; there is a very limited flow of pop culture products from Pop Culture China into Japan.[15] For these Hong Kong pop culture fans, their self-conceptualization is one that is not Japanese-centered or Japanese-chauvinistic. Said one such Japanese fan:

> Hong Kong is apparently similar to Japan in terms of physical appearance, but I realized that its culture is actually completely different from ours. [This is clearly illustrated by the fact that] Hong Kong has also achieved a high economic development, but retains the vitality that Japan has lost. (Iwabuchi 2004: 165, original parenthesis)

They see Hong Kong's capitalist modernity not only as "contemporaneous" to Japan's—"apparently similar"—but also as "different" and better—"retains vitality"—within high capitalist economic development.

Even while a minority of Japanese who are fans of Hong Kong pop culture are willing to accept Hong Kong as coeval with Japanese modernity, and are even willing to accept that about some other East Asian locations, the rest of Asia remains behind and backward in relation to Japan along the single dimension of capitalist consumer modernity. China, having only opened up to capitalist consumerism in the past two decades, is clearly among the "backward" nations in the eyes of media consumers in the "advanced" societies. This is brutally expressed by a Singaporean East Asian Pop Culture fan:

> Interviewer: Could you elaborate on why you would not want to be like the Mainland Chinese?
>
> Respondent (a 24 year old, Singaporean Huaren male): Okay, I am not trying to be nasty here but I do not really think well of the Mainland Chinese. The images that they portray are not as good as the Japanese and even if the Mainland Chinese try to be fashionable, the results can be quite disastrous. In school, I see the Mainland Chinese with long and dyed hair and although they do not look good, they are still okay but once they open their months, that's it, because everything is ruined. They talk loudly in Mandarin with a weird accent. My impression of the Mainland Chinese is that they are rough, loud and crude people and I am glad that neither the Japanese nor I (in some sense) look and behave like them. (Chua 2002: 38).

This Singaporean Huaren's very self-conscious and discriminatory exclusion of the mainland Chinese, in spite of a supposed ethnic affinity, and his claimed similarity to the Japanese in spite of ethnic and national differences, signifies an "Asian" identity constituted in terms of a developed capitalist consumerist culture.

Audiences of East Asian Pop Culture in the constituent locations apparently view each other in the terms of a fixed reference: a linear temporality on the single dimension of capitalist, consumerism-driven modernity. Along this dimension, Japan has remained at the most developed end, while less economically developed countries, such as China and Vietnam, take up the rear.[16] This explains the general structure of respective audiences' gazes: in the nostalgic gaze of the Japanese audience, Japan's past is the present of the rest of Asia, ideologically enabling the Japanese fans to retain their self-centeredness. However, Japan's position is no longer uncontested, as Korea and Hong Kong would both claim a coeval position. The future-oriented gaze of Taiwanese audiences watching Japanese television dramas illustrates that the present of Japan is the future of the rest of Asia where capitalist consumerism is less developed, leading the latter to desire, identify and embrace Japan as a representation of the future. Finally, this linear temporality of capitalist, consumerist modernity has also enabled pop culture fans in developed capitalist economies—Japan, South Korea, Taiwan, Hong Kong and Singapore—to distance themselves from their counterparts' media products from less developed economies which are perceived as "backward" and even "embarrassing"; others who are nevertheless also "Asians." This linear placement of regional audiences by other regional audiences, which is structurally homologous to the relative placing of the respective national economies, raises questions of whether a "pan-East Asian identity" has been emerging, or indeed is even possible, among the regional audiences of the same pop culture products.

## Pan-East Asian Identity

Studies of regional transnational audiences of East Asian television dramas suggest that there are instances in which the audiences do derive and/or impute a common or pan-East Asian cultural identity on themselves and the characters on screen, and by extension, with the culture of the people in the production location. A sense of cultural proximity, reinforced by the relatively similar physiognomy, is engendered when the culture of the production location is "absorbed" into the audience's own culture; e.g., Huaren audiences see Korean culture as very similar to their own culture. However, an equally common practice of the transnational audience is to invoke particularistic features of cultural representation on screen, so as to distance themselves from the culture of the production location, thereby rejecting any assumption of a shared culture and identity. The same audience is adept in quick-switching between these two practices. This intermittent process is further complicated by the unequal economic development between the production and reception locations. This unequal status leads those who are in advanced consumerist societies to distance themselves from, and discriminate against, those who are playing catch-up within the region. Taking these points together, it would seem that while a pan-East Asian identity among regional audiences of East Asian television dramas based on cultural proximity is a possibility, such an identity would nevertheless be very unstable.

At the individual level, identity is not permanently fixed but is an unending process of layering and interaction with a constant stream of cultural knowledge acquisitions. The result is an "identity" that is always multiple, complex, open to changes and contextual strategic use. Knowledge of pop culture can, of course, be part of the constellation of acquisitions and inputs into an individual's identity formation. However, in contrast to inputs such as nationality, gender, ethnicity, profession and age—which are involuntary and their inscription on individuals is institutionally (re)enforced and, therefore, socio-politically consequential to the individual—pop culture consumption as a leisure activity is largely voluntary and residual, with no social institutions enforcing compliance or dishing out payoffs that would institutionalize such practices as a process of engendering identity. Furthermore, several features of pop culture contribute to the dilution of its possible effects on stable identity formation for the leisure audience. The effect of pop culture on the leisure audience is ephemeral, changing rapidly with the latest trends and icons, both in terms of objects and artists. Although such consumption can be a major part of one's everyday life, as ex-audience members may recall (often fondly), its "lasting" effect on identity formation is difficult to establish.

Of course, the possibility of determined, even obsessive, consumption of East Asian Pop Culture, as with any other form of leisure, should not be precluded. For the relatively small number of truly avid fans, consumption of pop culture might be transformative of their personalities, life trajectories and identities. For example, one cannot deny the possibility that many middle-aged Japanese women may have permanently changed their attitudes towards Koreans as a consequence of watching the Korean television drama, *Winter Sonata*, and idolizing its star, Bae Yong-joon.

Beyond individual identity, history stands in the way of any emerging pan-East Asian identity among the regional transnational consumers of East Asian Pop Culture. The history of Japanese colonization in Korea and Taiwan and its military invasion of the rest of East Asia, including China, has not been entirely forgotten or forgiven, especially since this history has been consistently used by the colonized and invaded nations to generate local nationalism and to justify an antagonistic stance toward Japanese regional economic dominance in particular. Within this context, Korean and Taiwanese nationalists who recall Japan colonialization see the popularity of Japanese pop culture in Taiwan as a cultural form of "neo-imperialism."[17] On the other hand, right-wing Japanese nationalists have actively promoted anti-Korean Wave pop culture, including *manga*, that borders on being "hate" literature, to avoid the contamination of a superior national culture. The possibility of a pan-East Asian identity will inevitably run up against this regional history of past antagonisms and into a wall of dominant and deeper national identity that is buttressed by political institutions and which serves as a reservoir of cultural repertoires that absorbs and is modified by each new knowledge input.[18]

## Conclusion

East Asian Pop Culture as a cultural economy is based largely on the consumption of Japanese and Korean pop culture by the large regional Huaren population. Korean and Japanese television dramas and films are regularly dubbed and subtitled into different Chinese languages, and while the translated products are routed through different paths, they eventually reach all the major Huaren predominant locations. Dubbing and subtitling into different Chinese languages are processes that "domesticate" the Japanese and Korean dramas for the Huaren audience. Particular features of the dramas are invoked to reinforce this domestication; for example, heavily family-centered themes in Korean dramas are read as similar to, if not the "same" as, the predominant attitudes in "Chinese culture," with a distant reference to a shared Confucian ideology. Finally, the relatively similar physiognomy of East Asians obviously facilitates Huaren audience's identification with the characters on screen, which engenders in them a sense of cultural proximity, of being "Asian."

However, beyond this abstract sense of Asianness, particularistic narratives, activities and features are used by same Huaren audience to distance themselves from the foreign culture represented on screen. For example, Japanese dramas are read as too "Japanese," too "Western" and too "liberal," all the values that are deemed undesirable by conservatives among the female Huaren audience, regionally. This distancing from the foreign weakens the possibility of a pan-East Asian cultural identity which may be engendered by the sense of "(East) Asianness" felt by the Huaren audience's reception of Japanese and Korean television. In addition, transnational audiences in different parts of East Asia also differentiate between regional locations and place themselves, relative to each other, along a linear trajectory of capitalist consumerist modernity—Japan in the lead and China at the rear, with Korea, Hong Kong, Taiwan and Singapore in the middle with relatively equal development. This linear placement affects the attitude of regional transnational audiences towards each other, disrupting likely ground for a common "Asian" identity. Parenthetically, this reference to capitalist consumerism takes the target of identification for East Asians beyond the regional into a global comparison which might account for the common popularity of American pop culture, especially films, in Asia; comparative analysis of how East Asian regional audiences receive American pop culture remains an under-researched area. Finally, as mentioned, the possibility of an emergent "pan-Asian" identity deriving from a shared consumption of East Asian Pop Culture will unavoidably come up against the history of regional conflicts, national identities and national political interests, all of which mitigate against the emergent possibility; this is an issue that will be further discussed in Chapter 7.

# 6

# Layers of Audience Communities

With new technologies, the reception/consumption of pop culture has become a highly individualized activity. Listening to music has been highly individualized since the development of the now defunct Sony Walkman, which was replaced by a great variety of small portable gadgets including mobile phones. Television watching is less and less a shared activity among family members as individuals, especially youth, move to watching television on personal computer screens and again, mobile phones. Nevertheless, beyond the individualized watching and listening, aficionados of pop culture continue to seek out similarly inclined individuals with whom to exchange information and share the pleasures of consumption through different communication modes and material objects, fan clubs being the most conventional organized form. With the Internet, fan clubs have become less dependent on face-to-face interaction and are now also free from the constraints of a physical space. They have become transnational, a transformation that befits the increasingly global flows of pop culture that facilitate transnational fans. Perhaps, because this transformation is still a relatively new phenomenon, few "have considered the significance of fan culture on an increasingly global scene, fostered in particular by the advent of the internet as a tool for intercultural, and potentially worldwide, fan activity" (Darling-Wolf quoted in Chin 2010: 211).

However, as mentioned in Chapter 2, it is generally true that for a show watched by millions each week "maybe two to three hundred participated regularly in the many fan activities" (Bird 2010: 91). Statistically, the number of passive consumers in the leisure and entertainment audience of pop culture overwhelms the number of passionate members who are "hyperactive" aficionados and join fan clubs. Indeed, the popularity of an artist is dependent on the statistically large numbers of leisure and passive consumers rather than the passionate few. Studies of audience communities have been largely restricted to fan communities, without any attempt to theorize the possibility of community formation among this larger passive audience. Qualification for "membership" to a larger potential "community" is no more than the casual act of listening to or watching a particular piece of pop music or television program. Spatially, the geographical boundaries for this larger potential passive audience community would be equivalent to the distribution and circulation radius of the pop culture product in question. However, it stands to reason that, unlike the active fans, the potential community of the passive audience, who by definition do nothing beyond watching the television programs, would not achieve transnational connections. The conceptual question is how this statistically overwhelming presence of a passive audience can be transformed into an audience "community" or "communities." This chapter examines the two levels of audience communities within East Asian Pop Culture—the potential for a locally-grounded passive audience community of imported foreign pop culture and the transnational activities of avid fan communities. Methodologically, it is essential that the chapter draw on existing empirical research that analyzes events in East Asia Pop Culture that are germane to the conceptual possibility of constructing an abstract composite configuration of the different layers of communities in both its local and transnational dimensions.

## Occasioned Communities

As mentioned, the index of popularity of any pop culture item, be it an artist or genre, is the statistically large number of passive audience/consumers for whom pop culture is a leisure and entertainment activity. Their interests and audience reception habits may be casual or more involved, and the greater the level of involvement, the more appropriate the label of "fan." For the more passive audience, listening or viewing is largely a private activity performed at home or increasingly while in transit to places via a mobile communication device. They are literally grounded and local. Such an audience would not be concerned about others who share the same interest, and would not make an active effort to engage with fellow audience members or consciously seek to be part of a larger audience community. Without any active promoter or organizer, the potential community of passive leisure consumers remains for the most part a latent possibility, invisible. The question is through what processes and institutional mechanisms can this statistical presence manifest itself as a community?

One mode of realizing this larger community of consumers has already been presented in Chapter 2 on Pop Culture China; that is, the generation of occasional community mediated by the newspapers and other print media. The "popularity" of an artist or a drama is obviously and significantly both a cause and a product of media attention and coverage—newspapers, magazines, television, radio and advertising. "Hot" artists or programs are engendered by all the constitutive components of the multimedia-culture industry. For example, at the peak of the popularity of Japanese trendy dramas: *China Times*, Taiwan's most widely circulated newspaper, produced an entire page every week devoted to discussions of Japanese television dramas. Following this lead, other publishers began to target the young

Japanese television drama fans, which "led to the popularization of a new genre of writing, which combines information on Japanese TV dramas with discussions about Japanese fashion or lifestyle;" consequently, "Japanese TV dramas and other inter-referential texts bind together to create a 'mega-text'" (Lee M.T. 2004: 133).[1] Indeed, part of the large leisure audience is generated by the media coverage that creates a snowballing effect that boosts a product's popularity.

Any item in this mega-text could serve to realize the potential community of leisure consumers. As suggested in Chapter 2, the entertainment page of the Singapore national Mandarin newspaper can be conceptualized as a proxy map of East Asian Pop Culture. Geographically, the boundary of "East Asian Pop Culture" is defined by the places that appear regularly in the reportage; namely, the production centers of Seoul, Tokyo, Shanghai, Beijing, Hong Kong, Taipei and Singapore. The bounded page-space is "peopled" daily with images and information of East Asian artists: Bae Yong-joon in Seoul, Faye Wong in Shanghai, Wong Kar Wai in Hong Kong, Jay Chou in Taipei. These individuals inhabit the daily pages at unpredictable intervals, more frequently in the rising phases of their careers and with a diminishing presence when they are on the way out. The entertainment page is read by an unknown multitude of readers, who are also unknown to each other. When two or more readers happen to be present at an occasion/event and they participate in free flowing conversation, exchanges concerning any one of the items reported on the page make manifest the silent presence of other readers/audience members. A "community" of at least two persons is instantiated. When the occasion is over, the community is also dissolved. Such occasioned community of leisure audience members during personal, face-to-face, casual encounters is unavoidably small in scale and a weak form of community formation; it is ephemeral and does not register with anyone but the co-present conversationalists. Such a "community of consumers" of East Asian Pop Culture is an "occasioned" and "occasional" community, befitting the practices—including the "gossipy" character of the print media reports—of the overwhelming majority of leisure consumers, whose interest is in entertainment, rather than having a preoccupation in their everyday life as is seen with an avid fan.

A stronger expression of an occasioned community is the uncoordinated meeting of disparate individual audience members during a public appearance of a pop star. The statistical presence of a large number of individuals is transformed into a "crowd," whose social character is neatly deconstructed by Slater, following Walter Benjamin, as consisting of "people moving about according to their own self-determined logic" coincidentally "turning their gaze towards a particular focus"—"a spectacle, an event, an object of interest or desire" (1993: 190). A crowd can be completely incidental as in a traffic accident drawing in curious passers-by, or organized by a common focus. These crowds as the materialization of a community of consumers are common occurrences in East Asia; an artist is mobbed upon arrival at the airport or at the venue of a public appearance. Such a crowd-community, however, is likely to be constituted by both a mix of avid fans and members of the leisure audience.

This mode of materialization of an audience community has a socio-cultural impact for two reasons. First, the individuals that gather, without any prior organization, become aware of others who share the same passion, and hence gain a subjective, individualized realization of being part of a community, however ephemerally, with the others. Second, the constituted crowd is inevitably transformed into a "spectacle" by media attention. The write-ups and photographs transform the event into a media phenomenon—a second order spectacularization—that further fuels the artist's popularity, attracting a greater audience, if for no other reason than the curiosity generated by the media fuss. An example that shows the visual impact of such crowds of audience and the way in which the mass media presents them as spectacle can be found in the reception in Taipei and Tokyo of Bae Yong-joon, the male actor who had the lead role in the television drama, *Winter Sonata*, the first mega-hit Korean drama in Japan (Mōri 2008: 129). In Taipei:

> On 20, 21 and 22 August in 2005, all the major newspapers in Taiwan, including *Apple Daily*, *China Times*, *United Daily*, and *Liberty Times*, used the bulk of their entertainment page to cover this event [Bae's visit to Taiwan]. The coverage was image-centered. Different sized brightly colored pictures were arranged disorderly to create a sense of uncontrollability and excitement, like a noise disrupting the banality of everyday life. Even the headlines were colored bright red, blue, green, and yellow as a contrast to the sobriety of the serious economics and politics pages. The noisy pictures, which are about and of the body, can be divided into two categories. The first category contains the bodies of the irrational and overjoyed fans crowding and squeezing, even stepping on each other, competing for Bae's attention, or better yet, his physical touch. Headlines such as "Fans Thrilled Out of Control to Have Handsome Bae's Hugs" (*Liberty Times*, 22 Aug 2005), "Crossing the Ocean to Pursue Bae Yong-jun, Fans Offer Loads of Gifts" (*Liberty Times*, 20 Aug 2005), "People Wall Crumbled Down with the Arrival of Handsome Bae; 66 Year-old Grandma Tripped in the Crowds at the Bottom of Human Pyramid but Still Insisted on Chasing after Bae" (*China Times*, 20 Aug 2005), "Come and Take a Picture with the Water Cup that Bae Just Drank From" (*China Times*, 20 Aug 2005), "Hard to Say Good-bye to Handsome Bae, the Airport is Wild and Chaotic" (*Liberty Times*, 22 Aug 2005). These headlines, with the use of different colors, while describing the popularity of Bae, convey the craziness and childishness of these Korean drama fans. Both the headline and pictures make these fans and their behavior into a spectacle for the consumption and entertainment of the general public. However, with

the spectacularization of these images as out of control, these female Korean drama fans are also constructed as the Other of bourgeois rationality—a bunch of brainless bodies driven by desires, fantasies and illusions. (Yang 2008: 209–210)

A similar reception was recorded in Japan:

> A critical moment in the *Winter Sonata* phenomenon came on 3 April 2004. On that day Bae Yong Jun arrived at Tokyo International Airport. Five thousand fans, mostly middle age women, gathered to welcome him. This was exceptional, considering that five hundred fans came to the airport when footballer David Beckham arrived in Japan. This particular news shocked the Japanese people and the *Winter Sonata* and Yon-sama phenomenon drew great attention as a new boom. (Mōri 2008: 130)
>
> *Winter Sonata* is important because it made middle-aged women, roughly between 30 and 70 years old, visible as its audience . . . The Yon-sama phenomenon and its relation to middle-aged women has been reported in the mainstream media seriously, as well as contemptuously, almost everyday. For instance, on 29 August 2004, some TV chat shows reported pejoratively that fans organized birthday parties in different Korean BBQ restaurants in Tokyo to celebrate Yon-sama's birthday. This is one of the examples that show how the media deal with *Winter Sonata* and the Yon-sama phenomenon, focusing on fans that were sometimes described merely as a stupid audience. On the other hand, there are other media which look at middle-aged women in a more sympathetic way. A weekly journal AERA analysed more seriously what was happening to middle-aged women through detailed research and concluded that *Winter Sonata* provided a new sensation to women who were not happy in Japanese patriarchal society. In any case, the drama made middle-aged women a central topic in popular television culture for the first time. (Mōri 2008: 131)

It should be noted that in both instances the mass media coverage is extremely anti-women in its rhetoric; this is an issue that will be taken up in the next chapter.

Finally, there is the concert, which is intentionally organized and thus is not a spontaneous occasion and is likely to be attended by fans. Nevertheless, the element of an occasioned community of audience is not absent. Each individual concert attendee is there because of his/her own self-defined "relationship" with the performer, and is driven by his/her own private desires and adorations. However, their co-presence at the concert and the collective outpouring of affection for the same performer generates a sense of unity that is simply but fully expressed by one fan thus: "I was sitting on the mezzanine, watching this tiny person perform on stage. But I was elated. My goodness, so many people were singing the same song with me" (quoted in Tsai, 2008: 223). Here, the individual audience member's awareness of being part of a much larger, if anonymous, community is driven home.

## Fan Clubs of East Asian Pop Culture

An avid consumer of a particular genre of objects will often seek ways to intensify the pleasure of consumption through active engagement with others who are similarly disposed. This applies to pop culture consumption. The most conventional means to facilitate active engagement with other avid consumers is to join a "fan club." A fan club organizes the avid consumers who share an affection for a particular performance artist, drama or genre of pop culture into a "community." It can be organized as a "local" or an "international" club; furthermore, fan clubs from different locations can be linked up transnationally through different channels of exchange and communication; international and transnational fan clubs can be organized with greater ease nowadays through the Internet. One should not be misled by the term "fan club" into believing that the clubs are always organized by fans for fans, as they are often established by the artist and his/her production company as a means of sustaining fans' interest in order to extend the longevity of the artist's popularity, which is essentially an ephemeral phenomenon.

## Fan Communities across National Spaces

The transnational flows of East Asian Pop Culture across the region obviously provide the empirical conditions for the possibility for organizing audience communities that cut across national and cultural boundaries and spaces. Interestingly, these transnational audience communities often materialize and are brought into relief when an artist becomes entangled with larger political issues. This is nicely illustrated by two instances in the recent history of East Asian Pop Culture, researched by Tsai (2008).

The first case is Chang Hui-mei (Ah Mei), an aboriginal Taiwanese singer, who was hugely popular in Pop Culture China (Moskowitz 2010: 81–83). In 2000, she sang the national anthem of the Republic of China (Taiwan) at the inauguration of the elected president, Chen Shui-bian, leader of the Democratic Progressive Party which espouses independence for Taiwan from China. She was immediately made a site for the enactment of "Taiwan Straits" politics. The Chinese government immediately forced sponsors within the country to cancel her endorsement contracts, removed and suppressed all her images from public places and imposed a ban on her performances. The government clearly realized the impact of denying any Chinese language(s) artist access to its massive consumer power.[2]

According to Tsai, Chang's fans in Beijing took "a more pro-active stance toward building networks, which included the setup of a large fan organization in

China. In the absence of a promotional industry, the fans took on the promotional tasks themselves, staging sales events for Chang outside the biggest record shops in town and approaching shoppers with self made gifts" (2008: 228). Tsai also provided an illustrative instance of the connections, online, between Chang's fans in the China and Taiwan:

> Since 1999, S1's [a fan] in-depth writing and multi-media presentations of Chang's performances have made her website an inviting forum of exchange. This is also how her interactions with several veteran Chinese fans began. They exchanged and commented reflectively on each other's writing about Chang's music. S1 surprisingly felt at ease in communicating with a group of young people who were interested in discussing Chang's music and still possessed a knowledge of classical Chinese literature. Once a staff member in a large fan organization in Taiwan, S1 now keeps a distance from other fan groups mainly because of the failure to evolve into a more open-minded community. Besides, she is deeply affected by the Chinese fans' raw passion and urgency to introduce Chang's music to a broader audience. (2008: 231)

It was more than two years before Chang Hui-mei, endearingly known to her fans as Ah Mei, was able to perform in Shanghai again. However, her much anticipated concert in June 2004 in Hangzhou, near Shanghai, was canceled because of safety concerns. "Outside the venue, a group of self-identified 'patriots' held a banner that read 'Pro-Taiwan Independence Green People [the symbolic color of supporters of Taiwan independence] Not Welcome'" (2008: 220–221). She managed to hold a successful concert in Beijing in the following month.

The second instance concerns Korean television drama star, Song Seung-heon (宋承宪). In 2004, it was found that he had "manipulated medical records to dodge conscription" (Tsai 2008: 221). Song immediately owned up to the misdeed, apologized to his fans and the nation and was willing to abide by government order. He was then filming, in Australia, the music video for the much anticipated television drama *Sad Love Story* (*Seulpeun Yeonga* 悲伤恋歌 2005). He immediately returned to Korea once the video was completed and right away began his two-year military service. However, between the breaking of the news and his induction, there was a concerted letter writing campaign, in part instigated by Song's production company, among Song's fans in Korea, Hong Kong, Taiwan and China to the Korean government to permit Song to complete the much anticipated drama before his service.

Obviously, the immediate concern of the East Asian transnational fans was to drum up support for Song. However, knowing the futility of challenging the conscription and not wanting to antagonize the military authority or Korean masculinity, the fans took a non-confrontational stance. As one fan noted, "respecting the decisions of the Korean government was also a measure to protect Song from sinking into deeper water;" thus, the "'United Support Letter' issue by five fan organizations from Taiwan, China and Hong Kong prior to Song's return to Korea adopted a non-confrontational and non-imploring tone to influence the resolution of the crisis" (Tsai 2008: 236). According to Tsai (2008), the letter begins by empathizing with Song's suffering from the overwhelming publicity. It then describes how encounters with Song's work in the Korean Wave had led the overseas fans to new experiences like travelling and taking an interest in Korean culture. Praising his professional ethics and giving nature, the letter states the fans' unwavering stance behind his courage to tell the truth and closes with a warm and firm stance to stand by him throughout the hardship (2008: 238).

Strategically, the letter did not make any demand of the Korean government; it did not even suggest any desired outcome. The request for postponing Song's conscription was reserved for a subsequent mass letter writing campaign, a request that had some public support in Korea, which weighed "the cost of Song's contribution to *hallyu* [Korean Wave] against the gain of his immediate draft" (Tsai 2008: 239). The campaign was to no avail and there was a "dramatic gathering of hundreds of women from Korea, Japan, Taiwan and Hong Kong to send Song off outside the Chunchon preparatory camp on the morning of 16 November 2004" (Tsai 2008: 237).[3]

In these two instances, fans of a specific artist were literally powerless against a state that had done their idol wrong. The strategies of protest were devised out of this position of powerlessness. The first was to ignore the state legal restrictions and risk potential criminalization by contravening the official ban. The second was to take the role of a supplicant to avoid incurring the wrath of the state which might be counterproductive to the purpose at hand and, in addition, to play up to the interests of the state directly, appealing to "Song's contribution" to the Korean Wave, something that the Korean government actively promotes as an export industry and form of cultural diplomacy. These instances give us glimpses into the larger issue of the unavoidable entanglement of pop culture and national politics in East Asia, a subject to be discussed in the next chapter.

## 2PM

Organized expressions of affection and support for wronged idols are not only directed at governments. Reflecting the radical increase in consumer power, the transnational organization of fans' protests has also been directed at producers of pop culture, and with far greater effect. A case in point is the organized protests by fans of the Korean boy-band 2PM[4] against their producer, JYP Entertainment, at multiple sites across East Asia.

2PM, a seven member boy-band, debuted in 2008. All members were in their twenties, five were Korean, one was Thai and the lead singer was the

American-Korean Park Jaebeom, fondly known as Jay Park to fans. The group was incubated and managed by JYP Entertainment (JYPE), a Korean talent company. Typically such companies recruit young talent early and invest in long periods of training in singing and dancing before presenting the talent to the public.[5] Given the substantial money invested, recruits are generally bonded to the company by very long contracts, in excess of ten years is not uncommon, with highly disadvantageous conditions for the artist, so much so that these contracts have come to be known as "slave contracts" in Korea.[6] Sometime in his first year in Korea as a trainee, Park, who was kept socially isolated by JYPE, posted on his personal Myspace account some angry and negative comments about his alienation in Korea including "I hate Korea." Someone hacked into his account, extracted the negative comments and posted them on the Internet site, BBS, in early September 2009. The comments were rapidly reproduced and spread across the Internet, creating a media event. The negative comments were read as "anti-Korea" and a national "betrayal." Park accepted responsibility for his teenage words and repeatedly asked for forgiveness but the attacks continued relentlessly. Four days after the outing of the comments, he "resigned" from the band and returned to America. The official statement from JYPE was that Park resigned of his own volition and the company had to honor his decision.

Korean fans immediately organized themselves into the "2PM Fan Union" and issued a statement that declared a total boycott of all JYPE products (including those of its subsidiary company SK Communications), all companies that advertised and sponsored JYPE events and also vowed not to read any Internet postings of advertisements and products that were endorsed by the remaining members of 2PM. A demonstration of more than two thousand fans was held outside the JYPE office.[7] Fans kept up an exchange of views, information and emotions about the event on the Internet; exchanges that contributed greatly to the sense of solidarity among the fans.

Soon, transnational fans in East and Southeast Asia—Taiwan, Vietnam, Thailand and Singapore—responded by joining the boycott of JYPE products and organizing their own protest activities in their respective locations; some were members of the International 2PM Fan Union, which putatively had members from seventy countries.[8] Like the Korean fans, many penned songs and filmed support messages on video for Park which they posted on the Internet; by early October it was reported that there were more than one thousand fan videos on YouTube. In Bangkok, Thailand, where JYPE was hoping to generate substantial profit from 2PM product sales because one of the band members was Thai, a flash mob of more than one hundred turned up and performed a very well coordinated group dance at the open space in Siam Square, the premier public space in the shopping district. In Singapore, a group of forty teenage fans, mostly female, held a demonstration called the "Jay-Walk" procession; the pun is intended in a city where jaywalking is a punishable but seldom enforced offence. They carried placards reading "We Will Wait" and calling for Park's return and marched down Orchard Road, also in the premier shopping district. For a city where public demonstrations are illegal without police permission, this was an extremely rare event for any Singaporean, let alone school-aged teenagers. Apparently they had applied for a permit to hold the demonstration but were told by the police that no permit was required as the demonstration was not "political" in nature.

JYPE and the six remaining members of the band decided to continue the band without Park, begging the fans to stop their boycott, but to no avail. Things came to a head in late February 2010 when JYPE terminated Park's contract with the company, with the consent of the six remaining members. According to the company, even after Park returned to Seattle, he was kept in the loop of all the band's activities and of plans for re-launching the band in Korea in February 2010. On December 22, 2009, Park apparently telephoned the company representative to confess to some repetitive misdeeds in his personal life. These deeds were so "serious" that the company, after discussing the matter with the rest of the band, decided that Park could no longer return. The company subsequently terminated its contract with Park, without demanding any financial compensation to which it might be entitled. Subsequently, many of Park's protesting supporters started posting online the trivial "private problems" of other band members that were only known to fans. Meanwhile, Park kept his silence and uploaded a video on YouTube in which he recorded an English language song in a washroom. The recording attracted a huge number of hits and he started direct communication with fans on the Internet.

The power of transnational fans can be gleaned from the fact that the company and the rest of the band held a conference in Seoul on March 7, 2010 to answer all questions that the angered fans might have. Up to one hundred Korean and overseas fans were invited. During the conference, the company and the rest of the band refused to disclose the nature of Park's misdemeanor under repetitive questioning from the fans, insisting that only Park himself could disclose the details. Judging from the transcript of the conference posted on the Internet, the fans were less than pacified.[9] The fans have since become indifferent to the issue and have largely stopped boycotting the remaining members of 2PM and JYPE; instead they want to focus their energy on supporting Park's endeavors to return, as promised.[10]

## The Internet Sub-Fans

Obviously, none of the activities discussed above that cross national and cultural boundaries could have been organized with equal speed and efficiency without new communication technologies and the Internet. In addition to the strategies used by adoring fans of specific artists, the Internet has also been used by a different category of fans who operate beneath the radar of the state and the profit of the producers. These online communities are known as "sub-fan" groups.[11] The basic activities of a sub-fan are recounted by Hu with reference to the Japanese television drama, *Pride* (*Puraido* 2004):

> In January 2004, a Hong Kong fan, R, who is a skilled Japanese speaker, did the Chinese subtitling for *Pride*—a few days after the original broadcast in Japan... She thanks T and A for their supplies of the raw material ... and when she made a mistake in the subtitling, she took care to insert a correction by thanking another fan for pointing out the mistake—The version of R's Chinese subtitling of *Pride* was extremely popular in the Hong Kong newsgroup through its online circulation by means of BitTorrent ... [T]he marketing of another version of *Pride* produced by a Taiwanese-base leading pirated-Japanese-VCD company seems to be threatened, because R's version has already been so widely circulated among Chinese fans through the Internet... The inner passions for drama, fan friendship and performance/self-expression are displayed in the context of this Chinese translation/subtitling; being "acknowledged by a community of the like-minded is a characteristically romantic structure of feeling."[12] (Hu 2005: 177–178)

As translating and subtitling work in East Asian television drama is almost always from Japanese and Korean into the written Chinese script, the largest number of sub-fan groups is to be found in the Huaren population, especially in China. The overwhelming majority of the members of these groups is hewn from China, with some from Hong Kong and Taiwan and a few individuals from elsewhere in the global Huaren population. In a survey of seventy-two sub-fan groups, Hu (2009: 210–212) listed twenty-seven groups that specialize in animation subtitling, six in Japanese drama, eight in Korean drama and seven groups, run by fans of particular artists, in Korean and Japanese variety shows; the remaining specialize in subtitling English language, including American, and Thai language films and drama. The emergence of these groups in China is partly because of the absence of any legal access to the television programs. For example, according to Laikwan Pang writing at the end of the first decade of the twenty-first century, Japanese anime producers have not been very interested in the China market, as evidenced by the absence of official distributors in China, and "no feature-length anime films have been shown on official Chinese screens," consequently, "if an anime online or on disc has Chinese subtitles, it is almost certainly a bootleg" (2009: 122). This may also explain why the largest number of sub-fan groups is to be found in animation subtitling.

Obviously, sub-fan groups are highly organized and disciplined in discharging their work/responsibilities. Broadly, Hu (2009: 185, my translation) has outlined the organization of subtitling work by a sub-fan group for Japanese dramas thus:

first, as soon as a new drama is broadcast, someone is responsible for immediately locating its source, downloading it and sending it to a group that is responsible for constructing subtitles. Each forty-five minute episode will take approximately three to four hours to translate. For speed, three or four people will collaborate on each episode, each being responsible for eleven to fifteen minutes of the video file. After that, corrections to the translations are made by language professionals. Meanwhile, all the advertisements are removed from the file. The corrected subtitles are then pasted onto the screen, taking care to match the sound track. The finished product is finally uploaded. The ideal schedule is to take no more than eight hours from the time of original broadcast to complete and upload the subtitled episode. Speed is not only of the essence because the subtitled episode would have to be posted before the subsequent episode is broadcast; speed is also a matter of pride and self-satisfaction for individuals in the group which operates on high speed broadband Internet systems. Overwhelmingly, members of a sub-fan group are university students in their twenties, or those who have just recently graduated. Given the heavy commitment of time and effort, continuing participation becomes uncertain once an individual starts working. Indeed, dropouts are frequent; the average active participation period for an individual is approximately three years. Consequently recruitment for members/workers for every function in the production chain is a constant endeavor. New recruits have to be tested for language proficiency, trained and must be available to immediately replace anyone who drops out due to changing circumstances.

The case of sub-fan communities is clearly a case in which the audience are concurrently consumers and producers of culture. The drive to organize and participate in the different steps and functions of a coordinated division of labor—recruiting, downloading, distributing the translation work to be done, uploading and reposting—may not be entirely motivated by passion for the drama but also by a sense of achievement and self-worth. Their individual and collective labor, voluntary and without pecuniary reward, is purely for the benefit of anyone in the cyber-virtual world with the know-how to download the uploaded programs, people who are therefore largely unknown to the workers themselves. The products of their labor lie beyond the clutches of the profit-oriented original producers and their distributors in the regime of intellectual property rights. The same products also often fly under the radar of the censorship constraints of the nation-state. Unlike the self-serving profit motive of pirating enterprises, the sub-fan community labor is, above all else, a "labor of love," an "affective" labor.

## Affective Labor

In the above analysis of audience communities, the focus is on audience activities that are external to the media text but also beyond the conventional activities of fan clubs. A noted and significant difference between East Asian Pop Culture fans and those in the West is their respective attitude towards their objects of adoration. Chin (2010: 212–213) summarizes the difference in these terms: Western fans "exhaustively discuss the texts and the meanings they might derive from the characters and the texts" while East Asian fans seek "intimacy," i.e., personalized relations with the actors. The idea of "intimacy," drawn from Yano's (2004) analysis of Japanese fans of *enka* music, is also applicable to fans of contemporary pop culture stars. This is encapsulated in the fans referring to the adored artist as their "idol" (*ouxiang* 偶像), a term used throughout the region. "Intimacy" includes more conventional aspects such as the consumption of material objects to support the artist, the gathering of little-known knowledge of the artist's personal life and seeking meetings with the artist in different settings. One aspect of this "intimacy" that warrants elaboration is what Yano calls "surrogacy;" that is, a fan sees him-or herself as a bodily "substitute," a surrogate, for the artist (2004: 46). At the most mundane level, this is expressed by singing the idol's songs during karaoke sessions or mimicking the idol's fashion sense and behavior after closely studying the idol.

At the more abstract level, this surrogacy appears to translate into a "moral" obligation to behave in a way that is not potentially damaging to the reputation of the idol, as a fan's behavior is seen as "equivalent" to that of one's idol. Kim Hyun Mee argues that Korean fans "try to maintain 'grace' as fans that are worthy of the star's status by abstaining from talking back or cursing when attacked by rival fan clubs, upholding order and calm, and cleaning up after events. It is through such processes that they believe they can construct true fandom" (2004: 44). Similar decorum has been found among Singaporean fans of Mandarin pop music (Soh 1994). In the case of Song Seung-heon, discussed above, the supplicant stance taken by his fans so as not to antagonize the Korean state is, of course, also part of a strategic consideration of not wanting to jeopardize the possibility of the success in their appeal for the postponement of Song's military service. Finally, there is also the potential cost to the idol in this fan-idol relationship. Jung (2011) found that middle-aged Japanese fans of Bae Yong-joon identified so strongly with their construction of him as a "gentle," "pure" and "polite" figure, drawn largely from their first exposure to him in the television drama *Winter Sonata*, that they "straight-jacketed" him and became unable to accept him in the role of the rogue which he played in *Untold Scandal*, which was a box office success in Korea but did poorly in Japan (Jung 2011: 44–63). The fans were also unable to accept, without a large amount of rationalization, the new muscular body image that he developed in his more recent metamorphosis (Jung 2011: 68–71).

Intimacy is a mode of expression of the "affective" labor of fans, as conceptualized in the seminal work of Grossberg (1992) on fandom. The above cases of transnational audience communities, which form around both particular stars as objects of adoration and specific pop cultural genres in the case of Japanese television dramas, provide an opportunity to examine the consequences of the affective labor on material capital. In the cases of Chang and Song, the affective labor that transnational fan communities undertook to promote and protect their idols are productive labor inputs in promoting the products of their idols and material capital. The affective labor of the fans thus translates directly into a form of "immaterial labor"—"labor that produces the informational and cultural content of the commodity" (Lazzarato 1996: 133)—which is generative of material capital and financial gains for the production company.[13] Chang's China fans directly engaged in the sale of her albums, risking running foul of the law. Song's production company was behind the various phases of the fans' protest campaign, as the success of the campaign would have enabled it to finish the planned drama.

Significantly, technologically savvy transnational fans are fully aware of this transformation of their affection into capitalist profits. Consequently, the transnational fans of 2PM included in their boycott not only products of JYPE and its sponsors but also "clicking" on any of the items on the Internet that had to do with 2PM-without-Park. Boycotting fans of Park were not to search, read, circulate, broadcast or respond in any way to any information and content on 2PM-without-Park because such activities on the Internet not only help to advertise the remaining group but could also be harvested by the company as consumer information to form a database for designing future products that target the fans as consumers. The Internet boycott disrupted an important part of the overall marketing strategy that had been enabled by developments in information technologies and were available to JYPE.

As sub-fan communities have short-circuited the profit returns of producers, they may be said to have also successfully resisted the appropriation and transformation of their affective labor into profit by production companies. Unfortunately, the uploaded and freely distributed subtitled programs produced by sub-fan groups are not always the end of the line for the program. Life continues in two possible directions. First, profit-driven pirates have no qualms about downloading, copying and selling the sub-fan subtitled product in the market. Consequently, production companies are increasingly refusing to distinguish sub-fan activities from piracy for profit. They have in recent years been more vigilant in policing free-downloading and file-sharing activities, equating them with criminal piracy and prosecuting such practitioners in court to protect their copyright. Second, as sub-fan affective labor helps to disseminate and thus popularize a particular program or genre of pop culture, generating further consumption of the products, their affective labor is part of the "pull" activities that have popularized Japanese animation not only in China but also in the United States, the biggest market for Japanese animation (Leonard 2005).

## Conclusion

With the national and cultural boundary-crossing of East Asian Pop Culture becoming part of the regular diet of regional media consumers, national and transnational communities of audience/consumers have emerged, ranging from different types of "occasioned" communities to highly organized transnational fan communities that engage with the national politics of different countries as necessary. Of particular interest are the sub-fan organizations that operate beneath the radar of government censorship and profit concerns of the producers of pop culture. Significantly, while all these beyond-the-text activities of communities of consumers are motivated by their affective labor and are engendered by their love of the pop culture, stars and genres, they still unavoidably get appropriated and transformed by the producers into profit, even the sub-fan organizations cannot ultimately escape this fate.

# 7

# Pop Culture as Soft Power

The emergence of a loosely integrated East Asian Pop Culture economy since the beginning of the 1990s has, as might be expected, led governments in the region to think about using their pop culture exports as resources to positively influence the opinions and attitudes of the transnational audiences in the export destinations. In an age when the use of military power among responsible states as members of the international community is progressively receding, this desire to seek influence through "culture" is conceptualized as an exercise in "cultural diplomacy" or "soft power." As the flows of pop culture products have hitherto been very unequal, with Japanese and Korean pop culture flowing into Huaren communities across the region and very little reverse flow, unsurprisingly, it is the two major exporting countries that have been the first to think out loud and explicitly formulate soft power strategies to influence the regional Huaren audience. This initiated a discourse on regional soft power competition, particularly between Japan, Korea and China. The aim of this chapter is not to critique so as to further develop a better definition of the concept of soft power. It has a more modest and substantive concern, which is to organize the knowledge drawn from empirical research on the transnational reception of East Asian Pop Culture to assess the "efficacy" of pop culture as a resource and an instrument of soft power that can be wielded by the regional powers to pursue their desired goal of positive influence.

Power, in Weberian terms, is the ability to get others to do things that they may not be willing to do. The idea of soft power was developed by American political scientist Joseph Nye who argues "[a] country may obtain the outcomes it wants in world politics because other countries—admiring its values, emulating its example, aspiring to its level of prosperity and openness—want to follow it;" thus, "[s]oft power rests on the ability to shape the preferences of others" (Nye 2004: 5). He further suggests that one of the resources for the exercise of soft power is "culture"—"[c]ulture is the set of values and practices that create meaning for society ... It is common to distinguish between high culture such as literature, art, and education, which appeals to elites, and popular culture, which focuses on mass entertainment" (Nye 2004: 11). In contrast to hard power, as seen in the use of the military and economic forces, which extracts compliance through coercion and direct sanctions, soft power supposedly achieves its goals of influencing others through different modes of persuading the other that your views on the situation at hand are attractive views and they should or do indeed desire the same thing as you. Soft power supposedly succeeds by "attraction"—making one's culture attractive to the target audience (Nye 2004: 6).

In the US case, according to Nye, soft power has been developed through culture, ideology or political values, and foreign policy. In political ideology, the US has consistently promoted the universalization of liberalism, championing individual freedom and rights in contrast to the constraints of social institutions. Freedoms are immediately appealing to any individual, while the fact that social constraints and a sense of responsibility for others are necessary for social stability requires some degree of abstract reflection. If the successes of the US in foreign policy are increasingly difficult to find, the promotion of liberalism can be said to have been immensely successful since the end of the Second World War. By the end of the twentieth century, it has become conventional and commonsensical to think of liberal democracy—a conjugation of two separate political ideas—as the most developed stage of a modern polity, such that it is difficult for most people to imagine what a non-liberal democracy would look like.

In culture, American capitalists were among the earliest to invest in mass entertainment and consumer industries, realizing that the best way to absorb both the products of industrial mass production and the increased leisure hours of industrial workers was to correspondingly increase the consumption capacity of the working class. Furthermore, "increased consumer need would lash workers ever more firmly to their jobs" (Cross 1993: 39). Given this first mover advantage, the US is now the world's number one exporter of mass entertainment pop culture—music, films, television programs and formats—and the number one exporter of mass consumerism; the US holds the largest number of global brands, although actual production is outsourced to developing countries with low labor costs. The success of American pop culture and consumerism is reflected, according to Nye, "in general polls [which] show that our popular culture has made the US seem to others 'exciting, exotic, rich, powerful, trend-setting—the cutting edge of modernity and innovation,' such that 'people want to partake in of the good life American-style'" (2004: 12). However, there are no guarantees that expending soft power resources will produce the desired influence on the target population; the success or failure of soft power is highly contextual and "attraction and rejection of American culture among different groups may cancel each other out" (Nye 2004: 13).

## Evidence of Popularity and Influence

To achieve soft power, the exported pop culture must be able to shift its audience's perceptions, preferences, interpretative frameworks and emotions, i.e., a set of cognitive processes, towards a generally positive disposition and attraction to the exporting country, which is the applicant of soft power. Procedurally, the nation exporting the pop culture may have extensive control over the level of resources expended; for example, financial and infrastructural support for the cultural producers at home and efforts to promote the pop culture products in export destinations. Its control over the channels via which the resources are funneled in the export destinations are checked at two points: first, distribution and circulation of pop culture is dependent on local agents, distribution networks and local consumer practices and second, export volumes and contents are subjected to local government regulations, such as import quotas and censorship regimes, in the export destinations. Finally, the exporting country has no control at all over how its pop culture will be received and, therefore, in what ways the target audience could be influenced. This crucially means that it has no control over the cognitive processes of the transnational audience. Given this lack of control over influence, the effectiveness of pop culture as soft power can only be verified and substantiated by empirical evidence of audience behavior subsequent to reception; there should be evidence of changes in attitude in the audience towards the exporting nation. In the case of East Asian Pop Culture, as the previous chapters have demonstrated, there is indeed evidence that Japanese and Korean pop culture have influenced and engendered attitudinal changes among the transnational audience in different constituent locations.

Undoubtedly Japanese television "trendy" or "idol" dramas were regionally popular throughout the 1990s. These were displaced and replaced by Korean television dramas by the end of the decade. Japanese and Korean pop music have more limited penetration—they fill "a niche in the market" (Pease 2009: 155; see also Otmazgin 2008)—into the regional Huaren market, which is still dominated by Chinese language music, particularly Cantonese pop and, increasingly, Mandarin pop. Illustrative of the regional popularity of Korean drama are the ratings of the concluding part of the earlier mentioned *Jewel in the Palace*, in Hong Kong. Aired on May 1, 2005, this last episode garnered forty-seven percent of the total television audience that evening, the highest recorded in Hong Kong television history. *Jewel* was also dubbed in Mandarin by a Taiwan station and was subsequently broadcast in Singapore and China to equally enthusiastic receptions (Leung 2008). In Japan, it was the urban tragic-romance drama *Winter Sonata* which had the highest audience rating. Screened in 2003, it was the first mega-success for a contemporary Korean drama that was brought to the television screen in Japan.

Beyond registering mass popularity, there is evidence that Japanese and Korean pop culture exports have in fact shifted transnational audience sentiments in favor of the two countries. As pop culture genres have different audience demographics, influences vary across age groups. For example, the cognitive and ideological effects of Japanese and Korean pop music on their respective young audiences in Taiwan and China are encapsulated in the media labels *harizu* (哈日族) and *hahanzu* (哈韩族)—a tribe that suffers from Japan/Korea mania/fever or a tribe that identifies with Japanese/Korean culture (Ko 2004: 108; Lee M.T. 2004: 133; Pease 2009: 158); *ha* (哈) is a Taiwanese colloquial term for "yearning," "desire," "admiration" and "being interested" (Lee 2009: 121). As shown by Pease (2009), young audiences for Korean pop music in China evaluate Korean pop music positively and are simultaneously critical of Chinese pop music and cultural practices in China:

> Their [boy band High Five of Teenagers, H.O.T.] behaviour and songs are really a model for youth. Korean singers are fashionable and have vigour, and don't just rely on packaging (in fact, I think Koreans on the whole are very plain). Their dance is the highest level in Asia. We all see that Japanese music is on the wane, while Korean is flourishing. The Chinese mainland is so inferior there is no possibility; the HK/Taiwan singers obviously sing covers for their main songs; their decline is obvious.
>
> The reason China's music is less exciting is connected to the size of its population (like most of its problems). China overemphasizes totality: they want the whole, not parts. Clearly in pop music, if you want to write a song that everyone likes, of whatever status or age, there is going to be less creative power, it's not so rich. (Two fans quoted by Pease 2009: 159)

The influence of Korean drama is best illustrated by the middle-aged female Japanese audience. Japanese cultural studies scholar, Yoshitaka Mōri's observation about the changes in his mother is worth quoting extensively here:

> During the 2004 New Year's holidays, I watched the whole series of *Winter Sonata* with her. The drama was, in fact, more interesting than I had expected. However, what interested me more was the way in which she talked about the drama and the hero, Bae Yong Joon (nick-named Yon-sama, [Prince Yon] in Japan), as if she were a girl. I found that she exchanged information about the drama through the internet or over tea meetings with her friends. She became interested in Korean culture and even travelled to Korea. I started to wonder why *Winter Sonata* fascinated her so much, why Bae Yong Joon could change her idea on Korea, and what will happen to her during and after the Korean Wave? (2008: 127–128)

As mentioned in the last chapter, when Bae arrived in Tokyo on a promotional tour, more than five thousand middle-aged housewife fans turned up at the airport to welcome him. This event was transformed into a media phenomenon. However, instead of being reduced in media reports to a "mindless" crowd; they insisted, "we believe that it is 'we' who manipulate the media" through their performances as fans (Mōri 2008: 137). Many began to learn the Korean language and study Japanese-Korean colonial history. Many expressed a desire to be "cultural bridges" to ameliorate the underlying animosity between the two nations, a legacy of the colonization of Korea by Japan for almost fifty years, and began by changing their attitude by giving greater and friendlier attention to the long discriminated against Korean diasporas in their midst (Iwabuchi 2008). These are significant ideological and behavioral shifts because for many of these Japanese women, until the joint hosting of the World Cup in 2002, which brought modern urban Korea onto Japanese media screens, Korea was just an underdeveloped, ex-Japanese colony and primarily a sex tour destination for Japanese men.

Beyond the specific fan groups and their positive attitudes towards exporting nations, there is also anecdotal evidence that Koreans have benefited in a more diffuse way. A Korean woman living in Singapore said, "In the past, taxi drivers would ask me whether I was from Japan. These days they and other local people would greet me in 'An-nyong haseyo,' adding that Korean women are the most beautiful stock in Asia, or asking whether I can provide them with Bae Yong Jun's photo" (cited in Shim 2007: 75). Such diffused improvement in attitudes toward the presence of overseas Koreans in other parts of East Asia, the positive attitudes of the young mainland Chinese audience for Korean pop music, the radical transformation of attitude seen in the middle-aged Japanese women watching Korean television dramas and similar shifts among Taiwanese audiences of Japanese pop culture, provide the empirical ground for the idea that pop culture products can act as a channel for the soft power of the exporting nations.

## The Industry's Promotion of Japanese and Korean Content and the Rhetoric of Soft Power

Although Japanese pop culture was the first wave to hit the region, Japan did not appear to try to capitalize on this to expand its soft power until the late 2000s. Ironically, *manga* producers and some academics have been well aware of this potential for some time. Tezuka, arguably the "founder" of postwar *manga* and creator of "the first serialized television animation in Japan in 1963" (Shiraishi 1996: 237) wrote in 1983:

> [Animation has become] Japan's supreme goodwill ambassador, not just in the West but in the Middle East and Africa, in South America,

> in Southeast Asia, even in China. The entry port is almost always TV. In France, the children love watching *Goldorak*. *Doraemon* is huge hit in Southeast Asia and Hong Kong. Chinese youngsters all sing the theme to *Astro Boy*.[1] (Quoted in Leonard 2005: 288)

Drawing on the popularity of *Doraemon* as indicative of its cultural resonance and attractiveness throughout Asia, Shiraishi has argued that despite American domination in "image-based culture products," "Asian regionalism has its own undeniable and important contemporary popular culture" (1996: 235). Furthermore, *Doraemon*'s popularity in Asia speaks directly to Nye's mistaken view that "Japan is a 'one-dimensional' economic power marked by a cultural insularity that robs it of relevance for other societies" (quoted in Shiraishi 1996: 234). A little more than ten years after Nye's negative assessment, Japan's soft power resources were all too obvious to American journalist Douglas McGray. He noted "Japan's growing cultural presence [regionally and internationally] has created a mighty engine of national cool," "[n]ational cool is kind of 'soft power'" and that "while Japan sits on that formidable reserve of soft power, it has few means to tap it" (2002: 7). Referring directly to the presence of Japanese pop culture in East Asia, Otmazgin comes to a similar conclusion: "there is no conversion of [soft power] resources to diplomatic power, there is no creation of any substantial 'spheres of influence' for Japan" (2008: 75).

The Japanese government's failure to mobilize soft power resources to exercise more cultural influence globally was due to the absence of supporting public policies. Apart from requiring the publicly funded—through user licensing fees—NHK (Nippon Hōsō Kyōkai, Japan Broadcasting Corporation) to serve the nation and broadcast to Japanese living overseas, and incidentally, to foreigners, the government did not get involved with the media industry in general, let alone pop culture which it regarded as mere entertainment. Arguably, the reluctance of Japanese producers to aggressively export their products into the region may be due to lingering memories of the Japanese wartime atrocities in Asia, which acted as a check on Japan's regional political ambitions. Furthermore, Japanese belief that its culture is unique and its language impossible for others to master would imply a belief that its pop culture is unlikely to be accessible abroad.

The government's attitude was matched by the apparent disinterest Japanese pop culture producers had in overseas markets, particularly during the heyday of the bubble economy when culture producers appeared to be content with the high-spending domestic market. The producers' attitude appeared to be a mixture of all three of Leonard's strategies of ignorance: "uninformed ignorance" where producers "ha[ve] no idea what is going on," "strategic ignorance" whereby producers do "not wish to authorize the use" of their products because to do so might jeopardize future negotiations, and "dismissive ignorance" where the producers choose to "ignore the use ... because responding to [it] would only waste company time" (2005: 287–288). Thus, as we have observed, the circulation and popularization of Japanese television dramas in the early 1990s in East Asia was a result of Taiwanese and Hong Kong promoters, first through illegal means and subsequently through proper licensing. This is a combination of uninformed and strategic ignorance. Meanwhile the popularity of Japanese anime and *manga* in mainland China is unmistakable, yet until today Japanese animation still does not have official distributors there (Pang 2009), this is clearly a case of dismissive ignorance.

Against this background, McGray's (2002) vague concept of "Japan's Gross National Cool" provided just the right catchword for a 180-degree change in the Japanese government's cultural policies, from non-intervention to active engagement with recreation and entertainment industries, wrapped within the language of "soft power" and national interest. Leheny provides a string of examples: "the Ministry of Foreign Affairs has also begun to incorporate soft power into its lingo, though it is careful about suggesting that Japan is trying to exercise power over its neighbors;" the "Japan Foundation refers to 'Gross National Cool' and suggests that Japan's cultivation of its cultural resources can improve its 'national image' and thereby strengthen its global hand," this rhetoric supplanted the earlier one of cultural exchange for "mutual understanding;" "economic policymakers have seized on soft power as a crucial wedge for funding and supporting their efforts to promote Japan's 'content industries,' supplanting policy interest in communication infrastructure;" "METI [Ministry of Economics, Trade and Industry] aims at ensuring that Japanese content creators and providers—anime, J-Pop, film studios, game developers, toy producers, and virtually any other entertainment industry capable of catching global attention—remain competitive over the long term." The aggregate effect is a "broad governmental acceptance of the Gross National Cool core: Japan has become hip and fashionable specifically because it has changed into something different" (2006: 226–228). Concretely, the government passed several laws and plans in the early 2000s to increase financial and other administrative support for the media industry: The Fundamental Law for the Promotion of Culture and the Arts in 2001; the Plan for Promoting Japanese Film and Image Media, and the First Basic Policy for the Promotion of Culture and the Arts in 2002; the Content Promotion Law in 2004 and the Second Basic Policy in 2007.[2]

As listed on the official website, the mission of the Creative Industries Promotion Office, under the Ministry of Economics, Trade and Industry, sums up the plans and strategies of the Japanese government at the end of the first decade of the twenty-first century:

> 1. The government's "New Growth Strategy" and "Industrial Structure Vision 2010" expect that Japan's cultural industries, such as design, animation, fashion and movies will become a strategic sector that drives the nation's future economic growth.

2. Under the single, long-term concept of "Cool Japan," the Creative Industries Promotion Office will promote these cultural industries in cooperation with the private sector by facilitating their overseas expansion and human resource development.

3. More specifically, as a section within METI dedicated to measures to promote cultural industries, the Creative Industries Promotion Office will work with related ministries and Japanese/foreign private organizations to plan and implement inter-ministerial measures, such as helping these industries cultivate overseas markets, disseminating relevant information in Japan and abroad by hosting domestic and international events, and developing creative human resources through collaboration with universities and human resource matching programs.[3]

Beyond this promotion of the image-media industries economically, the promotion of Japanese pop culture, particularly *manga* and anime, globally became a personal mission of Taro Aso when he was the Minister of Foreign Affairs, before becoming the Prime Minister in 2008. His (2006) explicit justification of why pop culture is an effective instrument of soft power to be deployed in international diplomacy is perhaps the most coherent statement from a senior politician from East Asia and is worth quoting extensively. For him, a *manga* enthusiast, "cultural diplomacy that fails to take advantage of pop culture is not really worthy of being called 'cultural diplomacy.'" The reason is the world is now in "an era in which diplomacy at the national level is affected dramatically by the climate of opinion arising from the average person. And that is exactly why we want pop culture, which is so effective in penetrating throughout the general public, to be our ally in diplomacy." The beginning of the twenty-first century is "a point where culture made in Japan—whether anime and manga or sumo and Japanese food culture—is equally able to nourish the people of the world, particularly the younger generation. We [the Japanese Ministry of Foreign Affairs and Japanese culture industry practitioners] would be remiss not to utilize these to the fullest." Strategically, in addition to the expected call for a closer working relationship between the government and the cultural industry sector, he announced the inauguration of an annual International Manga Award for non-Japanese *manga* artists. Finally, in 2009, just before he was voted out of the prime minister's office, Aso announced in the annual government budget plans for heavy investment in Japan's soft power industries, with the aim of producing 500,000 jobs within a twelve-year period. This plan did not survive his departure.

Indeed, the popularity of and push for Japanese pop culture export into the region, as Iwabuchi points out, plays into the hands of Japanese nationalists, who "easily translate this spread of Japanese popular culture to other parts of Asia into the 'Asia-yearning-for-Japan' idea, which confirms [for the nationalists] the shift of power from the United States to Japan that took place in the 1990s," implying a "newly generated Japan's claim for its cultural superiority through asserting commonality with other Asian nations" (2002b: 66). He further points out that this nationalist attitude is a reformulation and extension of a historically deeper "ambivalence of the Japanese conception of 'Asia,' a cultural geography that offers Japan at once a shared identity with other parts of Asia and is also the source of Japanese feelings of superiority" (Iwabuchi 2002b: 66); a sense of superiority that underwrote Japan's attempt to colonize the rest of Asia during the Second World War into an Asian "co-prosperity sphere" under Japanese imperial leadership.[4] This often thinly veiled sense of superiority quickly ran up against antagonistic regional political sentiments, as demonstrated by the reception that greeted Aso's initiative. The International Manga Award, won by mainland Chinese artists in the first two years, was criticized by Chinese media as Japanese nationalist hubris; they questioned the "right" of the Japanese to judge, singularly, who is the world's best *manga* artist.

In contrast to the non-interventionist stance of the Japanese government before the 2000s, the Korean government has taken an active role in the development of the media industry since the end of the 1980s. According to Shim (2010), immediately after the demise of military-authoritarian regime of Chun Doo Hwan (全斗焕) in 1987, the television industry was liberalized. State-ownership of Munhwa Broadcasting Corporation (MBC) was transferred to an independent Foundation for Broadcast Culture to become a fully commercial media company that derives its revenue totally from advertising, without government subsidy or intervention. In 1991, the private broadcasting network Seoul Broadcasting System (SBS) was established. To develop an audience base, the new station launched a "'television drama offensive' with drama as its core programming" (Shim 2010: 123), as drama is the most popular genre for the domestic Korean audience. The other two stations, Korean Broadcasting System (KBS) and MBC, stepped up to the competition. The result was a "drama war." In the same year, the government imposed a compulsory outsourcing scheme on the television stations, requiring each to purchase a fixed quota of dramas from independent producers. This led to a proliferation of independent production houses of varying size and scale, competing to sell their products to the three networks. In 2008, the quota for outsourced dramas reached forty percent for KBS and thirty-five percent each for MBC and SBS (Shim 2010: 128). Competition led to an increase in quantity, quality and responsiveness to audience demands. The keenness of the competition can be surmised from the fact that the three networks air as many as thirty dramas per week. These dramas constitute the stock that is selectively exported to the rest of East Asia.

At the same time, with the forced opening of its domestic market to direct Hollywood distribution in 1988, the market share of domestic films sank from just below fifty percent to twenty percent in 1994, with Hollywood making corresponding gains (Shim 2006: 31). Television was similarly facing external challenges with the establishment of cable services and "the spill over of satellite broadcasting, such as NHK Satellite and Star TV" (Shim 2006: 31). Facing this, the government established the "Cultural Industry Bureau within the Ministry of Culture and Sports in 1994 and instituted the Motion Picture Promotion Law in 1995 in order to lure corporate and investment capital into the local film industry" (Shim 2006: 32). This strategy fumbled almost as soon as it started because the 1997 Asian financial crisis caused the Korean multinational corporations to pull out of the film industry. However, in its wake it left behind high quality professionals at every stage of the production process, from production financing to filmmaking. These independents successfully produced several commercial hit, blockbuster films, including international box office successes such as *Shiri* and *Joint Security Area*. These blockbuster films were very successful in East Asia, which accounted for sixty percent of their overseas sales (Shim 2006: 34).

The Koreans are anxious to ride on the popularity of their pop culture to develop their soft power regionally; this was a notable regional phenomenon almost immediately after the Korean Wave. This is all the more attractive, if not necessary, given Korea's weaker economic and political position in the world relative to Japan and China. As Korean scholar Lee Geun suggests: "even if Korea is the thirteenth largest economy in the world as of 2008, possessing a world-class military, it cannot compete with other advanced industrialized countries in the area of hard power;" however, with the "recent blossoming of its cultural potential in the name of the Korean Wave, Korea can and needs to develop its soft power and soft power resources as Korea's political and economic instruments of high significance" (2009: 85).

Furthermore, given its history of colonization by Japan, the Korean cultural nationalist voice is more assertive than the Japanese who were historically the aggressor. The Korean Wave was seen euphorically by Korean nationalists as a breaking out of a position of regional cultural marginality—which was a result of having been "oppressed for over 5000 years" (Kim Han-gil quoted in Cho 2005: 158)—and a chance for the "internationalization" of "Korean" culture to occur (Cho, 153):

> For those of us who have eulogized the aesthetics of living in seclusion for a long time next to a powerful country, the spread of our cultural products throughout the world these days cannot but be good news ... the news that Joint Security Area has earned about two million dollars in Japan is proof that the foreign competitiveness of Korean films has vastly improved. Above all, it appears that the Korean temperament is touching people's hearts around the world ... We can now say that what is Korean is, in fact, international. (A Korean journalist quoted in Cho 2005: 153)

As Cho remarks, sarcastically: "To the people of 'a marginal country,' who had for so long lived under the oppressive culture of other countries, the news that their own culture was influencing other countries' cultures could have been nothing other than amazing and wonderful" (2005: 173–174). Soft power is to be built on this foundation of acceptance.

Just as in Japan, the intensification of pop culture production and distribution dovetails very well with the growing cultural industries in Korea. Cho summarizes succinctly the frenzy of discussion between government and cultural industry entrepreneurs:

> Proposals for dismantling the "barriers to maintaining the Korean Wave" included developing a stronger strategy for continuous distribution through larger scale production, regulation of content quality, and *delinking the Korean Wave from nationalistic fervor*. Export-oriented government officials and businessmen had in common their concern about a lack of a coherent policy or strategy. A "cultural engineering mindset" was emphasized over and over in their discussion of how to produce and sell competitive cultural content. (2005: 160, emphasis added)

Again, as in Japan, if not to a greater extent, the Korean Minister of Culture and Tourism, Kim Hang-gil, pronounced that the government "will actively support the penetration of our culture into foreign markets" (quoted in Cho 2005: 160). However, the explicit reference to the need to "delink" pop culture export from "nationalist fervor" signaled the Korean government's awareness that nationalistic rhetoric and zealousness may incur the wrath of the people and government of the target nation and cause political and economic backlash. We need to turn attention to the potential obstacles to positive reception of the exported pop culture, which is essential to the transformation of pop culture into a resource and instrument of soft power.

## Obstacles Noted in Audience Studies: A Summary

In the previous chapter, it was shown that real time reception by audiences suggests there are hurdles or obstacles to identification with on screen characters, actions and narratives in foreign films. Some of these obstacles bear reiteration here. First, a common explanation for the popularity of Japanese and Korean dramas in East Asia is their "cultural proximity," ostensibly because of their shared Confucian values, which is radically reduced to patriarchal family relations (Lin and Tong 2008).[5] A survey by Korean media scholars Kang and Soo (2009), shows that the family institution is portrayed very differently in dramas from different parts of East Asia: Korean dramas are the most patriarchal, with parents constantly intervening in their adult children's affairs; Taiwanese dramas have vestiges of patriarchy; with communism's emphasis on gender equality, dramas from mainland China have more egalitarian relations between spouses and between parents and children; and finally, in Japanese urban dramas family is almost completely absent and instead individualism rules. This finding casts serious doubt on the assumption of cultural proximity through a shared Confucian patriarchal family, even if it cannot be ruled out completely.

Second, Korean and Japanese television dramas, a major pop culture genre for export, are dubbed and subtitled into Chinese languages and redistributed throughout Pop Culture China. As discussed in Chapter 5, reception of foreign dramas is a fragmentary process of intermittent moments of identification and distancing with what is on screen. More importantly, audience reception analysis shows that cultural particularities, i.e., foreign cultural elements, tend to cause audiences to distance themselves from what is on screen. For example, Singaporean audiences distance themselves from the portrayal in Japanese trendy dramas of "loose" sexuality, and a Hong Kong woman comments, "[Korean television dramas'] kind of life and death love story will never happen to me ... those things are too tiring to me, I may not do that!" (Lin and Tong 2008: 113). In such instances, the specificities of "Korea/the Korean" and "Japan/the Japanese" are seen as different/distant and are thus points used for rejection by transnational Huaren audiences. Furthermore, with specific reference to Japan, such audience distancing/rejecting of "Japaneseness" disrupts the above-mentioned simplistic Japanese nationalist reading, and cultural imperialist dreaming, of the popular reception of Japanese television dramas in East Asia as the rest of Asia desiring Japan. This raises additional doubts regarding "cultural proximity" and the likelihood of a positive influence of Korean and Japanese television dramas on Huaren audiences.

Third, empirical studies of Singaporean audiences of Japanese television dramas show that identification with characters and narratives on screen are highly abstract. They claim understanding and identification with what is on screen on either/both the basis of being "human" in general (MacLachlan and Chua 2004: 166–167) and being "Asian" specifically. It would appear that the "attractiveness" of what is on screen may not be Korean or Japanese but what is already the audience's "own." Hence, they do not necessarily see themselves as being positively influenced by the foreign dramas. Finally, there is empirical evidence that regional youth audiences are largely attracted by the capitalist consumer culture showcased in the Korean and Japanese urban dramas (Thomas 2004). Similarly, it has been argued that the attraction for the audience in China to Japanese "trendy" dramas "arises from the yearnings of the new bourgeois classes in China for a wealthier and more open lifestyle just around the corner" (Leheny 2006: 230). Identification at this level is therefore with capitalist consumer modernity rather than any particular national culture or Asian value.

In summary, while there is evidence that Korean and Japanese television dramas have engendered positive attitudes among their respective transnational East Asian audiences towards the two countries, there is equally compelling evidence that the particularities of Korean and Japanese cultures as represented on screen are also sources of disaffection for other East Asian audiences. In short, there is no guarantee that the popularity of the pop culture will result in a positive disposition toward the exporting nation, the outcome which the expenditure of pop culture as soft power aims to achieve.

## Transnational Pop Culture Meets Nationalism

No one wants to be the target of other's power, hard or soft. Indeed, penetration of pop culture into another country is almost always resented as "cultural contamination," "cultural imperialism" or "cultural hegemony." Politically, "soft power can be counter-productive" (Otmazgin 2008a: 75). Consequently, proponents of using pop culture as soft power are explicitly aware of the need to be circumspect with reference to the feelings of the target audience both as a population and as a nation. Despite this, the penetration of transnational pop culture into national territories in East Asia has engendered resentment and backlash from the importing or receiving peoples/nations. To examine this development it is necessary to delineate some contextual elements in the target nation.

An empirical issue in the study of pop culture concerns the difficulties in getting an accurate quantitative number of actual consumers of a particular product. All measures are at best by proxy, such as box office takings, television ratings and numbers of books/DVDs sold; all of which are undoubtedly unable to register the level of actual popularity, especially in these days of rampant piracy, Internet downloads and file-sharing. However, no matter how popular a pop culture product is in a particular location, its total audience population, aggregating both avid fans and the leisure entertainment audience, is definitely much less than the non-audience population locally. (Recall here the conceptual distinction between "pop" and "popular" culture made at the beginning of this book.) The social space of media pop culture is part of but definitely not equivalent to the larger popular culture. The difference in the size of the audience and non-audience populations locally is an important contextual obstacle to the efficacy of pop culture as soft power resource for the exporting country.

Within the larger popular culture sphere, the non-audience may coalesce into an occasioned community to confront the audience of imported pop culture in numerically grossly uneven contests. In such confrontations the non-audience can and will readily use their overwhelming demographic majority to "anoint" themselves as "the people," giving themselves an abstract symbolic unity, and turn the contest into one of "defending" the "national" culture against foreign cultural "invasion" or "imperialism," often with the complicity of not only local pop culture producers but also the state. This ability to evoke nationalist sentiments is contextually facilitated by the historical-political animosities between East Asian nations, for example, Japan's fifty-year colonization of Korea, Japanese atrocities during its undeclared invasion of China in the 1930s, including the Nanjing Massacre, and the ongoing "cross-straits" stalemate between Taiwan and China. Three instances in the recent history of East Asian Pop Culture illustrate this issue of politics against imported pop culture.

First, recall here the case, analyzed in the previous chapter, of Taiwanese aboriginal singer Chang Huimei being made a site for the enactment of the "Taiwan Straits" politics by the Chinese government. For segments of the China population, her performance at the 2000 Taiwan president's inauguration ceremony had marked her as an "enemy" of a unified Chinese nation. In 2004, her sold out concert in Hangzhou was canceled by local police because a group of self-proclaimed "patriotic" Chinese students protested at the concert site, with a banner that read "Pro-Taiwan Independence Green People [the symbolic color of supporters of Taiwan independence] Not Welcome" (Tsai 2008: 221). Labeling themselves as patriots, the protesting students had claimed for themselves the position as representatives of the "nation." While empirically such "nationalist" claims by the protesting students who were part of the non-audience might be spurious, it is the type of claim that will never be ideologically/discursively available to Chang's fans in China, thus leaving them impotent to fight back on the national stage.

The second instance is anti-Korean sentiments that emerged as a consequence of the success of Korean pop culture in Taiwan. Here, not only can the *han* (韩) in Korean Wave (韩流) also be transliterated as "cold current" (寒流), but the local media, including specialized magazines and newspapers dedicated to the business community, went further and referred to the popularity of Korean pop culture as the "invasion of the Korean Wave." The military metaphor of "invasion" suggests a "violation" of Taiwanese national territory. The Taiwanese pop music industry was particularly incensed. On the day Bae Yong-joon arrived in Taipei, in 2005, to promote his movie *April Snow* (外出), leading Taiwanese rock musician Wu Bai (伍佰) organized and staged the *Taike* (台客) Rock Concert, which prominently featured a rap song, "The Invasion of the Korean/Cold Wave" that was laced with obscenities against Korean culture generally, and Bae in particular. The lyrics also insult the overwhelmingly female audience of Korean drama and Bae, chastising them for their supposed naivety, gullibility and even stupidity in their hankering for "love" and "romance" as depicted in the dramas.[6] This highly gendered discourse about Korean drama consumption displaces the female fans' voices to the margins and argues they should not be entertained at the level of the serious, masculine business of running the national economy and polity. The genesis of the term *taike* preceded the rock concert. It is an ironic phrase that addresses local

Taiwanese as guests, *keren* (客人), a highly politically and emotionally charged reference to the way Hokkien/Minnan speakers have been suppressed and marginalized by the Kuomintang government in the past. Under that repressive regime, locals became "outsiders/guests" in their own homeland, Taiwan. This self-referencing as a "guest" is thus politically motivated, re-inscribing the conventional marginality as a source of pride and identity, as an act of resistance and rebellion against the Kuomintang regime. Yang (2008) points out that such self-referencing was extensively used by local musicians in politically alternative music in the late 1980s. However, once the Democratic Progressive Party (DDP) came to power in 2000, the enemy of *taike*, the Kuomintang, had been defeated, leaving its "alternative" status potentially politically vacuous, unless and until it could find a new target. This it did in Korean pop culture. The rock musicians and fellow *taike* travelers attacked imported Korean pop culture in the name of promoting and protecting the "national" culture against Korean cultural invasion, thinly veiling their own economic self-interest. Evoking the nation provides the ideological discursive space for mobilizing the non-consumers of Korean pop culture to join, not only in resisting the invasion of the foreign but also in the revival and revitalization of local Taiwanese culture. The sign of the "nation" has again been usurped by the non-consumers of Korean pop culture to exclude fans of Korean pop culture as cultural "traitors" of the nation.

The third instance is the emergence of the *Manga Kenkanryū* (Anti-Korean Wave Manga), in 2005, in Japan, when the Korean Wave was booming. Liscutin has undertaken a detailed textual and visual pictorial analysis of the *manga* and a summary of its general message:

> *Kenkanryū* is presented as an oppositional vision to an allegedly blind enthusiasm for things Korean among Japanese followers of the "Korean Wave." It seeks to counteract this infatuation by providing "the truth" about Korea, its history, culture, and Korean claims against Japan for restitution. Putting its premise—"When you know [about] Korea, it's only natural that you become Anti-Korean!"—into action, *Kenkanryū* aims to educate its readers on a wide range of misdemeanours allegedly committed by Korea, which it describes as [a] "thoroughly depraved nation." The manga seeks to demonstrate that "anti-Japan" sentiments and protests in Korea lack any legitimate historical basis, and that "correct" historical knowledge would enable Japanese people to be proud of their country's present and past achievements and thus fortified, to take a firm stance against any kind of "Japan-bashing" by their Asian neighbours. (Liscutin 2009: 172–173)

Obviously touching a nerve, the first volume of the *manga* was followed by two sequels in the next two years, with a total sale of 800,000 copies to date. Observes Liscutin, "The breathtaking impact of *Manga Kenkanryū*, is demonstrated less, however, by its sales figures than by the extensive pro-*Kenkanryū* movements that rapidly spread on various Japanese and global Internet sites" (2009: 173).

In all these three instances, the pop culture sphere rubs up against the larger public sphere of which it is a part. In every case, the ensuing contest is ideologically unequal, reinforced by the unequal size of the non-audience versus the audience of imported pop culture. The sign of the "nation," and with it the imagined national public space and national culture, is discursively/ideologically and strategically only available to the non-audience population. The self-proclaimed patriots are able to wield the sign of the nation as an oppressive power to label, marginalize and silence the local audience of imported media products as "less" than nationalistic, as "cultural traitors," who are thus to be politically/morally excluded from "the nation." The self-proclaimed protectors of the local/national usually have the implicit or explicit blessing of the state because such mobilization is good for nationalism. Thus, instead of containing the demonstration against visiting foreign pop stars, the state cancels the visits or the concerts, ostensibly for the safety of the stars; as in the case of Chang Huimei in Hangzhou, China. The confluence of interests between the anti-foreign non-audience activists and the state makes the target/importing nation an inhospitable location for the exercise of soft power from exporting nations. The situation is aggravated in East Asia where the flows of pop culture products are hitherto grossly unequal, from Japan and Korea into Pop Culture China.

## Reality Check Beyond Pop Culture

Generally, a country's presence in another has many fronts and it is nearly impossible for the country to coordinate the actual practices on all fronts to consistently project a positive image of the nation. The unavoidably contradictory or conflicting practices across the different fronts mean that the attractiveness of the foreign presence is always in flux and locals have uncertain feelings about it. The changing fortunes of the US global presence in different parts of the world at different times readily attest to this. The case of Korean dramas in Vietnam is instructive here. Korean dramas are popular among Vietnamese youth because scenes of urban Korea with its beautiful youth and rich consumer culture represent the future to which they aspire. So much so that, according to Ngo and Truong (2009), many Vietnamese women are willing to marry Korean men.[7] Beyond the television screen, transnational Korean manufacturing companies are major employers of cheap, sweatshop Vietnamese labor, particularly women, who may also be the audience for Korean dramas. Industrial relations in these oppressive and exploitative industries have been very tumultuous, with frequent violent confrontations between the workers and employers, including the burning down of factories. Their work experience under Korean male managers will undoubtedly serve as a reality check, dispelling any illusion that all Korean men are gentle, accommodating and loving like the male characters they see on screen. The negative effects of this on the efficacy of Korean soft power can be readily imagined.

## Enter Mainland China

As argued, given the unequal flow of Korean and Japanese pop culture into Pop Culture China, the soft power ambition of both Japan and Korea are clearly aimed at the regional Huaren audience population, the most important segment of which is in mainland China. Obviously, China is not going to sit idly by while its media space is inundated by imports from all over the world. It is only a matter of time before it enters the fray and fights for its space in the regional and global media markets and for the communist party-state to stake its place in soft power diplomacy. Indeed, both President Hu Jintao and Premier Wen Jiabao have explicitly stated the need for China to "raise our nation's cultural soft power."[8]

"Soft power" has become a preoccupation in China, not only for the party-state leaders but also for intellectuals and the Chinese media. In a search in the China National Knowledge Infrastructure, "the largest and most comprehensive database of Chinese journals and periodicals," for full articles on soft power, Li found that "[f]rom 1994 to 2000 there were 57, from 2001 to 2004, there were 212, from 2005 to 2007, there were 942" (2008: 5). In a survey of these writings, Li found that, thematically, the writers frequently invoke "traditional Chinese culture" as a resource for soft power, "on the premise that it boasts a long history, a wide range of traditions, symbols and textual records," and its emphasis on "harmony" (和) is appealing to others in this "era of cultural diversification and globalization" (2008: 6). Further, "traditional Chinese culture" has been influential throughout East Asia for millennia and, finally, there is evidence of the merits of traditional Chinese cultural values which is to be found in the socio-economic successes of East Asian "dragons" and, now, the success story of China's own economy. This may account for the rapid proliferation of state-sponsored Confucius Institutes in many of the major cities in Asia and Europe. This evocation is not without critics who argue that the so-called "traditional" Chinese culture is now too hybridized and "reshaped by the revolutionary experience of the CCP [Chinese Communist Party]," and besides, it contains too many "backward" elements for others to be interested in it.

A second element that the Chinese writers consider as a soft power cultural resource is China's own experience in the development of a market economy, i.e., China's rise as a development "model" for others to learn and emulate. Again, this evocation is equivocal; many are doubtful because "Chinese development is not completed yet, [so] it is too early to conclude that there has been a unique Chinese model of socio-economic development" (Li 2008: 12). Along with these two major themes, Chinese scholars "focus on anything that would be helpful in boosting China's international influence, ranging from traditional Chinese medicine to the story of China's economic success to sports culture to educational exchange programmes" (Li 2008: 10).

However, one thing is clear, given China's recently acquired economic and military power, which finesses its claim to a future as a "global" power, it is thinking about "soft power" in terms of global influence. Its ambition and desire to acquire soft power is deemed a necessary complement to its newly acquired hard economic and military power. Within this ambition is "notable Chinese discontent about losing competitiveness in the international trade of cultural products" (Li 2008: 7) including movies, popular music, television programs, fast food and fashion, primarily to the US globally and, one might add, regionally to Japan and Korea. In these and other cultural areas, such as intellectual property rights and patents, China suffers from a general "deficit in cultural trade" (Li 2008: 11). In the face of the inundation of consumer goods and pop culture from the rest of the world, Chinese leaders could not fail to notice that it is way behind in the global competition for the production of pop culture.

Since the marketization of the economy in 1978, the media sector, like all sectors in China, has been undergoing radical structural transformation. Space does not permit a detailed discussion of the changes, nor is it necessary for the purpose at hand. Broadly stated, the media industry that had been under state control since the establishment of the communist party-state in 1949 has been "commercialized." With marketization or economic liberalization, state subsidy as the only source of revenue for the industry was removed. While ownership remains in the hands of the state, in order to police and regulate the political content of media products, each unit in the media industry has to generate its own operating revenue from the marketing of its products. The consequences are profound, as itemized by Chan (2010: 206): (i) the emergence of a media market which has moved away from the purely propagandist and didactic function it had in the past and in which media products are traded commodities, the success or failure of which is dependent on audience reception or ratings;[9] (ii) revenue is dependent on profit from products and advertisements, thus indirectly giving rise to the emergence of an advertisement industry; (iii) while the state will not relinquish ownership of media companies, other related and ancillary businesses are allowed to be privatized, "as in the case of Hunan Broadcasting Group, which privatized its advertising and other business operations," even production can be outsourced to/from private production houses[10] and; (iv) the arrival of foreign capital in search of joint production with state media companies, since sole ownership is not possible, especially after 2001 when China joined the World Trade Organization, membership to which required China to open its domestic market.

With specific reference to television, the most important and ubiquitous medium of communication in a country which still has a huge illiterate population, there has been a proliferation of stations. The number of stations expanded from a mere 32 in 1975 to 202 in 1985 and 980 in 2000, with a corresponding expansion of relay stations, from 12,159 in 1985 to 42,830 in 2000 (Chang 2002: 11), reaching almost ninety percent of the population of more than 1.3 billion. Along with the entire media industry, television transitioned from being overwhelmingly an instrument of political propaganda to having a proliferation of programs that are aimed at providing mass entertainment, of which serial dramas make up a very important genre, generating a very large quantum of the total advertising revenues.[11] This proliferation and diversification of mass entertainment programs has been fed in part by imported programs, while the domestic industries step up the pace of production to fill the content demand generated by a constantly rising number of cable and satellite relay stations and program timeslots. The proportion of imported programs shown in 2002 reveals that the major locations exporting to China are Hong Kong (40.7%), South Korea (20.5%), Taiwan (12.9%), Japan (7%) and Singapore (2.1%); the only other foreign country with significant exports to China is the US (11.9%) (Chan 2010: 210). This distribution attests to the presence of an East Asian Pop Culture sphere.

Until the early 2000s, China had been and remains essentially a location of consumption of East Asian Pop Culture. This began to change by the end of the decade. The popularity of Korean television dramas, especially, has spurred the commercialized, state-controlled media industry to think competitively, deploying various strategies simultaneously. First, since the 1980s, China has been quite successful in exporting historical dramas and dramas based on Chinese literary classics, such as the *Water Margin* (*Shuihu Zhuan* 水浒传 1981). Capitalizing on this, it successfully marketed several historical dramas through the 1990s till mid-2000; for example, *Romance of the Three Kingdoms* (*Sanguo Yanyi* 三国演义 1994), *Yongzheng Dynasty* (*Yongzheng Wangchao* 雍正王朝 1999) and *Kangxi Dynasty* (*Kangxi Dadi* 康熙大帝 2001) (Keane 2008: 150–151). These dramas were successfully sold at reasonably high prices to Taiwan and Hong Kong stations. In 1998, the Hunan Satellite TV Station production, *Princess Huanzhu* (*Huanzhu Gege* 还珠格格) "was the first Mainland Chinese drama to achieve success in Korea, although broadcast after 11 pm on SBS due to Korean Broadcasting Commission's foreign content restrictions" (Keane 2008: 151–152). Finally, and intriguingly, Chinese military dramas seem to have a market in Korea and Japan. Of the more than seven hundred hours of dramas sold to Korea, "the most tradable category being military offerings such as *The Eighth Army* (*Balu jun*), *The Long March* (*Changzheng*), *The DA Regiment* (*DA shi*) and *Peaceful Time* (*Heping shidai*)" (Keane 2008: 152). In addition, *Drawing Sword* (亮剑), *Soldiers Sortie* (士

兵突击) and *My Colonel and My Corps* (我的团长我的团) were sold to Japanese stations (Xu 2010).

These exports are miniscule when compared to the increasing volume of television dramas produced in China with contemporary urban themes that remain largely without any external market. This is because these dramas still have to either stay broadly within the party-state socialist ideology or deal with issues of concern to the ongoing transformation in the country itself.[12] For example, the genre that has the family as a main theme deals with "emotional anxieties faced by the less well-off in an increasingly aggressive and individualistic society where morals and family values, whether traditional or socialist, have collapsed," but "more often than not, the resolution of these conflicts promotes a more traditional and conservative moral outlook in which harmony and stability prevail" (Kong 2008: 83). The transformed television industry is therefore caught between the need to generate revenue from the export market and being shackled by the political ideological control of the state. Thus, judging from the record of sales to the regional market, Keane rightly concludes that "Mainland Chinese producers have established a foothold [in the East Asian regional market] and in some way broken down stereotypes of Chinese dramas being boring and ideological' (Keane 2008: 152). At the end of 2009 further measures of commercialization were undertaken to "revitalize" the cultural industries by "lowering the threshold for private and foreign investment in state-owned media companies, tax breaks and setting up a cultural industries investment fund," as well as "nurturing cultural talents, improving intellectual property rights protection laws and cracking down on piracy" (Goh 2009). In spite of this, Goh—a correspondent for Singapore's *Straits Times*—noted that "the missing ingredient in this grand plan, however, is the expansion of space for creativity through looser government control" (Goh 2009). Whether China will become a major player in the regional television drama market, as the others are doing, remains a long-term goal and possibility.

In addition to the Japanese and Korean interests in using soft power to influence the audiences of pop culture, China is also motivated to export its pop culture for another reason. As mentioned above, China scholars see "traditional" Chinese culture as a soft power resource because it has influenced the rest of East Asia for millennia. In the same vein, China sees itself as the birthplace of an East Asian civilization and thus considers itself responsible for the "proper" historical accounting and interpretation of what is "root" or "traditional" East Asian culture. This ideological motivation has been agitated and continually fuelled by what are, to the Chinese, the audacious cultural claims of the Koreans. For example, in the regionally widely popular Korean drama, *Dae Jang Geum*, acupuncture, conventionally considered part of traditional Chinese medical practice, was portrayed as a Korean indigenous practice. Chinese netizens have also been incensed by UNESCO acceding to the Korean claim that the "rice dumpling festival" is part of a Korean cultural heritage. The Chinese, of course, see the festival as part of their annual calendar of festivals, the *Duanwu* Festival (端午节), commemorating the self-sacrifice of a loyal official, Qu Yuan (屈原). These Korean gestures have motivated the Chinese to "rectify" the historical misrepresentations (Xu 2010). This is the context that provides the Chinese government and its state-owned media industry with the rationale and motivation to establish themselves as custodians of what is "traditional" Chinese culture, elements of which were also historically part of the larger East Asian traditional culture, to "recentralize" Chinese culture in China.

In the regional contest for soft power China has one trump card, namely, its potential market of 1.3 billion, which every conceivable producer of commodities, including pop culture, can ignore only at its business peril. To gain access to this market, it is necessary to get past the obstacles of state bureaucracies and state-owned media industries, which also control the exhibition channels on both big and small screens, political ideological control and state-imposed annual import quotas. In the interest of reducing the investment risk, regional production companies from Hong Kong (Chow and Ma 2008), Taiwan (Chen 2008) and, increasingly, Japan and Korea (Lee D.H. 2008), have been entering into co-productions with Chinese companies so as to bypass all the official obstacles. In the case of Taiwan, the pressure for co-production is practically unavoidable because its pop culture cannot be exported directly, neither can it be broadcast directly into China; co-production agreements have to be conducted through non-government private companies. A less cumbersome alternative is for Taiwanese production companies to relocate to China; Chen reports that "numerous drama producers who formerly worked with the three Taiwanese terrestrial stations [TTV, CTV and CTS] have relocated to China" (2008: 183).

In the case of Hong Kong, Yeh observes that the huge market is so enticing that "Hong Kong directors such as Stanley Kwan and Stephen Chow moved their productions across the border so they could directly tap into the mainland market" (2010: 193). The 2003 Closer Economic Partnership Agreement has significantly reduced the barriers to Hong Kong pop culture crossing into China. Among other favorable conditions, the agreement permits Hong Kong films, including co-productions, to be counted as domestic Chinese releases and thus exempt from the foreign film quota. The new partnership has impacted on the media industries on both sides of the border. For Hong Kong, co-productions have injected new financial resources into a weakening film industry; this is particularly significant in the production of costly blockbusters. For China, co-production has introduced new aesthetics into the commercial entertainment elements of mainland Chinese pop culture production, which had hitherto been laden with staid and unrealistic themes of socialist selflessness in the interest of the masses and the nation.[13]

Whether it is through co-production or relocation, the collaborative efforts have, to a certain extent, resulted in a "reintegration" of three major Pop Culture

China locations—China, Taiwan and Hong Kong. As producers from all three locations have the same enlarged Huaren market in view, this reintegration makes financial sense. It enables the sharing of resources in developing "profitable dramas that conform to the taste of the ethnic Chinese market" (Chen 2008: 183). Relocating production to China also has the added advantage of making it easier to shoot on location for Chinese languages films and television dramas, especially for *wuxia* and historical genres. Such location shoots not only avoid the construction of expensive sets in studios but, in addition, lend authenticity to the film or drama as it features the "real" China, the "actual" place where the events on screen supposedly took place. The combined financial benefits and authentic spatial effects clearly contribute to the re-inscription of the centrality of China as the center of all things Chinese, including of course "Chinese" culture (Chow and Ma 2008). This is precisely the ideological desire of the contemporary Chinese government and its state-controlled media industries.

The shortcut into the China market through co-production or relocation unavoidably comes with constraints on the product content as the main market is now China itself, where the state continues to maintain strong ideological control on content, even as it liberalizes the economics of the media industry. Even in the instances of collaboration with Hong Kong or Taiwanese companies, the Chinese partners tend to predominate in the decisions on content. For example, the Taiwan–China co-produced *She is from the Sea* (她从海上来 2004), "a literary drama based on the autobiography of novelist Eileen Chang, could not attain approval for broadcast [in China] due to controversial and different interpretations of Eileen Chang's work in China" (Chen 2008: 184). Obviously, such political-ideological intervention of the party-state often seriously affects the financial bottom-line of China's regional media producers.

The pressure for co-production has intensified for Korean independent television drama producers since 2006, when the State Administration of Radio, Film and Television in China announced its intention to impose an annual quota on Korean drama imports. However, in the end, it is still the potential profit that can be gained from the China market that is the most important inducement for co-production: "For Korean co-producers, these projects represent a way to access audiences not only in Mainland China, Hong Kong, and Taiwan, but also in Malaysia, Singapore, and other countries where a large Chinese diaspora lives. These vast Chinese media markets offer a way for the co-producers to maximize financial resources and ensure large returns on their investments" (Lee D.H. 2008: 196). Access to the China market has also become more urgent as signs of an ebbing interest in Korean dramas are appearing, with "some [Chinese] viewers finding the pace of Korean drama too slow and the narratives too predictable" (Keane 2008: 151). In 2006, "the four most popular dramas purchased by provincial stations" were all Hong Kong dramas (2008: 151), even if China remains one of the most important markets for Korean dramas.[14] In the co-productions thus far, the content of the dramas produced in China seems to be more significantly determined by the tastes of the Chinese audience, as these dramas have had difficulties attracting sizable Korean audiences or finding Korean stations which would buy them (Lee D.H. 2008).

One imaginable and potentially positive outcome of all the co-production activities is the possible emergence of "pan-East Asian" cultural content, which might reduce the cultural distances and could circulate popularly between and within the constituent countries in the region. While this remains a logical possibility in the long term, the immediate term seems to undoubtedly favor China on account of its market and, if anything, seems to reduce the likelihood of the emergence of a common cultural product. This is demonstrated in Yeh's (2010) study of the Hong Kong-based film company Applause, founded by Peter Chan Ho-sun, a Thai-Chinese, in 2000.

From the start, Chan's aim was to "build a unified Asian marketplace," to this end, "Applause employs folklore together with [East and Southeast] Asian genre conventions, regional marketing, creative collaboration, and industrial alliances to create multiple trajectories of production, consumption and distribution" (Yeh 2010: 192). It was especially successful in the horror film genre—*The Eye* (2002), *Three* (三更 2003, co-directed by Nonzee Mimibutr, Kim Ji-woon and Peter Chan) and *Three ... Extremes* (三更2, 2004, co-directed by Miike Takashi, Park Chan-wook and Fruit Chan). The last two illustrate Chan's business and production strategies:

> Both are portmanteau films that include contributions from three different countries, styles and directors. The material and the market are tripled: three directors, three territories, three scary stories. In the sequel, *Extremes*, Miike Takashi, the Japanese cult director known for shocking genre experimentations, contributed his short, *Box*. Each of the films has regional and genre variations, comprised of supernatural visitations, nocturnal chills, and psychological thrills. Two of the shorts in the portmanteau films were furthermore spun off into feature-length horror films, *Going Home* (Peter Chan) and *Dumplings* (Fruit Chan). Both films won awards in Hong Kong and Taiwan for their distinctive treatments of the horror genre. This recognition showed that Applause's pan-Asian strategy of repackaging genre films can even pay off in prestige, an important value added to the company's branding and visibility. (Yeh 2010: 191–192)

Too big and too tempting to be ignored, Applause decided to enter the China market. In the process, it had to abandon its strengths in the horror and eroticism genres, as horror and "spirits" films were banned in China until 2008, when the first Hong Kong/China/Singapore co-production "horror/spirit" movie, *Painted Skin*

(画皮), was released to great box office success. Applause switched its focus to undertake big budget blockbuster films, with capital injected from mainland Chinese film enterprises. Its first film was *Perhaps Love* (2005), a musical. Yeh noted that Peter Chan retained a pan-East Asian orientation, "he mixed and matched pan-Asian ingredients with Chinese elements with respect to talent, locale, and narrative, creating a film that would interlock market segments and territories" (2010: 194); specifically, Taiwan-Japanese Takeshi Kaneshiro, Hong Kong's Jacky Cheung (张学友), Chinese actress Zhou Xun (周迅) and Korean television star Ji Jin-hee (池珍熙), with dances choreographed by Bollywood's Farah Khan, adding a South Asian element. However, the film was essentially aimed at the Chinese audience and thus, was set in pre-communist revolutionary Shanghai, "with glamour, nostalgia and a touch of decadence" (2010: 194). The "film grossed a disappointing $7 million worldwide, barely more than half of Applause's previous hit, *The Eye*" (Yeh 2010: 194). Yeh sees in this instance, an eclipse of "pan Asian cinema" "from regional consolidation to a mainland orientation in hopes of exploiting the China market" (2010: 194), where transnationality might "be more acceptable if it were subsumed to nationality" (2010: 195). Drawing from this case study, Yeh's final prognosis is that an integrative "pan East Asian" cinema has been deferred, for how long is anyone's guess.

The dynamics that have been playing out since China liberalized its economy and media industry without giving up political-ideological control of media content, and inevitably undermining the party-state's soft power ambition as a result, has ironically been articulated by Korean observers as the Korean Wave hit China:

> What China undoubtedly dreams of doing is transforming itself into a "global cultural center." For China, it is not just about escaping the status of a cultural colony; it is about becoming a cultural center. China is waiting for the day when it can control the world's cultural flows not politically, but as a cultural superpower. For China, Korea is a stepping stone towards this goal. If China emerges as a new cultural furnace, it will most likely mean East Asian's emergence from cultural colonialism [to Western culture] ... We need to view the Korean Wave not in terms of market expansion but as an opportunity to establish an identity. Through the Korean Wave, we must create a sense of cultural solidarity with China and use that position to raise the status of East Asia vis-à-vis Europe and United States. (Im Jin-mo quoted in Cho 2005: 157–158)

Here it is clear that the centrality of China in any idea of a "pan-East Asia" is conceded while the desire and hope for a pan-East Asian cultural identity, through transnational pop culture, is kept alive. This position recognizes that in the long run the current unequal flow of soft power influences from the other regional constituent nations, especially Japan and Korea, into China could be reversed and the better strategy, for Korea at least, is to seek accommodation.

## Conclusion

Undoubtedly television and films have a consequential impact on their audiences. For one who does not have the opportunity to travel, "knowledge" of a foreign land is often wholly derived from its representations on big and small screens. This ability to influence undergirds the proposal that pop culture can be transformed into resources and instruments of "soft power" through which the exporting nation can influence their target audiences/consumers. However, substantively and analytically, how this influence can be achieved remains an empirical issue that is seriously under-examined. In the context of a regional pop culture economy in East Asia, three countries—Japan, Korea and China—are vying to increase their regional soft power through the export of pop culture. Existing empirical studies of audience reception of television dramas have shown that the audience is a fragmented figure, intermittently identifying with and distancing itself from what is on screen. The result is an absence of sustained influence, positive or negative; the exporting nation's hope for positive influence on the audience in the target nation is thus not guaranteed. Furthermore, the overwhelmingly much larger non-audience of foreign pop culture could be readily mobilized, firstly, against its importation and, secondly, to confront the audience of imported products, in the name of "protecting" the domestic, "national" culture, with the tacit or explicit support of local culture producers and the state. Such possible backlash requires the exporting nation to tread softly with its soft power ambitions. Finally, empirically, market considerations have greatly impacted the regional pop culture economy. While the media industry in each country will undoubtedly continue to produce pop culture for its domestic audience, which is usually its most significant market, the same media companies will also have to pursue transnational co-production and distribution opportunities to enlarge their revenues. Here China, with its promise of 1.3 billion consumers, is drawing in regional producers with different co-production arrangements. The consequence is that the Chinese government, through its state-controlled media industry, appears to be gaining in determining the content of transnational productions in the region and with that, the ongoing accumulation of regional soft power resources, if not influence. At the regional level, one could argue that the historically deeper structure of Pop Culture China is re-asserting its dominance, after a brief two decades of being submerged by Japanese and Korean pop cultures, while groups of committed fans, operating in different modes on the Internet, continue to go under the radar of both the competing nation states and capitalist profits.

# Conclusion

The emergence of an East Asian Pop Culture stands significantly in the way of complete hegemony of US media culture, which undoubtedly continues to dominate the entertainment media globally. Indeed, at the beginning of the twenty-first century, discussions on media in East Asia have displaced concern with the "cultural imperialism" of the West, namely of the US, to focus instead on the celebration of the "arrival" of East Asian pop cultures in the global entertainment market; however, traces of this debate, albeit reconfigured in terms of the hegemony of multinational media corporations rather than nation-states, continue (Shi 2008). Several achievements mark this sense of "arrival." The earliest East Asian entries into the global pop culture entertainment markets were probably Japanese animation, *manga* and video games. According to Iwabuchi (2002: 257), these products were "culturally odorless" because they contain little explicit Japanese content; animation and *manga* figures have always been intentionally devoid of Japanese features and resemble no particular ethnic group. Nevertheless, they were recognizably "Japanese" because of the highly stylized renderings of the characters; the term *anime* refers exclusively to either Japanese or Japanese-inspired animation. These products continue to be the mainstays of Japanese pop culture export to the world. Since the 1990s, Chinese and Korean cinemas have entered global circulation, in both art house film festivals and commercial markets, and are juxtaposed against Hollywood's global dominance. Beneath the global scale, since the mid-1990s, the most significant pop culture genre to circulate transnationally within East Asia is serialized television dramas, streaming routinely into homes throughout the region—Japanese television dramas throughout the 1990s, followed by Korean television dramas in the early 2000s. The commercial success of these television dramas is, practically, an exclusively regional phenomenon as they have no market in the West, except among East Asian diasporas watching DVDs or licensed cable channels in their adopted land.

## Singapore: Signifier of East Asian Pop Culture

The transnationalization and regionalization of East Asian Pop Culture is most visible in Singapore because it is primarily an import and reception/consumption location of East Asian programs, as the small, multiracial and multilingual domestic population on this island-nation is unable to sustain a large media industry of its own. In the 1950s, when communist China was closed to Hong Kong producers, Singapore was also a point of redistribution for Hong Kong cinema throughout Southeast Asia. In the 1950s and 1960s, movies in Cantonese, Hokkien and Mandarin from Hong Kong and Taiwan were regular offerings in local Singaporean cinemas. Often funding for the films would come from Singapore through presale arrangements between Hong Kong producers and Singaporean and other Southeast Asian cinema owners.

In the mid-1970s, when television was still new and had low production capacity, Singaporean television screens were filled with television dramas imported from Hong Kong's TVB. Singaporeans were introduced to the now global movie star, Chow Yun Fat, on the small screen in the serial drama, *Man in the Net*, in which he played a Chinese migrant struggling to survive in Hong Kong. At the same time, the Singaporean audience was also watching Chinese costume dramas with themes drawn from the "traditional" family politics dictated by the Confucian principle of filial piety, particularly those based on the popular romance novels by the female Taiwanese writer Qiong Yao. Since then, Hong Kong and Taiwanese dramas of all genres have become an integral part of the daily programming of Singapore television stations. The circulation of Hong Kong and Taiwanese movies, television dramas and pop music in Singapore substantiates the incorporation of these locations with the predominant Huaren population into a loosely integrated cultural economy, which can be discursively designated as Pop Culture China.

Japanese action movies were popular in Singapore in the 1960s but the flow was disrupted as the Japanese movie industry fell into decline (Yau 2005). Japanese screen products returned in the 1990s, with what has come to be called "trendy" television dramas—melodramatic romance among young urban(e) professionals. Japanese export of these trendy dramas to the rest of Asia was largely serendipitous. Japanese television dramas were "imported" through informal channels into Taiwan, including via Taiwanese business people going to Japan who returned with DVD-sets of the dramas with the purpose of public screening, so as to feed the demands given the explosion of unlicensed satellite television stations caused by media liberalization in the late 1980s. From there Japanese trendy dramas spread to Singapore. However, by the end of the decade, Japanese trendy dramas had all but disappeared. Significantly, by the new millennium, the Japanese government's push to lend financial and institutional support to the development and export of its pop culture industries was primarily focused on animation and films, and television dramas are conspicuously absent from these efforts.

As Japanese television dramas lost their vitality and appeal at the end of the 1990s, Korean television dramas took over the space on the small screen. In contrast to the serendipity of the export of Japanese television dramas, the export of Korean television dramas is a well-executed national industrial strategy on the part of the Korean government. Correspondingly, the importing of Korean dramas became a strategy for new, smaller or marginal television stations to establish their presence among local audiences. Singapore is again a good illustrative example of this dovetailing of interests between Korean producer-exporters and local importers. In 1999, Singapore Press Holdings, the local monopoly newspaper publisher, ventured into commercial television with two free-to-air stations, one in English (Channel I) and the other in Mandarin (Channel U). The English language channel failed and was closed in less than two years. On the other hand, the Mandarin channel was able to carve out and take away a significant segment of the audience from the already established state-owned television station, through very heavy doses of Korean drama broadcasts. The popularity of the Korean dramas on Channel U pushed the state-owned Channel 8 to similarly import such series. Korean dramas became routine broadcasts by the early 2000s. Finally, the destructive competition for the same Korean dramas caused the two corporations to merge, with Channel 8 developing local drama and variety programs, and Channel U repositioning itself as the "Asian Pop Culture Channel" on which movies, television dramas and variety shows from Hong Kong, Korea and Japan are freely mixed into the daily offerings, interspersed with local news, talk shows and occasional variety or game shows, making it a signifier of the idea of an East Asian Pop Culture.

## Japanese and Korean Pop Culture: Similar Trajectories

The trajectory of entry of Japanese and Korean pop culture into Singapore was repeated in Hong Kong, Taiwan and China. In Hong Kong, where more than ninety percent of the local audience was already captured by the two free-to-air television stations, TVB and ATV, Japanese drama series were a significant vehicle for STAR TV, a cable television provider, to establish its presence in airspace and to garner its share of the local audience (Iwabuchi 2004: 7). In China, the dramas are mostly distributed by pirated VCDs and DVDs and, with increasingly sophisticated computer-mediated information technologies, circulated by sub-fan groups, who download, subtitle and upload for free distribution (Hu 2005: 176–180). By the early 2000s, Japanese dramas were either displaced or faced competition from Korean dramas. The inflow of Korean pop culture was so swift and noticeable that it came to be dubbed almost immediately as the "Korean Wave" (韩流) by journalists in China.

In 2004 and 2005, the most popular Korean drama series in East Asia was undoubtedly *Jewel in the Palace,* a fictionalized chronicle of the rise of the first female imperial court physician in the Choson dynasty during the fifteenth century. The "close" cultural affinity between the Choson dynastic period and Chinese history was an important bridge to its success. Practices such as the sharing of the same written calligraphic script and the use of herbs in traditional medicine facilitated the "indigenization" of the series for, and enhancing its popularity with, the Huaren audience. This is reflected in the way this drama traveled. First exported to Taiwan and dubbed into Mandarin, it was subsequently broadcast on TVB in Cantonese in Hong Kong, to record-breaking audience ratings; in 2004, the Hunan Satellite TV Station obtained the rights from the Taiwan distributor and broadcast it nationally in China and, finally, the drama was broadcast in Singapore on cable television and on the free-to-air Channel U; thus, completing the coverage of all points in Pop Culture China.

In contrast to the ease of penetration of Japanese and Korean pop culture into Pop Culture China, Japan is most resistant to the penetration of pop culture from the rest of the region. In the 1990s, there was a trickle of Hong Kong action movies, especially those of Jackie Chan, and almost no Korean imports at all. This situation exploded with the arrival of the Korean television drama, *Winter Sonata* in 2003; the drama, released in January 2002, had already gained popularity throughout Pop Culture China. The lead actor, Bae Yong-joon became the object of adoration of middle-aged housewives in Japan, their "Yon-sama," or "Prince Yon" (Jung 2011). After that, Japan became one of the leading importers of Korean pop culture in the region.

The trajectories of the popularization of Japanese and Korean television dramas across the region substantiate the presence of an East Asian Pop Culture sphere. The unequal flow of Japanese and Korean pop culture into Pop Culture China is a consequence of both industry structure and demographics. Structurally, Pop Culture China is a well-established production, distribution and circulation network that has a history stretching back to the late nineteenth century. Demographically, the relatively smaller consumer populations of Japan and Korea make routine dubbing or subtitling of Chinese-language(s) programs financially unviable. On the other hand, the massive Huaren population makes the dubbing and subtitling of Korean and Japanese programs a potentially lucrative business, as in the case of *Jewel in the Palace.* This configuration suggests that East Asian Pop Culture is a structural expansion of Pop Culture China that loosely incorporates Korean and Japanese pop culture into its extensive and established network. Meanwhile, within Pop Culture China, Chinese language(s) pop culture remains more widely consumed than Korean and Japanese imports, with occasional spikes generated by a very popular singer, film or drama from the latter.

## The Transnational Audience of Transnational Television

The emergence of East Asian Pop Culture provides an opportunity for examining the practices of transnational audiences, namely, local audiences receiving imported foreign pop culture products, where the culture in which the audience is embedded is different from the culture at the location of production. This "transnational" aspect is referred to as a matter of fact because it is commonly recognized that the global media culture is dominated by American products which are foreign to all locations but the US itself, yet it is a phenomenon that is curiously underresearched. It is argued that the serial nature of television drama draws an audience into an intimate virtual relationship with the characters in the drama, resulting in an active participation with what is on screen. This accounts for why the watching of television drama has conventionally been a fertile ground for audience reception studies. Transnational audience reception is no exception.

Within East Asia, Korean and Japanese dramas are routinely dubbed into Chinese languages to facilitate their reception in the regional Huaren audience. Dubbing is a process that "seeks to domesticate a foreign product and to make both the translator and the translation invisible" (Chaume 2004: 39). To this end, expressions and contextual references of the onscreen language which have no equivalent in the target language are substituted, and thus changed, with elements from the culture of the target audience. In this instance, Japanese and Korean television dramas are domesticated by the Chinese language and cultural context. This is in addition to the relatively similar physiognomy, a shared ideographic Chinese script, a common Confucian worldview—as illustrated in the Korean drama *Jewel in the Palace*—and a shared achievement of or desire for capitalist consumerist modernity (Iwabuchi 2002). However, the "foreignness" of imported dramas is a large part of the viewing pleasure for a transnational audience. Foreignness is preserved on screen through the various visual elements, especially those that signify "tradition," such as ethnic food and costumes or contemporary streetscapes of iconic or "slang" images (Khoo 2006) that are unmistakably metonymic representations of the foreign location. In audience reception, dubbed dialogue domesticates foreign television drama in order to facilitate identification while the visually exotic foreign items raise obstacles to identification.

Empirical investigations suggest that identification requires a certain order of abstraction: the most immediate level of identification is also at the most generalized and abstract level of simply "being human;" as seen in such comments from audience members as: "I understand the onscreen character because we are all humans" or "Love stories in big cities are more *real* for us. We are young. It is what we *dream* of" (Ko 2004: 123, original emphasis) or "The major attraction of *Tokyo Love Story* [a Japanese drama] to me is that it is not a story about somebody else.

It is a story about our generation, about us, about myself" (quoted in Iwabuchi 2002b: 146). In East Asia this abstract identification can take the form of "I identify with the character because we are Asians," affirming a sense of "Asianness" which implicitly invokes various cultural elements that can be claimed to be shared by East Asians, while simultaneously suppressing cultural differences between the production and consumption locations. All the variations of identification with what is on screen are ready-to-hand "repertoires of interpretation" (Hermes 1999).

Crucially, the factual foreignness/difference of the imported television drama is never erased but merely displaced to just beneath the surface of the abstract identifications. They emerge immediately, as soon as onscreen characters and actions are contrary to an audience's sentiment. Difference can be used by a transnational audience to distance itself from the culture of the location of production thus rejecting the "other," or can be received positively and engender a desire to embrace the "other." One particularly poignant instance of this is the changes the Korean television drama *Winter Sonata* wrought on its audience of middle-aged Japanese women. Many began to consider the possibility of becoming "cultural brokers" who could work on changing the image of Korea/Koreans in Japan and even improve the international relations between the two nations (Mōri 2008). Concretely, as tourists they transform Korea from a male sex-tourist site to a female tourist location of "friendship."

To generalize, what emerges is a picture of the transnational audience as a fragmented entity that intermittently identifies and recognizes difference and distances itself from what is on screen rather than holding a sustained and unwavering identification with or rejection of what is on screen. The factors that can be and are invoked—one can imagine for example, "global citizenship," gender and class—as grounds for identification are invariably abstract and contextual. Conversely, the factors that are invoked for distancing are more often than not culturally specific. This opens up opportunities for empirical investigations into how different historical, political, social and cultural factors can, and have been, evoked in different locations across different national, cultural and linguistic boundaries to anchor specific instances of identification/distancing.

The popularity of a pop culture item, such as a television drama, is the result of a mass audience who does nothing more than watch the show on television, although a relatively small number of dedicated fans will engage in beyond-the-text activities and practices. For the leisure entertainment audience, a possible "community" is latent and invisible until it is instantiated when two or more members happen to be co-present at a social occasion/event and, as part of the free flowing social conversation, they exchange impressions and opinions, i.e., they consider their shared knowledge concerning the latest television drama drawn from their watching and/or reading, and a "community of audience" instantly materializes. When the occasion is over, the community is dissolved. Such occasioned communities of audience are a grounded, incidental and face-to-face phenomenon and, one can imagine, ubiquitous although ephemeral. The ephemeral character does not amount to a stable "interpretive community" (Alasuutari 1999: 7).

In the case of fans, the Internet and new communication technologies have spawned new possibilities for fan organization across time and space. One of the most significant developments is the sub-fan communities of highly organized but de-territorialized, de-centralized and faceless organizations of highly skilled and highly dedicated individual transnational audience members engaged in downloading a program, subtitling it in good time and uploading it for distribution; a tightly coordinated sequence of activities that is accomplished smoothly for every episode of a particular drama series. The immaterial labor (Lazzarato 1996: 145) is done entirely for the pleasure of self-satisfaction, and for the benefit of others in the cyber-virtual world. It escapes the clutches of the profit-oriented producers and distributers and flies under the radar of censorship and other legal constraints of the nation-state. Another development made possible by the Internet is the engagement by fan groups in coordinated international petitioning of specific governments in the interests of their idols/stars. This is tantamount to "extraterritorial" intervention into the political sphere of the nation in question. Admittedly, it is difficult to imagine how such petitioning activities could have any significant impact on the nation's domestic politics.

## Pop Culture and Soft Power

Conventionally, the politics of transnational pop culture are framed within the terms of "cultural imperialism" on the one hand and "cultural security" on the other (Tomlinson 1997). Since the end of the ideological Cold War in East Asia that was initiated by the marketization of the economy in China, "ideology" has been displaced by the less politically-charged terms "culture" and "cultural imperialism," and "cultural security" has been replaced by "soft power" competition. The exporting and importing of pop culture has been transformed into an arena of such competition, as the potential use of military power between the region's competing nations recedes. In this competition, Korea is most anxious about the race because it is sandwiched between two much bigger powers—Japan whose animation and *manga* are globally distributed, and a rising China with a massive consumer market with expanding consumption capacity. It is already apparent that the size of this market has played to the advantage of China. Producers of pop culture, particularly films and television dramas, not only from Taiwan and Hong Kong but also Korea, are already heading to China to develop co-productions with Chinese media companies in order to escape any restrictions imposed by the government on foreign pop culture imports. In so doing, they subject the contents of the products to the ideological control of the Chinese state, which owns all media enterprises, even if they operate without state subsidy.

Getting beneath these four abstract concepts to the level of actual transnational audience practices, "politics" takes on a more personal character in East Asia, where fandom is oriented towards particular idols. As we have already seen in the instances of coordinated petitioning activities, the adoration of the fans can occasionally spill into the larger public political sphere of the location of production or the location of reception, or both. In the location of reception/consumption, members of the local audience of foreign pop culture are confronted by the overwhelmingly large population of compatriots who are not audience members. Activists against foreign pop culture could mobilize the large non-audience population to raise objections to its importation and to the presence of foreign artists in the country. In such mobilization efforts, such activists could position themselves as "defenders" of national culture and national interests, which simultaneously cast and politically marginalize the much smaller audience population as "cultural traitors." Ironically, empirical evidence suggests that the individual audience is often inclined to distance themselves and reject precisely the particularistic cultural elements of foreign pop culture, defying the label of cultural traitor. Nevertheless, in such instances, the state is often complacent and complicit regarding the activists invoking its name, as activists' "nationalist" protests are advantageous to the state. Arguably, such anti-foreign protests are part and parcel of the soft power competition conducted between states. Politics of consumption at the popular level is therefore inextricably intertwined with politics of soft power at the state and international levels.

## Conclusion

With the massive transformations in communication technologies that enable information to transcend all the constraints of time and space, it is entirely understandable that contemporary discussions of media industries will emphasize globalization and its potential cultural homogenization effects. Simultaneously, in reaction to the emphasis on globalization is the often rather shrill defense of the local as "resistance" to the global and its effects. Empirically, of course, given the reality that global capitalism no longer has any ideological and/or practical resistance and the oligopolistic formation that concentrates the media industries in the hands of a few global media enterprises, some homogenization of media culture around the world is unavoidable. This is most obvious in the selling of formats, usually developed in a few media centers and sold to any station that can afford the price.

However, what has also happened empirically, in the spaces between globalization and localization, is the regionalization of media industries. This is especially the case in television entertainment. Conventionally, local audiences favor local television programs over imported ones. However, the concept of the "local" can be rather elastic in cultural terms. "Local" is conventionally used to substantiate politically the result of artificial boundaries of geographically contiguous territory by nation-states. The artificial national boundaries are imposed on shared histories, shared cultures and shared languages, even the similar physiognomy, of people living in contiguous geographic spaces. The shared conditions constitute a loose "cultural proximity" that facilitates the boundary crossing of "local" television programs into spatially contiguous and historically and culturally proximate regions, engendering the regionalization of media culture. "Cultural proximity" however is not "cultural identity" but implies both elements of familiarity and foreignness/difference, and identification/distancing (or even rejection) by the local audience of culture products from its neighbors. The regionalization of East Asian Pop Culture is but one of the many identifiable instances taking place within Asia: other examples include the impact of Indian soap operas in South Asia (Fazal 2009: 49), Thai television dramas in mainland Southeast Asia (Jirattikorn 2008) and Malay language television dramas in archipelagic Southeast Asia (Weintraub 2011). The reception practices used by transnational audiences of these regional pop cultures may share similar structures of identification and distancing. The transnational fan activities and the politics that result from the contact between fans and the non-audience local population may share similar features of confrontation around the trope of nationalism, as each of these regions has its own historical legacy of regional conflicts and border disputes. Finally, each of these regionalizations has its own history of structural integration of the production, distribution and circulation processes. These are, of course, empirical questions, and the present study of East Asia Pop Culture will hopefully invite comparative analysis from researchers examining other instances of the regionalization of media elsewhere in the world.

# Notes

## Introduction

1.  There is a plethora of books that focus on different "national cinemas" from East Asia. An illustrative sample includes Shin and Stringer (2005) on new Korean cinema, Davis and Chen (2007) on post–New Wave Taiwanese cinema, Berry and Farquhar (2006) and Zhang (2004) on Chinese national cinema, and Morris, Li and Chan (2005) on Hong Kong films.

2.  Curtin (2003) provides a very concise history of the development of Hong Kong as a media capital in Chinese-language pop culture and notes the constant competition it faces from other contenders such as Taiwan.

3.  This is most apparent in the case of Chinese-language cinema, see Yeh (2010).

4.  Approximately seventy-four percent of the residential population of five million is ethnically Chinese, thirteen percent Malay, and nine percent Indian, with a very small percentage of others. English is the language of education, commerce, public administration and, increasingly, everyday life. Statistics from Advance Release of Singapore Population Census 2010, http://www.singstat.gov.sg/pubn/popn/c2010acr.pdf (accessed Sept 15, 2011).

5.  Liew (2010) provides a succinct account of the obstacles faced by Southeast Asian ethnic Chinese, including Singaporean, artists in the *Gangtai* entertainment industries.

6.  http://blog.tianya.cn/blogger/post_show.asp?BlogID=561820&PostID=6211910 (accessed Feb 22, 2011).

7.  See http://www.koreatimes.co.kr/www/news/include/print.asp?newsIdx=30480 (in Chinese, accessed Feb 22, 2011); http://tieba.baidu.com/f?kz=64514375 (accessed Feb 22, 2011).

8.  As the Malays of Malaysia and Indonesia are Muslims, comparative studies of pop culture across these two countries tend to focus on Islamic themes and issues, rather than on the Malay language; for example, the papers presented at the Conference on Islam and Popular Culture in Indonesia and Malaysia, University of Pittsburg, October 10–12, 2005; http://www.ucis.pitt.edu/asc/conference/indonesia/index.html (accessed Jan 31, 2011).

## Chapter 1

1. The term "idol" has become an adjective that characterizes a specific segment of popular culture products, as in "idol-drama."

2. There is a wealth of books on Asian national cinemas and auteur filmmakers, which are referenced throughout this book; for an example of an analysis of auteur filmmakers, see Teo (2005; 2007).

3. This "nostalgic" reading of other Asian pop culture may be read as a vernacular version of the historically deep-seated Japanese ideological tendency to place itself as the "leader" of the rest of Asia; see Ching (2000).

4. It has also been excluded from two major surveys in the field (du Gay and Pryke 2002; Amin and Thrift 2004).

5. See du Gay and Pryke (2002) and Amin and Thrift (2004).

6. Communication as a social process of encoding/decoding was proposed by Stuart Hall (1980); for a critique of parts of Hall's thesis, see Rajagopal (2001:10).

7. This is a case of what Lee and LiPuma (2002) call the "culture of circulation."

8. The historical conditions under which a location emerges as a "media capital," such as Hong Kong, are examined in detail by Curtin (2003).

9. "Ethnic" Chinese is a problematic category because "Chinese" is itself a multi-ethnic category. In this book, "ethnic Chinese" refers to Han Chinese, with all its different dialects or languages.

10. See the *Inter-Asia Cultural Studies* (2008) theme issue on Hou Hsiao-Hsien.

11. The television station, Channel U, which broadcasts in Mandarin, only produces its own news program and fills the rest of its twelve-hour daily airtime with variety shows and dramas from every production point in East Asian Pop Culture.

12. For a personal account of academic fascination with Japanese trendy drama, see Tsai (2003).

13. This Japanese view of themselves as being ahead of the rest of Asia is one of deep historical standing and prejudice; indeed, it was partially responsible for Japan's imperial and militarist ambition during the Second World War, see Ching (2000).

14. This was the first contemporary Korean drama to be brought to the television screen in Japan, by Nippon Hoso Kyokai (NHK) Station, to shore up its flagging audience base. The television station was so uncertain of the reception of the drama that it was screened in the late night (11 pm) program slot. Its popularity was thus entirely unexpected. *Winter Sonata*'s first broadcast garnered an audience of 9 percent; within the next two years, the drama was repeatedly screened on prime time, free-to-air channels, managing to capture a 17.6 percent audience rating (Fuyono 2004); around 40,000 DVD sets were sold, as of September 2003 (Han 2008).

15. During that time, Korea was under the repression of an authoritarian regime; the fact that Japanese pop culture was illegal generated additional pleasure in consumption, see Kim Hyun-mee (2002).

16. These figures were provided by Dr Shin Hyunjoon from the Institute of East Asian Studies, Sungkonghoe University, in personal communication, email dated February 4, 2010.

17. In contrast, Chinese historical dramas do circulate quite well within Pop Culture China.

18. Refer to Leong (2002).

19. Many of these series were based on the popular romance novels by the (female) writer, Qiong Yao.

20. It was also the very first popular Mandarin television drama to be screened in Indonesia after the lifting of the official ban on Chinese culture. It was alleged that the "*Meteor Garden* has turned many Indonesians on to anything Chinese" (Asmarani, 2002).

21. For a brief analysis of Ah-Mei's stage persona, see Moskowitz (2010: 81–83).

22. Some of the more domestically popular dramas are analyzed in Zhu, Keane, and Bai (2008).

23. On the other hand, Shaw Brothers, Malay Film Productions Limited, and Cathay-Keris Films were producing Malay-language films in Singapore. These studios closed after Singapore separated politically from Malaysia.

24. For a review of their earlier films, see Chua and Yeo (2003).

25. For a history of the Singapore film industry, see Millet (2006).

26. Refer to Lin (2010).

27. In response to the film being poorly received by the critics, supposed distributors Miramax delayed its scheduled American screening and subjected the film to edits. Miramax eventually sold the rights to Warner Independent who screened it to a poor response, relative to the former two films mentioned.

## Chapter 2

1. For a critical commentary on the use of the term "diaspora" to describe the dispersed overseas Chinese population, see Wang (2000).

2. See also the Special Issue of *China Quarterly* (1993) "Greater China," no. 136.

3. For a critical discussion on this imposition of a presumed shared Chineseness by self-interested others, see Ien Ang (2001).

4. This was particularly promoted under the Democratic Progressive Party (DPP) government, which championed Taiwanese independence, between 2000 and 2008.

5. To date, Curtin (2007) has provided the most comprehensive survey of the film and television industry in Pop Culture China.

6. In 2007, a textbook entitled *Pop Culture China! Media, Arts and Lifestyle* (Latham 2007) was published under a series called Pop Culture in the Contemporary World. This book sidesteps the transnational dimensions of Chinese-language pop culture and focuses only on pop culture in mainland China.

7. The 2010 film, *It's a Great Great World*, by Singapore filmmaker Kelvin Tong, set in 1950s/60s Singapore has multilingual dialogue—Hokkien, Cantonese, Teochew, Hainan, and Mandarin—on screen, reflecting the polyglot reality of the Singapore Huaren community at the time.

8. Parenthetically, it should be noted it is the multi-accented Mandarin dialogue of this film that inspired Shih (2007) to coin the term "Sinophone."

9. There are, of course, individuals who consider being "'culturally' Chinese" as their dominant personal identity regardless of nationality. These include many Huaren academics who are intellectually and emotionally heavily invested in overseas Chinese studies; for these individuals, nationality is incidental, cultural identity is everything.

10. Nevertheless, their places of origin are occasionally mentioned, perhaps as a reminder to regular readers or, more likely, as background information for a new generation of readers/audience.

11. As no major events took place during March 2010, examples had to be drawn from other times.

12. The inclusion of this Japanese actor is a reflection of the possibility of a larger construction of the popular culture sphere in East Asia, which includes Japan and South Korea, see Chua (2004).

13. http://koreajoongangdaily.joinsmsn.com/news/article/article.aspx?aid=2933181 (accessed Mar 9, 2011).

14. http://english.chosun.com/svc/list.html?catid=48pn=3 (accessed Mar 2–11, 2011).

## Chapter 3

1. I have left out on this particular occasion the language of the Hakka, who constitute a substantial proportion of the Taiwan population.

2. Hokkien migrants also constitute the majority of the Chinese immigrant population in Penang in Malaysia and Manila in the Philippines.

3. Many films from Taiwan are not released in the commercial movie houses in Singapore, although they are frequently included as "art" films during the film festival and are usually among the films that sell out. Often, commercial outlets will pick up the films for popular release based on their reception during the festival.

4. In Singapore, as a legacy of the British colonial negligence of public education, more than fifty percent of the adult population who is more than fifty years of age has less than a secondary school education. Refer to official census: http:www.singstat.gov.sg/pubn/popn/c2000adr/chap3.pdf (accessed Sept 20, 2011).

5. It should be noted that at the time *Money* was shown on the big screen the three main actors also appeared together, every Monday night, in a very popular local situation comedy in which one of them (the Mandarin speaker) cross-dresses as the mother of household. In a country in which homosexuality remains largely hidden from the public eye, this actor is the only one who appears in drag on public television, as a "woman/mother/old lady" without sex or sexuality.

6. The romanticizing of Hokkien is not restricted to the mass media. The present prime minister, Lee Hsien Loong, and his immediate predecessor, Goh Chok Tong, have been known to pepper their annual National Day Rally speeches with a few phrases in Hokkien to great effect. Such phrases never fail to draw laughter and applause from the audience.

7. For a debate on "the invention of Taiwanese," see the exchange between Chun (1998) and Wu (1998).

8. Indeed, it is a lesser language in Taiwan than the Japanese language as a consequence of close to fifty years of Japanese colonization of Taiwan. Many older, or elderly, Taiwanese can still speak Japanese fluently. Furthermore, some Japanese lexical items are mixed into Taiwanese conversational practices, but one almost never encounters two Taiwanese people conducting their conversation in Japanese.

9. In Singapore, the concept of a "dialect" or "language" is used to designate the difference between the official and written language of Chinese, and their spoken languages. Within the frame of the official and written, all Chinese languages other than Mandarin are rendered as "dialects," yet in the world of speech each of these "dialects" can operate fully as a language.

10. To date, Purushotam has provided the most comprehensive analysis of the politics of languages in Singapore, to which this discussion is indebted.

11. In May 2010, the minister of education announced that Mandarin would be given less "weight" in a student's overall academic achievement standing, which caused a storm of public outcry and led to a public petition and demonstration, very rare occurrences in this generally quiescent society, see Oon (2010).

12. However, with the introduction of paid cable television in 1995, which is owned by the state, Cantonese and Hokkien programs have been screened on cable channels, but the ban on public television continues.

13. I will have to depend on Taiwan researchers to analyze Taiwanese audience's reception of the very occasional Singapore films that are screened there.

14. Indeed, Taiwan Hokkien films are rare in Singapore, in part because of the no-dialect-in-mass-media policy that is still in place. However, when they are screened, as during the annual Singapore International Film Festival, Taiwanese films are often among the earliest to be sold out, which is indicative of their popularity.

15. Indeed, Hokkien films have to be occasional as the Singaporean audience seems to tire of them easily. For example, since the release of *Money* there have been several much better made Hokkien films which could not recoup their costs of production, including the above mentioned *Eating Air*, which was immediately picked up by international film festivals.

## Chapter 4

1. In recent years, there have been efforts to imagine Japan and Korea as multicultural societies; however, non-Koreans only constitute one percent of Korea's national population and in the case of Japan, a significant portion of so-called new immigrants are South Americans of Japanese descendant.

2. For example, Zee TV of India has found a ready audience among the Indian-Singaporeans, see Kaur and Yahya (2010); nevertheless, the Malay population has been known to watch Korean television dramas on a regular basis.

3. The Chinese-language schools in Singapore have used Mandarin as the language of instruction since the 1920s. Nevertheless, all the other Huaren languages were still being transmitted across generations and through the mass media until the government imposed a ban on the use of these languages, which led progressively to the decline of their use such that by now Huaren under thirty years of age are often unable to speak or understand any Huaren language other than Mandarin.

4. Malay is nominally the "national" language because it is the historical lingua franca of island Southeast Asia where Malays are the indigenous population.

5. In 2003, the EDB entered into partnership with both the National Geographic and Discovery channels, on a 50/50 partnership for a period of five years and a total of budget of thirty-five million US dollars, to finance documentary projects which are to be produced in Singapore. Technical professionals in production from both channels are brought in to work with local practitioners. These are "factual" documentaries with exotic "anthropological" themes not necessarily about Asian cultures, let alone contemporary Singapore. The well-financed, one-hour programs—which could cost up to one million US dollars per program, in contrast to about thirty-five thousand dollars per hour of local television drama—have been of very high quality, winning awards internationally and a few have even made their way into the prized US market.

6. No Singaporean singers or actors have ever made it big in the Anglo-American entertainment world.

7. For a detailed discussion of Khoo's films for an international audience, see Marchetti (2005); for a local comparative reading of the films of Neo and Khoo, see Chua and Yeo (2003).

8. Notable among these are Ann Kok and Bryan Wong, see Liew (2010: 192).

9. Mandarin music has long been dominated by romantic ballads. However, in recent years, some Taiwanese singers have used hip hop or rap rhythms with Mandarin lyrics, a combination that has proved to be very popular, see Felicia Seck Yen Yin (2004) and Moskowitz (2010).

10. The Lee Wei Song School of Music has since become a choice location for aspiring local singers and Lee Wei Song himself is now a much sought-after songwriter for Mandarin pop singers.

11. The rest of the four channels consist of one Malay-language channel, one channel for Indian languages, one arts channel and one regional twenty-four hour news channel, Channel News Asia. Of these, Channel News Asia is most successful regionally, see Yue (2006).

12. One Singaporean actress that has achieved some success through this mode of entry is Fann Wong, who played the Little Dragon Girl in a popular *wuxia* series and, in 2003, starred in Jackie Chan's blockbuster, Hollywood produced movie, *Shanghai Knights*.

13. For a detailed discussion of format sharing in East Asia, see Lim (2005).

14. A general conceptualization of the diasporic audience can be gleaned from Appadurai (1996).

15. See also Robins and Aksoy's (2006) analysis of diasporic Turks in Europe.

16. There have been instances where the non-Mandarin speakers, including non-Mandarin competent Huaren, complained of being deprived of the viewing pleasure of highly popular Korean television dramas because no English subtitles were provided.

17. In one instance, a Singapore tour group was persuaded by a member to change their designated ski resort to one that was featured in the very popular Korean drama, *Winter Sonata* (Foong 2003).

18. A politically very embarrassing instance attests to this: Senior Minister Goh Chok Tong has been quoted as saying of people in less developed countries: "Because they don't know what life is, they're quite happy. They wake up, they brush their teeth, then they'll farm, and then they'll sleep. But do you want it that way?" (Cheong 2011). The "rural" is often ideologically reduced to the "underdeveloped" and is used to refer to the pre-1960s past. In recent years it has been nostalgically re-inscribed as a place to escape to for its simplicity of life, if only temporarily; as a respite from the complexities and overcrowding of the city (Chua 1997).

19. Jung (2011) has demonstrated that the different Korean masculinities are embodied by different Korean actors and genres, of which "beautiful masculinity" is one category particularly appreciated in Japan.

## Chapter 5

1. The unevenness has become a source of complaint among media practitioners in China who see the popularity of Korean pop culture as "cultural invasion" (Foong 2005).

2. For greater detail on the idea of "dominant" meanings and the "encoding/decoding" process, see Morley (2003).

3. For a summary of the different theories of audience reception, see Eldridge, Kitzinger and Williams (1997: 125–133).

4. There is a very large body of literature on the encoding/decoding model that is well nigh impossible to review here; for a recent summary of some points of debate, see Morley (2006).

5. Cross-national joint productions of films among the East Asian locations have been on the increase in the past decade. However, unlike television programs, films tend not to be dubbed, thus increasing their "multi-Asian-language" character, including multi-accented Mandarin(s) in Chinese language films.

6. In addition to lip-synchrony, dubbing must also pay attention to "kinetic synchrony"—synchrony with body movements on screen— and "isochrony"— synchrony in the timing of screen characters' utterances (Varela 2004: 41).

7. Significantly, many in Singapore prefer the Cantonese to the Mandarin version because of the effect of the "greater authenticity" the colloquial expressions give, rather than the relative "stiffness" of the Mandarin version.

8. Interestingly, the popularity of *Jewel* reportedly exceeded that of the locally produced, large-scale period drama *Emperor of the Han Dynasty* (汉武大帝 2004) among the Chinese audience; according to one commentator, this is because the former series "resonates with modern viewers" (Foong 2005), implying the latter does not, presumably because it is too historical.

9. The researcher adds her commentary, which reinforces the sense that "we are all human" (Leung 2004: 94–95).

10. Similar sentiments against explicit sexuality in Japanese dramas are apparently held by Hong Kong Huaren audiences (Lin and Tong 2008: 103), who consider Japanese dramas to be closer to Western dramas than Hong Kong dramas in the attitudes they convey.

11. For an excellent discussion of the complex history of relations between modern Japan and the rest of Asia, see Sun Ke (2000).

12. This "superior" attitude was used to justify Japan's invasion of the rest of Asia during the Second World War.

13. As Thomas (2004: 178) observes, along with an imagined prosperity, there are also Vietnamese who see consumerism-driven capitalist modernization as "cultural contamination" and the destruction of wholesome local cultural practices. Ambivalence towards capitalist consumerism is pervasive in all developing societies, it is not limited to the Vietnamese (Chua 2000: 12–16).

14. Ko's emphasis on the youth audience possibly arose from a generational gap in the reception of Japanese television dramas in Taiwan. Harking back to the history of the Japanese colonization of Taiwan, older Taiwanese, particularly the intellectuals, are wary of yet another "invasion" of Japanese imperialism.

15. The smug sense of "elitism" is common among aficionados of marginal cultures.

16. East Asian pop music industries share a similar temporal placement in discussing the development of regional pop music (Pease 2009: 157).

17. A counter-sentiment has emerged in recent years in Taiwan. In the face of China's unyielding claim on Taiwan as a "province," some Taiwanese filmmakers have been using the island's Japanese colonial past as a marker to distinguish and distance the island from China. A very popular example of this genre is the film, *Cape No. 7* (海角七号 2008) by Wei Te-Sheng (魏德圣).

18. On the idea of social repertoires, see Taylor (2004).

## Chapter 6

1. Lee quotes the idea of the "mega-text" from Su (1999).

2. In 2004, it similarly canceled the already granted performance permits to a few Singaporean singers after the then-incoming prime minister of Singapore, Lee Hsien Loong, visited Taiwan in his "personal" capacity. http://www.china-embassy.org/eng/xw/t142816.htm (accessed Oct 12, 2011).

3. According to Tsai, the dramatic event was somewhat staged, "not only were reporters informed and played a part in this sentimental media event, some audience members from Japan were invited by a television company to observe the send-off" (2008: 277, endnote 24).

4. The information on 2PM is indebted to the research work of Lee Yumi, a Ph.D. candidate in the Cultural Studies in Asia program at the National University of Singapore and to Alyson Rozells, an events manager at the Asia Research Institute and a Korean Wave fan.

5. The mode of operation of the Korean talent companies is copied from the practices established by the Japanese company, Johnny Company, who is responsible for many of the regionally popular Japanese boy-bands, including SMAP (Chua 2005).

6. Lawsuits against the Korean entertainment agencies have been increasing in recent years; for example, three of the now disbanded five member boy-band, TVSQ, sued SM Entertainment, Korea's biggest talent agency to end their contract (Kim 2011).

7. http://www.allkpop.com/2009/09/2000_mobilize_at_jype_building_in_a_silent_protest (accessed Apr 23, 2011).

8. http://www.allkpop.com/2009/10/hottests_around_the_world_are_flashing_for_jaebeom (accessed Apr 23, 2011).

9. http://www.allkpop.com/2010/03/transcript-of-jypes-conference-about-2pm-jae-beom-pt-1 (accessed Mar 10, 2010); http://www.allkpop.com/2010/02/full-letter-from-jyp-entertainment-regarding-jaebeom (accessed Feb 28, 2010).

10. Jay Park visited his fans in Taipei, Shanghai, Hong Kong, Thailand, the Philippines and Malaysia in early 2011 and has plans to release a new album in Korea in the same year.

11. Sub-fan practices have already been found among anime fans in the US since the days of video types, see Leonard (2005).

12. Hu is quoting Streeter (2003: 649).

13. I owe this point to Lee Yumi in a written assignment she did for a course in Cultural Studies in Asia at the National University of Singapore.

## Chapter 7

1. For a detailed analysis on the popularity of *Doraemon* in Asia, see Shiraishi (1996). *Astro Boy* was the first foreign animation series to be broadcast in China (Shiraishi 1996: 268).

2. Japan's Agency for Cultural Affairs website on details of various policies regarding the promotion of Japanese culture: http://www.bunka.go.jp/english/index.html (accessed Apr 29, 2011).

3. http://www.meti.go.jp/english/policy/mono_info_service/creative_industries/creative_industries.html (accessed Apr 29, 2011).

4. Conversely, as Iwabuchi points out, instead of Asia desiring Japan, this situation is more symptomatic of the desire of Japanese nationalists to "return" to the embrace of Asia, a desire that was suppressed as Japan became culturally marginalized after being defeated in 1945, in the Pacific War (Iwabuchi 2002).

5. A more oblique criticism of the cultural proximity argument is the fact that Korean television dramas are also popular among Malays, who are Muslims, in Malaysia.

6. A transcription of the song is provided by Yang (2008).

7. Ngo and Truong have grossly simplified the complex issue of foreign brides, including Vietnamese brides, and why they marry low-income and rural Korean men who are unable to find partners in their local Korean society, although they do note that "the number of ill-treated and suicidal Vietnamese wives has continuously increased" (2009: 102).

8. See Hu Jintao's speech to the Seventeenth Communist Party Congress, 2007.

9. The American company, A. C. Nielson set up a rating service in China in 1999. CCTV also has "its own audience surveys and feedbacks to allocate primetime slots for various news and social programs" (Chang 2002: 20).

10. At the end of the 2000s, independent production remains a high risk business. Because of the difficulty of securing broadcasting time, joint productions with guaranteed screening are the preferred mode of operation (Xu 2010).

11. According to one estimate, in 2002, television dramas generated ninety percent of all the advertising revenues generated from television programming (Zhu, Keane and Bai 2008: 1).

12. Here it is opportune to point out that the party-state's interest in soft power is equally directed towards the domestic sphere in the pursuit of a "harmonious society," "a concept that the Hu–Wen leadership has proposed to tackle mounting domestic social challenges" (Li 2008: 14).

13. For detailed discussions on the new developments in the media industry of mainland China, see Xu (2010).

14. In that same year, the Taiwanese government restricted the airing of imported (read Korean) dramas between six and ten pm (Kim 2005: 198).

# References

Agost, Rosa (2004). "Translation in bilingual contexts: Different norms in dubbing translation." In Pilar Orero (ed.), *Topics in Audiovisual Translation*. Amsterdam/ Philadelphia: John Benjamin Publishing Company, pp. 63–82.

Alasuutari, Pertti (1999). "Introduction: Three phases of reception studies." In Pertti Alasuutari (ed.), *Rethinking the Media Audience*. London: Sage Publications Ltd, pp. 1–21.

Amin, Ash and Thrift, Nigel (eds.) (2004). *The Blackwell Cultural Economy Reader*. UK: Blackwell Publishing Ltd.

Andersen, Benedict (1983). *Imagined Communities: Reflections on the Origins and Spread of Nationalism*. London: Verso.

Ang, Ien (2001). *On Not Speaking Chinese*. London: Routledge.

Aoyagi, Hiroshi (2000). "Pop idols and the Asian identity." In Timothy J. Craig (ed.), *Japan Pop! Inside the World of Japanese Popular Culture*. Armonk, NY: M. E. Sharpe, pp. 306–326.

Appadurai, Ajun (1996). *Modernity at Large: Cultural Dimensions of Globalization*. Minneapolis: University of Minnesota Press.

Asmarani, Devi (2002). "Taiwan TV drama latest Jakarta craze; Series starring the four Taiwanese heartthrobs has made Indonesian teens lap up anything Chinese" in *The Straits Times*. Jun 21.

Aso, Taro (2006). "A new look at cultural diplomacy: A call to Japan's cultural practitioners." http://www.mofa.go.jp/announce/fm/aso/speech0604-2.html.

Bell, Daniel A. (2008). *China's New Confucianism: Politics and Everyday Life in a Changing Society*. Princeton: Princeton University Press.

Bell, Daniel A. and Hahm Chaibong (eds.) (2003). *Confucianism for the Modern World*. Cambridge: Cambridge University Press.

Berry, Chris and Mary Farquhar (2006). *China on Screen: Cinema and Nation*. New York: Columbia University Press.

Bird, S. Elizabeth (2010). "From fan practice to mediated moments: The value of practice theory in the understanding of media audience." In Birgit Bräuchler and John Postill (eds.), *Theorizing Media and Practice*. New York: Berghahn Books, pp. 85–104.

Chan, Felicia (2008). "When is a foreign-language film not a foreign-language film? When it has too much English in it: The case of a Singapore film and the Oscars," *Inter-Asia Cultural Studies* 9 (1): 97–105.

Chan, Joseph M. (2010). "Cultural globalization and Chinese television: A case of hybridization." In Michael Curtin and Hemant Shah (eds.), *Reorienting Global Communications: India and Chinese Media Beyond Borders*. Urbana and Chicago: University of Illinois Press, pp. 201–219.

Chang, Tsan-Kuo (2002). *China's Window on the World: TV News, Social Knowledge and International Spectacles*. Cresskill, NJ: Hampton Press.

Chaume, Frederic (2004). "Synchronization in dubbing." In Pilar Orero (ed.), *Topics in Audiovisual Translation*. Amsterdam and Philadelphia: The John Benjamins Publishing Company, pp. 35–52.

Chen, Kuan-Hsing (2000). "The formation and consumption of KTV in Taiwan." In Chua Beng Huat (ed.), *Consumption in Asia: Lifestyle and Identity*. London: Routledge, pp. 159–182.

Chen, Xiaoming (2000). "The mysterious other: Postpolitics and Chinese film." In Arif Dirlik and Xudong Zhang (eds.), *Postmodernism and China*. Durham: Duke University Press, pp. 222–238.

Chen, Yi-Hsiang (2008). "Looking for Taiwan's competitive edge: The production and circulation of Taiwanese TV drama." In Ying Zhu, Michael Keane, and Ruoyun Bai (eds.), *TV Drama in China*. Hong Kong: Hong Kong University Press, pp. 175–186.

Cheong, Natalie (2011). "A farmer's life deserves respect", *TODAY*, Apr 4.

Chin, Bertha (2010). "Beyond kung-fu and violence: Locating East Asian cinema fandom." In Jonathan Gray, C. Sandvoss, and C. L. Harrington (eds.), *Fandom: Identities and Communities in a Mediated World*. New York: New York University Press, pp. 210–219.

Ching, Leo (2000). "Globalizing the regional, regionalizing the global: Mass culture and Asianism in the age of late capitalism," *Public Culture* 12 (1): 233–257.

Cho, Hae-Joang (2005). "Reading the 'Korean Wave' as a sign of global shift," *Korea Journal* 45 (4): 147–182.

Chow, Carol and Eric Ma (2008). "Rescaling the local and the national: Trans-border production of Hong Kong TV dramas in Mainland China." In Ying Zhu, Michael Keane, and Ruoyun Bai (eds.), *TV Drama in China*. Hong Kong: Hong Kong University Press, pp. 201–215.

Chow, Rey (1995). *Primitive Passions: visuality, sexuality, ethnography and contemporary Chinese cinema*. New York: Columbia University Press.

Chu, Yiu-wai Stephen (2005). "Hybridity and (g)local identity in postcolonial Hong Kong cinema." In Sheldon H. Lu and Emilie Yueh-yu Yeh (eds.), *Chinese-Language Film: Historiography, Poetics and Politics*. Hawaii: University of Hawaii Press, pp. 312–328.

Chu, Yiu-wai Stephen (2007). "Before and after the fall: Mapping Hong Kong Cantopop in the global era," Working Paper No. 63, David C. Lam Institute of East-West Studies, Hong Kong Baptist University.

Chu, Yiu-wai Stephen (2008). "The Importance of Being Chinese: Orientalism Reconfigured in the Age of Global Modernity," *boundary* (2), Summer 2008: 183–206.

Chua, Beng Huat (1995). *Communitarian Ideology and Democracy in Singapore*. London, NY: Routledge.

Chua, Beng Huat (1997). "Nostalgia for the kampong." In *Political Legitimacy and Housing: Stakeholding in Singapore*. London: Routledge, pp. 152–167.

Chua, Beng Huat (ed.) (2000). *Consumption in Asia: Lifestyles and Identities*. London and New York: Routledge.

Chua, Beng Huat (2003). *Life is Not Complete Without Shopping*. Singapore: National University of Singapore Press.

Chua, Beng Huat (2004). "Conceptualizing an East Asian popular culture," *Inter-Asia Cultural Studies* 5: 200–221.

Chua, Beng Huat (2009). "Being Chinese under official multiculturalism in Singapore," *Asian Ethnicity* 10 (3): 239–250.

Chua, Beng Huat and Koichi Iwabuchi (eds.) (2008). *East Asian Pop Culture: Analyzing the Korean Wave*. Hong Kong: Hong Kong University Press.

Chua, Beng Huat and Yeo Wei Wei (2003). "Cinematic critique from the margin and the mainstream." In Chua Beng Huat (ed.), *Life is Not Complete Without Shopping*. Singapore: National University of Singapore Press, pp. 177–189.

Chua, Chyi Yih (2002). "'They look just like me': the appeal of Japanese boy bands among Chinese Singaporean Youths." Unpublished Honors thesis, Department of Sociology, National University of Singapore.

Chua, Chyi Yih (2005). "A 'New' Form of Travel: Johnny's Travelling Fan Club." Unpublished MA thesis, Department of Sociology, National University of Singapore.

Chun, Allen (1995). "From nationalism to nationalizing: Cultural imagination and state formation in postwar Taiwan," *The Australian Journal of Chinese Affairs* 31: 49–69.

Chun, Allen (1996). "Fuck Chineseness: On the ambiguity of ethnicity as culture and identity," *boundary 2* (23): 111–138.

Chun, Allen (1998). "The culture industry as national enterprise: The politics of heritage in contemporary Taiwan," and "Rejoinder to second look." In Virginia R. Dominguez and David Y. H. Wu (eds.), *From Beijing to Port Moresby: The Politics of National Identity in Cultural Policies*. Amsterdam: Gordon and Beach Publishers, pp. 77–113 and pp. 133–137.

Chung, Stephanie Po-yin (2009). "A Chinese movie mogul and the transformation of his movie empire: The Loke Wan Tho family and the Cathy Organization in southern China and Southeast Asia," *Asia Europe Journal* 7: 463–478.

Cross, Gary (1993). *Time and Money: The Making of Consumer Culture*. London: Routledge.

Curtin, Michael (2003). "Media capital: Towards the study of spatial flows," *International Journal of Cultural Studies* 6 (2): 202–228.

Curtin, Michael (2007). *Playing to the World's Largest Audience: The Globalization of Chinese Film and TV*. Berkeley: University of California Press.

Davis, Darrell W. and Robert Ru-Shou Chen (eds.) (2007). *Cinema Taiwan: Politics, Popularity and State of the Arts*. London: Routledge.

De Kloet, Jeroen (2000). "'Let him fucking see the green smoke beneath my groin': The mythology of Chinese rock." In Arif Dirlik and Xudong Zhang (eds.), *Postmodernism and China*. Durham: Duke University Press, pp. 239–274.

du Gay, Paul and Michael Pryke (eds.) (2002). *Cultural Economy: Cultural Analysis and Commercial Life*. London: Sage Publications.

Eldridge, John, Jenny Kitzinger, and Kevin Williams (1997). *The Mass Media and Power in Modern Britain*. New York: Oxford University Press.

Erni, John Nguyet (2007). "Gender and everyday evasions: Moving with Cantopop," *Inter-Asia Cultural Studies* 8 (1): 86–108.

Fazal, Shehina (2009). "Emancipation or anchored individualism? Women and TV soaps in India." In K. Moti Gokulsing and Wimal Dissanayake (eds.), *Popular Culture in a Globalized India*. London: Routledge, pp. 41–52.

Foong, Woei Wan (2003). "K-Mania still rules, ok?" in *The Straits Times*, Jan 4.

Foong, Woei Wan (2005). "Palace Malice; The Korean Wave—helmed by costume soap *Jewel In The Palace*—is seeing a backlash in China" in *The Straits Times*, Oct 16.

Fu, Poshek (2008). *China Forever: The Shaw Brothers and Diasporic Cinema*. Urbana and Chicago: University of Illinois Press.

Fung, Anthony Y. H. (2007). "The emerging (national) popular music culture in China," *Inter-Asia Cultural Studies* 8 (3): 425–437.

Fung, Anthony Y. H. and Eric Ma (2002). "Satellite modernity: Four modes of televisual imagination in the disjunctive socio-mediascape of Guangzhou." In Stephanie H. Donald, Michael Keane, and Yin Hong (eds.), *Media in China: Consumption, Content and Crisis*. London: Routledge, pp. 67–79.

Garfinkel, Harold (1967). *Studies in Ethnomethodology*. New Jersey: Prentice-Hall Inc.

Gellner, Ernest (1983). *Nations and Nationalism*. Oxford: Basil Blackwell.

Goh, Sui Noi (2009). "Chinese culture a hard sell," *The Straits Times*, Oct 28.

Grossberg, Lawrence (1992). "Is there a fan in the house? The affective sensibility of fandom." In Lisa A Lewis (ed.), *The Adoring Audience: Fan Culture and Popular Media*. London: Routledge, pp. 50–65.

Hall, Stuart (1980). "Encoding/decoding." In Stuart Hall, Dorothy Hobson, Andrew Lowe, and Paul Willis (eds.), *Culture, Media, Language*. London: Routledge, pp. 117–127.

Hall, Stuart (1994). "Notes on deconstructing 'the popular'." In John Storey (ed.), *Cultural Theory and Popular Culture: A Reader*. New York: Harvester Wheatsheaf, pp. 455–466.

Han, Benjamin Min (2008). "Reliving *Winter Sonata*: memory, nostalgia, and identity," *Post Script* 27 (3). http://www.freepatentsonline.com/article/Post-Script/191765321.html (accessed Jan 31, 2011).

Han, Seung-Mi (2000). "Consuming the modern: Globalization, things Japanese, and the politics of culture identity in Korea," *Journal of Pacific Asia* 6: 7–26.

Han, Sung-joo (1999). *Changing Values in Asia: Their Impact on Governance and Development*. Singapore: Institute of Southeast Asian Studies.

Hartley, John (1996). *Popular Reality: Journalism, Modernity and Popular Culture*. London and Sydney: Arnold.

Hermes, Yoke (1999). "Media figures in identity construction." In Pertti Alasuutari (ed.), *Rethinking the Media Audience*. London: Sage Publications, pp. 69–85.

Hu, Kelly (2005). "The power of circulation: Digital technologies and the online Chinese fans of Japanese TV drama," *Inter-Asia Cultural Studies* 6: 171–186.

Hu, Kelly (2009). "Chinese subtitle groups and the neoliberal work ethics" (in Chinese), *Journalism Research* 101: 177–241.

Iwabuchi, Koichi (1994). "Return to Asia? Japan in the global audio-visual market," *Sojourn* 9 (2): 226–246.

Iwabuchi, Koichi (2002). "From Western gaze to global gaze: Japanese cultural presence in Asia." In Diane Crane, Nobuko Kawashima, and Ken'ichi Kawasaki (eds.), *Global Culture: Media, Arts, Policy and Globalization*. New York: Routledge, pp. 256–274.

Iwabuchi, Koichi (2002a). "Nostalgia for a (different) Asian modernity: Media consumption of 'Asia' in Japan," *positions: east asia culture critique* 10 (3): 547–573.

Iwabuchi, Koichi (2002b). *Recentering Globalization: Popular Culture and Japanese Transnationalism*. Durham: Duke University Press.

Iwabuchi, Koichi (ed.) (2004). *Feeling Asian Modernities: Transnational Consumption of Japanese TV Dramas*. Hong Kong: Hong Kong University Press.

Iwabuchi, Koichi (2008). "When the Korean Wave meets resident Koreans in Japan: Intersection of the transnational, the postcolonial and the multicultural." In Chua Beng Huat and Koichi Iwabuchi (eds.), *East Asian Pop Culture: Analysing the Korean Wave*. Hong Kong: Hong Kong University Press, pp. 243–264.

Iwabuchi, Koichi, Muecke, Stephen and Thomas, Mandy (eds.) (2004). *Rogue Flows: trans-Asian Cultural Traffic*. Hong Kong: Hong Kong University Press.

Jirattikorn, Amporn (2008). "Pirated transnational broadcasting: The consumption of Thai soap operas among Shan communities in Burma," *Sojourn* 23 (1): 30–62.

Jones, Andrew F. (1992). *Like a Knife: Ideology and Genre in Contemporary Chinese Popular Music*. Ithaca, NY: East Asia Program, Cornell University.

Jung, Sun (2011). *Korean Masculinities and Transnational Consumption: Yonsama, Rain, Oldboy and K-Pop Idols*. Hong Kong: Hong Kong University Press.

Kang, Myungkoo and Soo Ah Kim (2009). "Representing families in popular television dramas in China, Japan, Korea and Taiwan." Proceedings of the Korean-ASEAN Academic Conference on Pop Culture Formations across East Asia in the Twenty-first Century: Hybridization or Asianization? Burapha University, Thailand, February 1–4, pp. 167–183.

Kaur, Arunajeet and Faizal Yahya (2010). "Zee TV and the creation of Hindi media communication in Singapore," *Sojourn* 25 (2): 262–280.

Keane, Michael (2008). "From national preoccupation to overseas aspiration." In Ying Zhu, Michael Keane, and Ruoyun Bai (eds.), *TV Drama in China*. Hong Kong: Hong Kong University Press, pp. 143–156.

Khoo, Olivia (2006). "Slang images: On the 'foreignness' of contemporary Singaporean films," *Inter-Asia Cultural Studies* 7 (1): 81–98.

Kim, Hyun Mee (2002). "The inflow of Japanese culture and the historical construction of 'Fandom' in South Korea." Paper presented at the International Conference on Culture in the Age of Informatization: East Asia into the Twenty-first Century, Institute of East and West Studies, Yonsei University, Seoul, Korea, November 16.

Kim, Hyun Mee (2004). "Feminization of the 2002 World Cup and women's fandom," *Inter-Asia Cultural Studies* 5 (1): 42–51.

Kim, Hyun Mee (2005). "Korean TV dramas in Taiwan: With an emphasis on the localization process," *Korea Journal* 45: 183–205.

Kim, Soyoung (2003). "The birth of the local feminist sphere in the global era: 'trans-cinema' and Yosongjang," *Inter-Asia Cultural Studies* 4 (1):10–23.

Kim, Sujeong (2009). "Interpreting transnational cultural practices: Social discourses on a Korean drama in Japan, Hong Kong and China," *Cultural Studies* 23 (5–6): 736–755.

Ko, Yufen (2004). "The desired form: Japanese idol dramas in Taiwan." In Koichi Iwabuchi (ed.), *Feeling Asian Modernities: Transnational Consumption of Japanese TV Dramas*. Hong Kong: Hong Kong University Press, pp. 107–128.

Kong, Shuya (2008). "Family Matters: Reconstructing the Family on the Chinese Television Screen." In Ying Zhu, Michael Keane and Ruoyun Bai (eds.), *TV Drama in China*. Hong Kong: Hong Kong University Press, pp. 75–88.

Kuo, Eddie C.Y., Quah, Jon S.T. and Tong, Chee Kiong (1988). *Religion and Religious Revival in Singapore*. Singapore: Ministry of Development.

Kwok, Jenny (2007). "*Hero*: China's Response to Hollywood Globalization," *Jump Cut: A Review of Contemporary Media*, 49: Spring.

Landler, Mark (2001). "Lee's 'Tiger,' Celebrated Everywhere but at Home," *New York Times*, Feb 27, B1, B2.

Latham, Kevin (2007). *Pop Culture China! Media, Arts and Lifestyles*. Santa Barbara: ABC Clio.

Lazzarato, Maurizion (1996). "Immaterial labor." In Paolo Virno and Michael Hardt (eds.), *Radical Thought in Italy*. Minneapolis: University of Minnesota Press.

Lee, Benjamin and Edward LiPuma (2002). "Cultures of circulation: The imagination of modernity," *Public Culture* 14 (1): 191–213.

Lee, Dong-Hoo (2004). "Cultural contact with Japanese TV dramas: Modes of reception and narrative transparency." In Koichi Iwabuchi (ed.), *Feeling Asian Modernities: Transnational Consumption of Japanese TV Dramas*. Hong Kong: Hong Kong University Press, pp. 251–274.

Lee, Dong-Hoo (2008). "From the margin to the Middle Kingdom: Korean TV drama's role in linking local and transnational production." In Ying Zhu, Michael Keane, and Ruoyun Bai (eds.), *TV Drama in China*. Hong Kong: Hong Kong University Press, pp. 187–200.

Lee, Geun (2009). "A soft power approach to the Korean Wave." Proceedings of the Korean-ASEAN Academic Conference on Pop Culture Formations across East Asia in the Twenty-first Century: Hybridization or Asianization? Burapha University, Thailand, February 1–4, pp. 85–96.

Lee, Keehyeung (2008). "Mapping out the cultural politics of 'the Korean Wave.'" In Chua Beng Huat and Koichi Iwabuchi (eds.), *East Asian Pop Culture: Analysing the Korean Wave*. Hong Kong: Hong Kong University Press, pp. 175–189.

Lee, Ming-tsung (2004). "Travelling with Japanese TV dramas: Cross-cultural orientation and flowing identification of contemporary Taiwanese youth." In Koichi Iwabuchi (ed.), *Feeling Asian Modernities: Transnational Consumption of Japanese TV Dramas*. Hong Kong: Hong Kong University Press, pp. 129–154.

Lee, Ming-tsung (2009). "De/re-territorialized Ximending: The imagination and construction of 'quasi-Tokyo' consuming landscapes" (in Chinese), *Router: A Journal of Cultural Studies* 9: 119–163.

Leheny, David (2006). "A narrow place to cross swords: Soft power and the politics of Japanese popular culture in East Asia." In Peter J. Katzenstein and Takashi Shiraishi (eds.), *Beyond Japan: The Dynamics of East Asian Regionalism*. Ithaca: Cornell University Press, pp. 211–233.

Leonard, Sean (2005). "Progress against the law: Anime and fandom, with the key to the globalization of culture," *International Journal of Cultural Studies* 8 (3): 281–305.

Leong, Anthony C.Y. (2002). *Korean Cinema: The New Hong Kong*. Victoria, British Columbia: Trafford Publishing.

Leung, Lisa Yuk-ming (2004). "*Ganbaru* and its transcultural audience: Imaginary and reality of Japanese TV dramas in Hong Kong." In Koichi Iwabuchi (ed.), *Feeling Asian Modernities: Transnational Consumption of Japanese TV Dramas*. Hong Kong: Hong Kong University Press, pp. 89–106.

Leung, Lisa Yuk-ming (2008). "Mediating nationalism and modernity: The transnationalization of Korean dramas on Chinese (satellite) TV." In Chua Beng Huat and Koichi Iwabuchi (eds.), *East Asian Pop Culture: Analysing the Korean Wave*. Hong Kong: Hong Kong University Press, pp. 53–70.

Li, Mingming (2008). "Soft Power in Chinese Discourse: Popularity and Prospect," Working Paper No. 165, S. Rajaratnam School of International Studies, Singapore.

Liew, Khai Khiun (2010). "'Symbolic migrant workers': Southeast Asian artistes in the East Asian entertainment industry." In Doobo Shim, Ariel Heryanto, and Ubonrat Siriyuvasak (eds.), *Pop Culture Formations Across East Asia*. Seoul: Jimoondang, pp. 181–208.

Lim, Wei Ling Tania Patricia (2005). "Formatting and Change in East Asian Television Industries: Media Globalization and Regional Dynamics." Ph.D. thesis, Queensland University of Technology.

Lin, Angel and Avin Tong (2008). "Re-imagining a cosmopolitan 'Asian us': Korean media flows and imaginaries of Asian modern femininities." In Chua Beng Huat and Koichi Iwabuchi (eds.), *East Asian Pop Culture: Analysing the Korean Wave*. London: Routledge, pp. 73–90.

Lin, Wenjian (2010). "Low ratings for local dramas," *The Straits Times*, Oct 29.

Liscutin, Nicola (2009). "Surfing the neo-nationalist wave: A case study of *manga kenkanryu*." In Chris Berry, Nicola Liscutin, and Jonathan D. Mackintosh (eds.), *Cultural Studies and Cultural Industries in Northeast Asia: What a Difference a Region Makes*. Hong Kong: Hong Kong University Press, pp. 171–194.

Long, Susan (2000). "Where Mr Cosmopolitan clashes with Mr Heartland," *The Straits Times*, Jan 9.

Lu, Sheldon Hsiao-peng (2001). *China, Transnational Visuality, Global Postmodernity*. Stanford: Stanford University Press.

Lu, Sheldon H. and Yeh, Emilie Yueh-Yu (eds.) (2005). *Chinese language film: historiography, poetics, politics*. Honolulu: University of Hawai'i Press.

Ma, Eric (2000). "Re-nationalization and me: My Hong Kong story after 1997," *Inter-Asia Cultural Studies* 1: 173–180.

Ma, Eric (2006). "Transborder visuality: The cultural transfer between Hong Kong and South China," *International Journal of Cultural Studies* 9 (3): 347–357.

MacLachlan, Elizabeth and Geok-lian Chua (2004). "Defining Asian femininity: Chinese viewers of Japanese TV dramas in Singapore." In Koichi Iwabuchi (ed.), *Feeling Asian Modernities: Transnational Consumption of Japanese TV Dramas*. Hong Kong: Hong Kong University Press, pp. 155–176.

Maliangkay, Ronald (2010). "The effeminacy of male beauty in Korea," *International Institute for Asian Studies (IIAS) Newsletter* 55: 6–7.

Marchetti, Gina (2005). "Global modernity, postmodern Singapore, and the cinema of Eric Khoo." In Sheldon H. Lu and Emilie Yueh-yu Yeh (eds.), *Chinese-Language Film: Historiography, Poetics and Politics*. Honolulu: University of Hawai'i Press, pp. 329–361.

Martinez, Xénia (2004). "Film dubbing, its process and translation." In Pilar Orero (ed.), *Topics in Audiovisual Translation*. Amsterdam and Philadelphia: John Benjamins Publishing Company, pp. 3–8.

McCarthy, Terry (1998). "In Defence of Asian Values: Singapore's Lee Kuan Yew," *Time Magazine*, May 16.

McGray, Donald (2002). "Japan's gross national cool," *Foreign Policy* 130: 44–54.

Millet, Raphaël (2006). *Singapore Cinema*. Singapore: Editions Didier Millet.

Mōri, Yoshitaka (2008). "*Winter Sonata* and cultural practices of active fans in Japan." In Chua Beng Huat and Koichi Iwabuchi (eds.), *East Asian Pop Culture: Analyzing the Korean Wave*. Hong Kong: Hong Kong University Press, pp. 127–142.

Morley, David (2003). "The nationwide audience." In Will Brooker and Deborah Jermyn (eds.), *The Audience Studies Reader*. London: Routledge, pp. 95–104.

Morley, David (2006). "Unanswered questions in audience research," *The Communication Review* 9 (2): 101–121.

Morris, Meaghan (2005). "Introduction: Hong Kong connections." In Meaghan Morris, Siu Leung Li, and Stephen Chan Ching-kiu (eds.), *Hong Kong Connections: Transnational Imagination in Action Cinema*. Hong Kong: Hong Kong University Press.

Morris, Meaghan, Siu Leung Li, and Stephen Chan Ching-kiu (eds.) (2005). *Hong Kong Connections: Transnational Imagination in Action Cinema*. Hong Kong: Hong Kong University Press.

Moskowitz, Marc L. (2010). *Cries of Joy, Songs of Sorrow: Chinese Pop Music and its Cultural Connotations*. Honolulu: University of Hawai'i Press.

Ngo, Thi Phuong Thien and Truong Thi Kim Chuyen (2009). "Effects of Korean movies on Vietnamese viewers." Proceedings of the Korean-ASEAN Academic Conference on Pop Culture Formations across East Asia in the Twenty-first Century: Hybridization or Asianization? Burapha University, Thailand, February 1–4, pp. 97–104.

Nye, Joseph (2004). *Soft Power: The Means to Success in World Politics*. New York: Public Affairs.

Ong, Aihwa (1999). *Flexible Citizenship: Mutations in Citizenship and Sovereignty*. Durham: Duke University Press.

Onn, Clarissa (2010). "Much ado about mother tongue," *The Straits Times*, May 8.

Otmazgin, Nissim Kadosh (2008). "Contesting soft power: Japanese popular culture in East and Southeast Asia," *International Relations of the Asia-Pacific* 8 (1): 73–101.

Otmazgin, Nissim Kadosh (2008a). "When culture meets the market: Japanese pop culture industries and the regionalization of East and Southeast Asia." In Shiraishi Takashi and Pasuk Phongpaichit (eds.), *The Rise of Middle Class in Southeast Asia*. Kyoto: Kyoto University Press, pp. 257–281.

Pang Laikwan (2009). "The transgression of sharing and copying: Pirating Japanese animation in China." In Chris Berry, Nicola Liscutin, and Jonathan D. Mackintosh (eds.), *Cultural Studies and Cultural Industries in Northeast Asia: What a Difference a Region Makes*. Hong Kong: Hong Kong University Press, pp. 119–134.

Pease, Rowan (2009). "Korean pop music in China: Nationalism, authenticity and gender." In Chris Berry, Nicola Liscutin, and Jonathan D. Mackintosh (eds.), *Cultural Studies and Cultural Industries in Northeast Asia: What a Difference a Region Makes*. Hong Kong: Hong Kong University Press, pp. 151–167.

Purushotam, Nirmala S. (1998). *Negotiating Languages, Constructing Race: Disciplining Difference in Singapore*. Berlin: Mouton de Gruyter.

Raghavendra, M. K. (2009). "Local resistance to global Bangalore: Reading minority Indian cinema." In K. M. Gokulsing and Wimal Dissanayake (eds.), *Popular Culture in a Globalised India*. London: Routledge, pp. 15–27.

Rajadhyaksha, Ashish (2003). "The 'Bollywoodization' of the Indian cinema: Cultural nationalism in a global arena," *Inter-Asia Cultural Studies* 4 (1): 25–39.

Rajagopal, Arvind (2001). *Politics after Television: Hindu Nationalism and the Reshaping of the Public in India*. Cambridge: Cambridge University Press.

Robins, Kevin and Asu Aksoy (2006). "Thinking experiences: Transnational media and migrants' minds." In James Curran and David Morley (eds.), *Media and Cultural Theory*. London: Routledge, pp. 86–99.

Seck, Felicia Yen Yin (2003). "Defying Oppression: new myth builders of the Chinese pop music industry." Unpublished Honors thesis, Department of Sociology, National University of Singapore.

Shih, Shu-Mei (2007). *Visual and Identity: Sinophone Articulations across the Pacific.* Berkeley: University of California Press.

Shim, Doobo (2002). "South Korean media industry in the 1990s and the economic crisis," *Prometheus* 20: 337–350.

Shim, Doobo (2005). "Globalization and cinema regionalization in East Asia," *Korea Journal* 45 (3–4): 233–260.

Shim, Doobo (2006). "Hybridity and the rise of Korean popular culture in Asia," *Media, Culture and Society* 28 (1): 25–44.

Shim, Doobo (2007). "Korean Wave and Korean women television viewers in Singapore," *Asian Journal of Women Studies* 13 (2): 63–82.

Shim, Doobo (2010). "Whither the Korean Media?" In Doobo Shim, Ariel Heryanto, and Ubonrat Siriyuvasak (eds.), *Pop Culture Formations across East Asia*. Seoul: Jimoondang, pp. 115–135.

Shin, Chi-Yun and Julian Stringer (eds.) (2005). *New Korean Cinema*. Edinburgh: Edinburgh University Press.

Shiraishi, Saya S. (1996). "Japan's soft power: Doraemon goes overseas." In Peter J. Katzenstein and Takeshi Shiraishi (eds.), *Network Power: Japan and Asia*. Ithaca: Cornell University Press, pp. 234–272.

Slater, Don (1993). "Going shopping: markets, crowds and consumption." In Chris Jenks (ed.), *Cultural Reproductions*. London: Routledge, pp. 188–209.

Soh, Seok Hoon (1994). "Fandom in Singapore." Unpublished Honors thesis, Department of Sociology, National University of Singapore.

Streeter, Thomas (2003). "The romantic self and the politics of Internet commercialization," *Cultural Studies* 17: 648–668.

Stronach, Bruce (1989). "Japanese television." In Richard G. Powers and Hidetoshi Kato (eds.), *Handbook of Japanese Popular Culture*. New York: Greenwood Press, pp. 127–166.

Su, Yu-Ling (1999). "Romance Fiction and Imaginary Reality: Reading Japanese Trendy Drama Socially." MA thesis of the Graduate Institute of Mass Communication, Fu Jen Catholic University, Taipei.

Sun, Ke (2000). "How does Asia Mean?" *Inter-Asia Cultural Studies* 1: 13–48 and 331–341.

Sun, Wanning (2002). *Leaving China: Media, Migration and Transnational Imagination.* Lanham: Rowan and Littlefield.

Tan, Sor Hoon (2004). *Confucian Democracy: A Deweyian Reconstruction*. Albany, NY: State University of New York Press.

Tan, Tarn How (2000). "Come, so you want to fight?" *The Straits Times*, Jan 8.

Tan, Yew Soon and Soh Yew Peng (1994). *The Development of Singapore's Modern Media Industry*. Singapore: Times Academic Press.

Tay, Jinna (2009). "Television in Chinese geo-linguistic markets: Deregulation, regulation and market forces in the post-broadcast era." In Graeme Turner and Jinna Tay (eds.), *Television Studies after TV: Understanding Television in the Post-Broadcast Era*. London: Routledge, pp. 105–114.

Taylor, Charles (2004). *Modern Social Imaginaries*. Durham, NC: Duke University Press.

Taylor, Jeremy E. (2008). "From transnationalism to nativism? The rise, decline and reinvention of a regional Hokkien entertainment industry," *Inter-Asia Cultural Studies* 9 (1): 62–81.

Teo, Stephen (2005). *Wong Kar-Wai: Auteur of Time*. London: British Film Institute.

Teo, Stephen (2007). *Director in Action: Johnny To and the Hong Kong Action Film*. Hong Kong: Hong Kong University Press.

Teo, Stephen (2008). "Promise and Perhaps Love: Pan-Asian production and the Hong Kong-China relationship," *Inter-Asia Cultural Studies* 9 (3): 339–340.

Tham, Irene (2010). "Local animators, look before you leap," *The Straits Times*, Nov 14.

Thomas, Mandy (2004). "East Asian cultural traces in post-socialist Vietnam." In Koichi Iwabuchi, Stephen Muecke, and Mandy Thomas (eds.), *Rogue Flows: Trans-Asian Cultural Traffic*. Hong Kong: Hong Kong University Press, pp. 177–196.

Tomlinson, John (1997). "Internationalism, globalization and cultural imperialism." In Keith Thompson (ed.), *Media and Cultural Regulation*. London: Sage Publications.

Tōru, Ōta (2004). "Producing (post)trendy Japanese dramas." In Koichi Iwabuchi (ed.), *Feeling Asian Modernities: Transnational Consumption of Japanese TV Dramas*. Hong Kong: Hong Kong University Press, pp. 69–86.

Toyoshima, Noburu (2008). "Longing for Japan: The consumption of Japanese cultural products in Thailand," *Sojourn* 23 (2): 252–282.

Tsai, Eva (2003). "Decolonizing Japanese TV drama: Syncopated notes from a 'sixth grader,'" *Inter-Asia Cultural Studies* 4 (3): 503–512.

Tsai, Eva (2005). "Kaneshiro Takeshi: Transnational stardom and the media and culture industries in Asia's global postcolonial age," *Modern Chinese Literature and Culture* 17: 100–132.

Tsai, Eva (2008). "Existing in the age of innocence: Pop stars, publics and politics in Asia." In Chua Beng Huat and Koichi Iwabuchi (eds.), *East Asian Pop Culture: Analyzing the Korean Wave*. Hong Kong: Hong Kong University Press, pp. 217–242.

Tu, Weiming (1991). "Culture China: The periphery as the centre," *Daedalus* 120: 1–32.

Tu, Weiming (1991a). *The Triadic Chord: Confucian Ethics, Industrial East Asia and Max Weber*. Singapore: Institute of East Asian Philosophies.

Turner, Graeme, Bonner Frances and Marshall David P. (2000). *Fame Games: The Production of Celebrity in Australia*. Cambridge, UK: Cambridge University Press.

Wang, Gungwu (2000). *Joining the modern world: inside and outside China*. Singapore: World Scientific Publishing.

Warde, Alan (2002). "Production, consumption and 'cultural economy.'" In Paul du Gay and Michael Pryke (eds.), *Cultural Economy: Cultural Analysis and Commercial Life*. London: Sage Publications, pp. 185–200.

Weintraub, Andrew N. (2011). *Islam and Popular Culture in Indonesia and Malaysia*. London: Routledge.

Wong, Ain-ling (2006). *The Glorious Modernity of Kong Ngee*. Hong Kong: Hong Kong Film Archives.

Wu, David (1998). "'Invention of Taiwanese': A second look at Taiwan's cultural policy and national identity." In Virginia R. Dominguez and David Y. H. Wu (eds.), *From Beijing to Port Moresby: The Politics of National Identity in Cultural Policies*. Amsterdam: Gordon and Beach Publishers, pp. 115–132.

Xu, Minghua (2010). "Globalization, Cultural Security and Television Regulation in the Post-WTO China." Unpublished Ph.D. dissertation, Department of Sociology, National University of Singapore.

Yang, Fang-chih (2008). "Rap(p)ing Korean Wave: National identity in question." In Chua Beng Huat and Koichi Iwabuchi (eds.), *East Asian Pop Culture: Analyzing the Korean Wave*. Hong Kong: Hong Kong University Press, pp. 191–216.

Yano, Christine (2004). "Letters from the heart: Negotiating fan-star relations in Japanese popular music." In William W. Kelly (ed.), *Fanning the Flames: Fans and Consumer Culture in Contemporary Japan*. Albany: State University of New York, pp. 41–58.

Yao, Souchou (2002). *Confucian Capitalism: Discourse, Practice and Myth of Chinese Enterprise*. London: RoutledgeCurzon.

Yau, Shuk-ting Kinnia (2005). "Interactions between Japanese and Hong Kong action cinema." In Meaghan Morris, Siu Leung Li, and Stephen Chan (eds.), *Hong Kong Connections: Transnational Imagination in Action Cinema*. Durham and London and Hong Kong: Duke University Press and Hong Kong University Press, pp. 35–48.

Yeh, Emilie Yeuh-Yu (2010). "The deferral of pan-Asian: A critical appraisal of film marketization in China." In Michael Curtin and Hemant Shah (eds.), *Reorienting Global Communication: Indian and Chinese Media Beyond Borders*. Urbana and Chicago: University of Illinois Press, pp. 183–200.

Yin, Kelly Su Fu and Kai Khiun Liew (2005). "Hallyu in Singapore: Korean cosmopolitanism or the consumption of Chineseness?" *Korean Journal* (winter): 206–232.

Yue, Audrey (2006). "The regional culture of New Asia: Cultural governance and creative industries in Singapore," *International Journal of Cultural Policy* 12 (1): 17–33.

Zhang, Yingjin (2004). *Chinese National Cinema*. London: Routledge.

Zhu, Ying, Michael Keane and Ruoyun Bai (eds.) (2008). *TV Drama in China*. Hong Kong: Hong Kong University Press.

# Index

\*    \*    \*    \*    \*    \*

## Pop Cultural Products